CAMBRIDGE LIBRARY COLLECTION

Books of enduring scholarly value

Egyptology

The large-scale scientific investigation of Egyptian antiquities by Western scholars began as an unintended consequence of Napoleon's invasion of Egypt during which, in 1799, the Rosetta Stone was discovered. The military expedition was accompanied by French scholars, whose reports prompted a wave of enthusiasm that swept across Europe and North America resulting in the Egyptian Revival style in art and architecture. Increasing numbers of tourists visited Egypt, eager to see the marvels being revealed by archaeological excavation. Writers and booksellers responded to this growing interest with publications ranging from technical site reports to tourist guidebooks and from children's histories to theories identifying the pyramids as repositories of esoteric knowledge. This series reissues a wide selection of such books. They reveal the gradual change from the 'tomb-robbing' approach of early excavators to the highly organised and systematic approach of Flinders Petrie, the 'father of Egyptology', and include early accounts of the decipherment of the hieroglyphic script.

Dendereh 1898

A pioneering Egyptologist, Sir William Matthew Flinders Petrie (1853–1942) excavated over fifty sites and trained a generation of archaeologists. This excavation report, first published in 1900, documents and illustrates the findings made at the cemetery of Dendera, until then neglected by archaeologists in favour of the more famous temple site. The work includes descriptions of the tombs and a chapter by Francis Llewellyn Griffith (1862–1934) on the inscriptions. Also covered are the pottery, funereal furniture and animal catacombs. The discoveries date from the Old Kingdom right through to the Roman period. The extensive section of plates includes plans of the tombs along with drawings and photographs of the many artefacts found within. Petrie wrote prolifically throughout his long career, believing that insights gained from his digs should be shared as swiftly as possible. A great many of his other publications – for both specialists and non-specialists – are also reissued in this series.

Dendereh
1898

W.M. Flinders Petrie

Cambridge
University Press

CAMBRIDGE
UNIVERSITY PRESS

University Printing House, Cambridge, CB2 8BS, United Kingdom

Published in the United States of America by Cambridge University Press, New York

Cambridge University Press is part of the University of Cambridge.
It furthers the University's mission by disseminating knowledge in the pursuit of
education, learning and research at the highest international levels of excellence.

www.cambridge.org
Information on this title: www.cambridge.org/9781108067270

This edition first published 1900
This digitally printed version 2013

ISBN 978-1-108-06727-0 Paperback

The original edition of this book contains a number of colour plates,
which have been reproduced in black and white. Colour versions of these
images can be found online at www.cambridge.org/9781108067270

DENDEREH. ARCHED PASSAGE OF ADU I., VI. DYNASTY.

DENDEREH

1898

BY

W. M. FLINDERS PETRIE, D.C.L., LL.D., PH.D.

EDWARDS PROFESSOR OF EGYPTOLOGY, UNIVERSITY COLLEGE, LONDON
VICE-PRESIDENT OF THE ROYAL ARCHAEOLOGICAL INSTITUTE, LONDON
MEMBER OF THE IMPERIAL GERMAN ARCHAEOLOGICAL INSTITUTE
CORRESPONDING MEMBER SOCIETY OF ANTHROPOLOGY, BERLIN
MEMBER OF THE SOCIETY OF NORTHERN ANTIQUARIES

With Chapters by

F. LL. GRIFFITH, M.A., F.S.A.,
DR. GLADSTONE, F.R.S., AND OLDFIELD THOMAS, F.Z.S.

SEVENTEENTH MEMOIR OF

THE EGYPT EXPLORATION FUND

PUBLISHED BY ORDER OF THE COMMITTEE

LONDON
SOLD AT
THE OFFICES OF THE EGYPT EXPLORATION FUND, 37, GREAT RUSSELL STREET, W.C.
AND AT 59, TEMPLE STREET, BOSTON, MASS., U.S.A.
AND BY KEGAN PAUL, TRENCH, TRÜBNER & CO., PATERNOSTER HOUSE, CHARING CROSS ROAD, W.C.
B. QUARITCH, 15, PICCADILLY, W.; ASHER & Co., 13, BEDFORD STREET, COVENT GARDEN, W.C.

1900

LONDON:
PRINTED BY GILBERT AND RIVINGTON, LIMITED,
ST. JOHN'S HOUSE, CLERKENWELL.

EGYPT EXPLORATION FUND.

CONTENTS.

LIST OF PLATES.

LIST OF EXTRA PLATES.

* The reference on p. 47 to XXVI.C should be to XXV.B.

DENDEREH.

INTRODUCTION.

1. Dendereh is to most persons only the name of a temple; one of the largest, best preserved, and most popular examples of Egyptian architecture, visited and admired by every tourist, a stopping-place of every steamer. The large volumes in which Mariette published the inscriptions, which had been uncovered by his direction, might be thought to exhaust what was to be done for Dendereh. But beside the temple there was a town, which is yet untouched, except by native diggers. And the inhabitants of this town were buried in a large cemetery on the desert behind the town, which had never been touched by scientific work. With the usual reckless wastefulness, dealers were allowed in the last few years to try plundering there; but happily their ventures were not fruitful, as they reopened already rifled tombs, and did not search for the external sculptures.

A cemetery of a nome capital, as yet unopened in modern times, was therefore a promising site for historical study. The town was known to be ancient, and there was the possibility of its proving to be prehistoric; there were many questions to be solved, and a fair prospect of results. I therefore applied, on behalf of the Egypt Exploration Fund, for permission to excavate at Dendereh, and westward as far as Hu. The first year our time was fully occupied at Dendereh itself, and the second year we extended our work along the desert to Hu.

Our party was happily composed. I had the advantage of the help of Mr. Arthur Mace, who was keenly interested in the work, and most painstaking and thorough in all that he did. In the latter half of our time we were joined by Mr. David MacIver, who came to Egypt mainly for anthropometric work, but had been well fitted for archaeology by working with Mr. Alfred Maudslay on Central American remains, and by familiarity with continental museums. These gentlemen, who were both Oxford men, have continued their work in the following year with good success. We were also joined by Mr. N. de G. Davies, who came mainly to practise on copying, and who did several large pieces of such work with accuracy; beside which he gave much time to clearing the cemetery of Ptolemaic times, and all the steles, labels, and amulets of that age come from his ground; while later on he excavated many of the eastern-most mastabas. My wife was with me all the time, helping in the surveying, cataloguing, and marking of the objects, and also drawing all the tomb plans here published. And at the last, Mr. Chas. Rosher was on the ground a week or two before I left, and continued work there afterwards for the American Exploration Society, during which he found some more tombs.

2. The cemetery extends from the back of the temple enclosure, up a gentle slope of desert for about a third of a mile, to a boundary bank which encloses it (see map, pl. xxvii.). Its length is undefined, but covers about two-thirds of a mile. Within that area of about a hundred acres there are six or eight large mastabas of brick still standing as high mounds, eighteen or twenty large mastabas denuded down to the ground, about fifty small mastabas, and many dozens of tomb-pits without remains of building around; all of the IVth to the XIth Dynasty. Toward the west end is a Ptolemaic cemetery with hundreds of burials; and some others of that age as secondary burials in the older mastabas. And all over the site, especially near the back of the temple enclosure, are great numbers of shallow graves of Roman age.

Thus the main periods of activity at Dendereh seem to have been from the VIth to the XIth Dynasty, and the Ptolemaic and early Roman age. Of the prehistoric there is nothing; of the flourishing XIIth Dynasty scarcely a single tomb, and none of importance; of the brilliant XVIIIth and busy XIXth Dynasty only two or three re-used tombs; of the XXVIth Dynasty two or three steles; and of the prolific age of Christian and Coptic remains scarcely a trace.

3. We had therefore here a good opportunity of lighting one of the dark periods of Egyptian history, the period of which scarcely any remains were yet known, from the fall of the VIth Dynasty to the rise of the XIIth. In this cemetery we have many noble buildings of the age of the Pepys, a great mass of sculpture leading on from that style until we meet with the names of Antef and Mentuhotep, and then not a single chip of working, nor a single name, of the already well-known ages that followed. For the first time we can trace that dark age through both in sculpture and pottery; and the value of this present work is essentially the clearing up of a period which has been as yet practically unknown.

4. Some mention should be made of the form in which the present results are published. It has been the excellent custom of the Exploration Fund to publish every inscription discovered during its work. It would be a misfortune were this custom to be dropped, as may be seen by the lack of information about discoveries made by the other nationalities working in Egypt, from whom the student is thankful to get some fragments of their results issued from various sources some years after discovery. He who gives quickly gives twice, and he who publishes fully and soon discovers double. Yet, with the best intention, the Fund was faced with a difficulty in the great quantity of inscriptions from Dendereh, of which most were formulae and repetitions; in fact, the sort of material which has lain for a generation past in museum magazines undescribed and uncatalogued. Coming from a locality exactly known, and forming part of a long series, it was of much value for comparison; yet of interest only to original students, and not to the public in general. To spend as much as would have issued the whole of this material in an edition of 2000 copies would have crippled the Fund for further research; and, as probably not fifty people would ever want or use the whole material, it would have been mere waste to issue so large an edition.

The course which has therefore been followed is to publish in the usual edition, issued to all subscribers, all material which can be of general interest; and to publish this in the best form, with photographic plates freely used, so as to show the important subject of style fully and unquestionably. And then to complete the issue of all the minor material in a smaller edition of 250 copies. These additional plates are all marked by letters, such as ii.A, vii.A, xi.A, xi.B, xi.C, &c. Hence it is clear when reference is made in the text, whether it be to plates in the volume, or to additional plates. Those who wish for the additional plates can have them on application at a small cost, just to cover the expense of printing. And they can be had either separately, or else bound interleaved with the plates of the volume, as desired. To any ordinary reader the half will be greater than the whole, as comparison can be more readily made between the striking and best examples of each style, when not mixed with inferior fragments. And to the student who desires to be exhaustive, every morsel of inscription is accessible. This course has saved some two hundred pounds in cost, without—it is hoped—sacrificing any of the usefulness of the publication.

The plates in the present volume are 14 photographic, and 24 lithographic. The additional plates, with lettered numbers, are 12 photographic, and 28 lithographic.

CHAPTER I.

TOMBS OF THE OLD KINGDOM.

5. The earliest tombs found in the cemetery form a small group, almost exactly behind the temple, in the centre of the cemetery (see map, pl. xxvii., "Abu-suten," or more correctly to be read as Suten·en·abu). The arrangement of the group can be followed in the plan on pl. xxviii., "Group of mastabas of III. or IV. Dyn." These tombs have, it will be observed, the old square wells leading to the sepulchre, such as belong to the IVth Dynasty; later the wells lengthen out north to south, to allow of long sarcophagi being lowered; and later still, toward the Middle Kingdom, they are lengthened from east to west. Each mastaba has one or two panelled imitation doorways, commonly called "false doors," on the east face; the whole of these tomb plans are here drawn with west side upwards. The well in each tomb leads down to a short passage turning southward—to left hand—so as to reach the sepulchral chamber, which was placed behind the stone false door, where the offerings were made for the deceased. In these, and all the plans here, the solid black is brickwork, the broken shade is gravel filling, and the chambers and wells are left white.

The earliest tomb is either the top one, that of Suten·en·abu, or the right-hand one. Probably Suten·en·abu is the earlier, as it is of a simpler type; the right-hand one having an enclosed chamber before the stone false door, which is divided from the enclosure by a front wall.

Starting therefore with the mastaba of Suten·en·abu (top one on pl. xxviii.), we see that it is formed by massive brick walls, filled in with gravel, forming a block of about 65 × 28 feet. There are two wells cut in the rock, which is of limestone, covered with ten to twenty feet of coarse rolled gravel from the Hammamat valley. The larger well is lined by a brick wall down the south side. Neither of the chambers below contained anything, except masses of bones of cows from late burials of the sacred cattle of Hathor. On the east face of the mastaba is a small false door of brick at the north end, which is usually the wife's doorway; and a large false door of stone at the south end, which was for Suten·en·abu himself. The plan of the stonework is shown by line shading. It was plain, with finely worked surfaces, bearing some traces of outline drawing, showing that there was an intention of sculpturing it. For this see view at base of pl. ii. At the back, filling the door space, was a figure of Suten·en·abu, and an elaborate carving of a doorway below it, shown at the top of pl. ii. Lastly, in front of the east face a wall has been built to enclose and protect it, with a doorway in front, a doorway at each end, and a narrowing of the space, which formed a small chamber just before the stone false door. The front doorway has been narrowed by a block on the south side, which is here left with a white space between it and the earlier side. This system of building a front wall to enclose the eastern panelled face of the mastaba is common here on all scales. Such a wall we usually termed the "fender," as it fended off visitors from approaching the tomb. Only one piece of pottery remained in this tomb, a large ring-stand, pl. xvi. 1.

Looking now at this sculpture of Seten en abu (pl. ii.), we see that it is undoubtedly of very early style. Hitherto we have had no figure sculpture of the IVth Dynasty except from Memphis, so that the style of Upper Egypt is unknown. But here we see such resemblance to the earliest Memphite sculptures known that we can hardly date it to any other period. The elaborately carved hieroglyphs, awkwardly sized and spaced, remind us of the panels of Hesy, or the tomb of Sokarkhabau. The elaboration of the false door pattern, with its band of diagonal work, is like the earliest tombs in the Louvre. The stiffness and clumsy pose of the figure is like that of the earliest mastabas; and the general air of un-mannered largeness and boldness belong to the oldest works from Saqqara. It is therefore akin to the work generally attributed to the IIIrd Dynasty (or even to the IInd Dynasty by some) rather than to the age of Khufu. This precious example of the art of Upper Egypt is now in the British Museum.

Next after this mastaba there seems to have been built the northern one, to the right hand, joining on to the end of the fender wall. Next, the one in front of Suten·en·abu, below it on the plan, which was shifted to one side, in order to leave a passage-way between it and the previous mastaba. Next, the smaller mastaba southward, to the left hand (No. 470), the face of which is in line with that last named. A flight of steps leads down before it to a small chamber under it; but this may more probably belong to an older tomb, over which No. 470 was built. Then No. 327 was built in front of this; and probably No. 472 was about the same age.

The northern mastaba contained no sculpture, although it is in good condition, and is still preserved some six feet high at the chamber. Only a slab, with a hollow for offerings, was in the chamber. The surfaces are all well finished, with fine smooth plastering. In the middle mastaba, before Suten·en·abu, nothing was found; both the front and the walls proving quite barren.

The chamber below No. 470 contained two of the usual very thick offering-cups, known in the early IVth Dynasty, as at Medum, see pl. xvi. 14, 15, and a small vase, xvi. 29. The pit 327, outside the small mastaba before No. 470, contained a contracted burial; and from other burials since discovered, it seems likely that this was that of a low-caste servant of the man who was buried in the small mastaba to which it belongs. The smallest square mastaba, No. 472, belongs also to this age, as shown by the pottery, pl. xvi. 15, 21, 26.

Before leaving this group we should notice a very interesting bowl which is photographed in pl. xxi., marked as "III. Dyn." It lay on the ground between the middle mastaba and No. 470, a narrow space only two feet wide, which was filled with clean, blown sand. Such a space must have been filled up within a year or two of the building, by the sand-laden winds; and it appeared never to have been disturbed. Hence this bowl is certainly as old as the mastabas, which seem to belong to the end of the IIIrd or early IVth Dynasty. It is much like the pieces found by M. de Morgan in a mastaba of the same age (*Recherches sur les Origines*, i., pl. xi.). It differs entirely from usual Egyptian pottery, and is evidently imitated from basket-work. Its source is probably Libyan, being akin to the prehistoric black incised pottery, and also to the incised bowls of the invaders of the XIIth Dynasty.

6. The next important tomb is the mastaba of Prince Mena, nearly a quarter of a mile west of Suten·en·abu (see map, pl. xxvii.; plan, pl. xxviii.). This is far more elaborate in plan than the earlier mastabas just described; and we learn from the inscriptions that it is as late as Pepy II. The stone false door is here in a chamber, which is entered from the east front. The large stone stele was found fallen forward in the chamber from its niche in the brickwork.

It is kept in Cairo, and photographed here in pl. i. Down each side was a narrow band of inscription, one given here at the base of pl. ii.A, and over the large stele was a round drum or roller, shown at the top of pl. ii. The eastern front had twelve small false doors along it: three south of the chamber door, and nine north of that, fenced by a fender wall in front, thus forming a corridor. Each of these false doors had a roller or drum over it, two of which are shown in the middle of pl. ii.A, with the inscription "Prince Mena." And over each drum was a large panel of sculptured stone in each doorway with a figure of Mena; of these five were recovered, three given in pl. ii., and two in pl. ii.A. These stones had all fallen down when the brickwork had decayed, and were found lying face down in the dust which filled the corridor. Above all these twelve false doors the mastaba had a stone cornice, the blocks of which had likewise fallen into the corridor. The inscription on these blocks is shown, re-arranged by Mr. Griffith, in the upper half of pl. ii.A. Beside these sculptures there was found in the corridor a slab of a man with his wife Nebt-atef, with incised inscription, and therefore not from a portal panel. Probably this showed Mena with his wife, and was let into the wall. Also in the corridor was an effaced inscription, reading both ways from a middle line, probably from the inscription over the entrance door, shown next below the small drums, pl. ii.A. Another block from a long incised inscription (shown at the left base of pl. ii.A.) was found outside the north end of Mena's mastaba, and may belong either to that or to Meru. This completes the external stone-work.

Of the form of the mastaba, an unusual feature is the open court at the north—right hand—end, the walls of which have a slope of about 1 in 5. It was entered from a western arched door, and had a bench running along the north and east sides, 23 to 24 inches wide and 30 to 34 inches high. From this court a flight of steps led up to the roof of the mastaba, of which ten still remained, and a continuation of the space which would have held sixteen more steps; as eight steps rise 58 inches, the twenty-six steps would rise 188 inches. This suggests that the mastaba was about 16 feet high, which seems very suitable to its length of 83 feet and width of 52 feet. The bulk of the mastaba was divided by cross walls, and filled in with gravel. The northern courtyard was also entirely filled with clean gravel, and seems therefore to have been intentionally filled up, and not merely choked with *débris* like the corridor.

Two wells, with their length from north to south, descended to two chambers on the south of them. One is here called the "well of offerings," as several large jars were found in it, but no sign of burial. The other is marked "sepulchre," as a short passage led to a chamber lined with stone slabs, which might rather be called a built sarcophagus. The sides were all painted, and are copied on pl. iii. by Mr. Davies, who spent some weeks mainly in recovering the design from the remaining traces, much having perished by efflorescence. The north, or entrance end, of the chamber was closed by two slabs, painted as doors (top right hand, pl. iii.), with the sacred eyes, one on each side. Around are the titles of Mena, who was director of the temples of the pyramids of Meryra (Pepy I.) and of Merenra. Along each side is a painting of a doorway highly decorated, a list of offerings, and drawings of offerings; and at the south end are other drawings of offerings, mostly perished. The long list of 8 × 17 offerings is repeated on a larger scale in pl. iv. Most of the stones were too much scaled and injured to be worth removal; but the two door slabs were brought away, and are now at Chicago. For the small copper objects found here, see the account of the tomb of Meru, sect. 7.

The access provided to the top of the mastaba by a staircase is curious. Similar access remains in the other large mastabas of Adu I. and Merra, and probably in that of Adu III. On the top of the rounded weathered mound of Adu I. there were, when I first went up it, many pieces of offering vessels of the Old Kingdom; those had been left there since the last offerings were made over five thousand years ago, disregarded by man, and too heavy to be removed by wind and weather. It seems then that offerings were made on the tops of mastabas, like the custom at Memphis in the same age. Perhaps there was access to the well of offerings to renew the food and drink there. Yet any way, this access to the top was not left unchecked later on, but was definitely closed by filling up the courtyard with gravel, and so completing the solid block of the mastaba.

7. Adjoining the mastaba of Mena on the north was a slightly smaller and less elaborate mastaba of Meru. The name was only found by occurring on a roller drum from a doorway. The plan is in externals much the same as that of Mena, with nine doorways north of the entrance, and probably three to the south. The principal interest was the group of funeral models in copper, and the beads, found lying on the floor of the sepulchre (see pl. xxii.), together with a vase (xvi. 31). These models are, apparently, the implements for the funeral ceremonies; the *hotep* altar on a framework, four vases to stand upon it, a hoe, and an axe, and a large fan-shaped cutting-tool at the top of the group. The head of the body had been to the north, but only the legs and a few vertebrae remained. The *hotep* and vases were together in the N.E. corner, with a small jar like xvi. 31; at the N.W. was a large jar of the type xvi. 30; the small jar xvi. 31 was near the knees; the axe on the shins; and the hoe and fan cutter together at the feet. As the body had been plundered, this may not have been the original distribution. A similar cutting-tool, axe, and hoe, together with a long piece of jointed wire, were found just outside the N.E. corner of the sarcophagus of Mena, under a pan inverted on the sand. Scattered with the tools of Meru were glazed beads, white (decomposed green?), and brown-black, imitating flies; these, with the end piece of a collar, are strung together in this group, pl. xxii.

Immediately in front of Meru is another mastaba of Zauta-Resa, from which some tablets and door drums are shown in pl. vii. His wife's inscription (which continued on a weathered chip) was "his wife, his beloved, the royal relative, priestess of Hathor Lady of Dendereh, Mer-rta." The form of the mastaba is evidently a copy of that of Meru.

At the north of Zauta-Resa another mastaba joined it, also of a Zauta. This was found by Mr. Rosher after I left. All of these mastabas are denuded to only about a foot high, and are covered with sand. In general I use here letters to distinguish between persons of the same name when their order is uncertain; but when the relative order is known, Roman numerals are used, as Adu I, II., III., IV.

In front of Zauta-Resa is a group of three joined mastabas, only one of which has a name, Zauta (B); see base of pl. xxviii. The mastaba is of the same type as Zauta-Resa; only a mirror was found in the tomb (pl. xx. 3); but a little tomb has been built into it later, the smaller well behind the chamber being only 20 inches deep, with brickwork doming over it, and a little false door niche being built just behind it. From a scarab found in this tomb it is probably of the XIIth Dynasty. To the north of this mastaba is part of the foundation of an unfinished tomb. The bases of the walls are laid out, but it has never been completed, as the long sloping trench cut in the rock to contain the built passage had no brickwork in it, but only rubbish. This trench is shown in outline on the plan, sloping down from the north to about fifteen feet deep at the south. A wall was built across it, to convert the south end into a well leading to the chamber, which opens from the south end. This was all plundered; but a small side chamber on the west of the trench (dotted in the plan) contained an untouched burial of a woman, with the group of stone vases and mirror photographed at the top of pl. xxi., marked VI. Dyn. At the upper left hand is a carved shell of translucent diorite, an alabaster vase in the middle, and a porphyry vase on the right. Below the diorite shell is a small bowl of diorite, a copper mirror in the middle, and a hard limestone cup with spout on the right. At the base are five small vases of alabaster and hard limestone. The form of the mirror is compared with others on pl. xx., marked "Group xxi. 2." These vases being well dated to the VIth Dynasty, serve as fixed points for comparing others.

Another early tomb is a square pit with traces of mastaba walls, far out by the telegraph poles; the plan is given on pl. xxviii., marked Tomb 524. From this pit come the large mirror in pl. xx., and an alabaster vase to the left of it. The burial was normal, at full length head north; the mirror by the head, the vase at the feet.

8. The mastaba of Adu I. is the largest and most elaborate in the cemetery. The plan and section are given on pl. xxix.; the entrance door in pl. ii.; the view of the entrance passage in frontispiece; the fresco on pl. v.; the cornice and a slab in pl. vi. The form differs from that of Mena and others in having a long sloping tunnel of entrance from the north, copied from the early mastaba and pyramid type. The east face has four portals south of the entrance, and nine to the north. In the first chamber is a fresco of Adu and his family fishing; from this we learn that he was director of the pyramid temples of Pepy I. and Pepy II. Two other chambers connect with this on the north, but contained nothing, except the tablet of Sekhet-hotep, pl. vi. On the south is the chamber of the great stela. Across the chamber lies a large flooring slab, with a little tank sunk in the floor for offerings, on the north of it. Above this slab stood the stele in a recess, but unhappily it had all been broken up for stone, probably in Roman times, and only a fragment served to show what fine work it had been. Another chamber opens out west of this, containing a shallow well, 40 inches deep, for offerings. Beyond this a block of brickwork had been built in, closing the connection with two other chambers. The further chamber, the S.W. one in the whole mastaba, had, however, been accessible by a stairway from the roof. In this chamber, or court, was a pit, 127 × 39 inches; this opened into a chamber on the east of it, which contained a sunk recess in the floor for a coffin. Here were found the top and base of a fine head-rest of diorite; also the limestone slab, with two model cups of obsidian, and the neck of a model vase of alabaster, shown on pl. xxi. 3. Such slabs with model vases and implements are already known in collections, but have not yet been dated, as this one is to the close of the VIth Dynasty.

The mass of the mastaba is formed of chambers, connected by narrow doorways for convenience during building, but all filled up with gravel filling to form a solid mass. A stairway led up to the top of this, as shown by steps from the side of the tunnel; and from the top other steps led down to the court at the S.W., which contained a subsidiary burial of a relative or chief man of Adu. Apparently a narrow passage had existed on each side of the tunnel, since filled up with brickwork, the joints being shown here by white lines left in the black mass. This narrow passage on the east had led into a long construction chamber; on the west it had led to two small construction chambers, one of which had a pit in the floor; nothing, however, was found in this pit.

We now turn to the sepulchre. The appearance of the mouth of the arched tunnel is shown at the foot of pl. ii., still partly crossed by the outer wall of the mastaba. This tunnel begins at the foot of the steps (see pl. xxix.) in a sloping face; and the outer wall and filling of cross passage were solid across it. Inside the tunnel was another cross wall, just before it opened into the pit, and the whole tunnel was filled with earth and hundreds of offering jars, shown on pl. xvi. 8. The tunnel was boldly arched with four rings of brickwork, laid on the slope in the greater part, and turning level where it joins the pit. The appearance of it from the pit is shown in the frontispiece, which is from a fully-measured sketch, as it was impossible to photograph in so narrow a space. This is the oldest arching yet dated, and shows that in brickwork the Egyptian would freely and boldly use arching in early times, as we already know that he did in the XIIth and and XIXth Dynasties. From the pit the tunnel goes on in the same line downward through the marl, which underlies the gravel, until it reaches the subterranean chamber. A small side chamber, on each side of the passage, contained broken pottery.

The sepulchral chamber was cruciform, lined around with sculptured slabs, roughly carved with offerings, and a long band of hieroglyphs, shown in pl. v.A. In the long stem of the cross the floor was formed by the massive lid of the sunken sarcophagus. This was found undisturbed in its place; and on clearing down to the north end of the sarcophagus—the only accessible part—that was found complete. It seemed as if the burial must yet remain untouched. We eagerly broke the lid, and looked in, only to find that some plunderer, who knew the exact plan of the place, had tunnelled from the outside straight to the sarcophagus, and had broken into it through its side under the floor, and extracted everything from it. I got into the hole, now under water, and felt over everything in the sarcophagus; brickbats and large flints showed only too plainly that the entrance had been forced through the foundation of the mastaba. The chamber is drawn in the section roughly curved in the upper part, as that is its present condition. The very coarse gravels and marl which formed the roof and sides have entirely caved down, and forced most of the lining forward, so that the chamber was filled with *débris*. We extracted all the sculptured lining, about 200 slabs, and handed them over to the Cairo Museum to be reconstituted; the continuity of the whole is shown by the inscription around it, in pl. v.A.

9. Next beyond this is another mastaba, nearly as large, and apparently later in development. This is of Adu II. The plan is on pl. xxix.; the cornice and some slabs of inscription on pl. vi.; the statue and two steles on pl. vii.; and the pottery on pl. xvi. 2, 4, 5, 6, 7, 19, 20, 23, 24. The changes from the previous plan are mainly in providing a large open court at the south end for the relatives, in making the tunnel much steeper so as to get to the full depth before reaching the well, and simplifying the internal construction by not making any brick walls except where needed to be seen.

The front has twelve false doors to the south of the entrance, and eighteen to the north, thirty in all, the greatest number on any tomb found in the cemetery. The entrance on the east was by a narrow passage, leading to a chamber, which seems to have contained a large stela in a niche, now empty; and a smaller niche of brickwork to the north end of the face, which was doubtless for the wife. We see from the two tablets found in this chamber (in pl. vii.) that Adu II. had a wife named Ana; the second well in the plan was therefore for the wife, and in the chamber below it we found a female skull of high class.

The entrance to the sepulchre was similar to that of Adu I.; but the tunnel is much steeper, so that it is only by notches on the floor that it can be descended without slipping. The roof is of brick arches, laid on a much flatter bed. In the lower part it was very difficult to distinguish the brickwork, as the ground was so damp that the pressure of the well and tunnel had united the bricks into a soft brown earth, similar to that which filled the passages. Passing the well, the chamber was reached. This was cruciform, like that of Adu I.; the walls lined with brick, and brick doming had formed the roof of the side recesses. Nearly all of this had fallen in, with much of the gravel above it, but we removed the *débris* and cleared the floor, without, however, finding any trace of a sarcophagus or of the burial. In the well was found the seated figure of Adu, shown in pl. vii. 1. Portions of the cornice inscription from the east front were found fallen below, and are shown in pl. vi. Also three slabs, and one corner-piece inscribed with titles of Adu, which are probably from an inscription of the doorway.

The minor burials about the mastaba are unusual. Just before the east face is a long pit, leading to a chamber under the wall, which is marked with shading in the solid black. This pit was untouched, and had a brick filling closing the entrance to the chamber. In the chamber was a coffin, 72 × 25 inches, plain box form, with traces of inscription on the white coating; inside it a female skeleton at full length, head north; under the head a stone block head-rest. Outside the feet of the coffin were two wooden statuettes, nearly consumed by white ants, and some small blue glazed beads with them. Along the east side of the chamber were four large jars, see pl. xvi. 20; and a pile of four bowls standing on two bricks, see xvi. 4. Two little pots were at the side of the coffin, see xvi. 2.

At the end of the stele chamber it will be seen that there is a brick blocking, which closed a doorway leading to the south court. In this court were nine separate burials. Only one was untouched, that reached by the southern stairway. In this was a box coffin, body full length, head north, normal, hands at sides, and by the head a red bowl, as xvi. 4. Outside the head of the coffin was a jar, as xvi. 20. On the body was a small ivory button near the throat, apparently the fastening of a cloak. It was engraved with a figure of a man, almost reduced to a geometrical pattern; it will be published afterwards in connection with other buttons for comparison, as it serves to date a whole class of such things. The other pits were mostly plundered; one contained three jars, see xvi. 19, and one small vase, fig. 23, with the legs of a female, judging by their slightness; head north. Another small vase, fig. 24, was in one of these tombs. On the centre of the floor of the court, probably thrown out of a tomb, were the two vases and the censer, xvi. 5, 6, 7, with a flint knife shown in pl. xx. The northern stairway led to a chamber with several jars and bowls of the same type as before; only a leg of an ox, and a few human bones, were left.

To the north of Adu II. were two other mastabas. One small one, marked Detiat (pl. xxx.), should read Degat; fragments from it are given at base of pl. vi.: and the drum with name is repeated in the group of various small blocks, pl. vii.A. The larger mastaba was partly traced, the rest having been destroyed: it belonged to Merru. The trench in the rock for the entrance had been emptied, and re-used for late Ptolemaic or Roman burials. A large sandstone coffin, lying on the stairway, had a rudely painted red inscription with blundered address to "the great god lord of Abydos, . . . Osiris prince of gods in the midst, Osiris P'ast urt. . . ."

10. The series of Adu mastabas continues with another behind Adu II., which is probably Adu III., shown in plan and section on pl. xxx. Here further development has taken place; the tunnel is as steep as in Adu II., but the difficulty due to the sliding thrust of the roof at so steep an angle is met by making the roof horizontal, and so forming a vaulted chamber with sloping floor for a tunnel. The courtyard for minor burials is given up, but such burials are thrust into the mastaba mass at irregular points.

The east face is covered with portals, divided by the entrance into nine to the south and thirteen to the north. The chamber has a niche for the great stele, now entirely lost, and another niche near the south end, with a low altar built in it for offerings. Some fragments of cornice were found from the east face, inferior in work to those of the predecessors (top, pl. xiii.); and one bit of a stele (pl. xiii.) gives the name Adu, as the second, or *nefer*, name of the owner.

The entrance to the sepulchre was with a slight slope downward at first, passing by a stairway ascending on the west—omitted by accident in the plan, pl. xxx. Then entering into the tunnel chamber by a low door, it went down a rough stairway, while the roof remained level over it, until the chamber was nearly fifteen feet high at the south end, where another low door led to the well. Thence a slight descent further led to the sepulchre; this was so greatly fallen in, that little of the original form could be traced. There was a wide passage, nearly as wide as the well; then a narrowing on the west; and then a turn westward, which had apparently been the chamber. The floor was piled so deep with fallen gravels, that it could not with certainty be found under the water which covered it.

The minor burials were in the S.W. part of the mastaba. The largest tomb was a stairway of rough steps leading to a small chamber in the gravel. At the head of the stairway was a pit for burial, apparently separate, with a wall between it and the stairs. The square pit most to the east was about seven feet deep; in it was a great quantity of pottery broken up, mostly bowls, such as in xvi. 3; and with these much linen cloth, and two large stone vases, one of porphyry, the other of alabaster. Both of these are now in the Cairo Museum, one kept in the division, the other appropriated out of our share. The other pits contained nothing.

This family may perhaps be completed by the tomb of Adu IV., which lay to the west of Adu III. The plan is at the end of pl. xxxv.; and the only fragment of inscription which dates it is from a door lintel, at the upper part of pl. xiii.; this was found in the long chamber. This tomb has probably been greatly altered, the two wells lying with length E. to W. seem almost to be of the XIIth Dynasty, and we cannot certainly date the square well and the other wells to the west. In the southern of the long wells was a burial of the XXVth Dynasty, with the fine stele of Mutardus, the singer of the temple of Hathor, shown in pl. xxv.

11. The only other important mastaba of the VIth Dynasty is that of Pepy-seshem-snefer, surnamed Senna. The plan is on pl. xxx.; the steles and cornice on vii. and vii.A; the pottery on xvi., figs. 33 to 37. The form is usual, except that the entrance is in the middle, which is rare, and thus there is an equal number of portals—eight—on each side of the entrance. The perfect condition of the slabs of sculpture (vii., vii.A) is due to their never having been built into the portals, for which they were intended; these square slabs were all found standing on edge, stacked against the wall of the chamber. Beside these uniform panels there is a piece of a relief panel (vii.); part of an incised stele, showing a man whose name is lost, with another named Pepy-mennu-nefer Senbat (vii., xiii.); a panel of a woman, Sentefsa (?) (vii.A); and a large quantity of the cornice, rather carefully but feebly sculptured (vii.A).

Other tombs which probably belong to the VIth Dynasty should be noticed here. Zauta A. is a large mastaba west of Adu I., and perhaps as early as that. The plan (pl. xxx.) is difficult to trace, as it is denuded away to below the sills of the doorways, and even no foundation is left in some parts. It seems to have had long chambers on the east; three shallow wells containing some broken offering bowls, as in Adu III.; and a sloping rock-cut passage leading to a small rounded chamber. Just inside the entrance, in the N.-W. corner, were stacked twelve pans of red pottery, more brown-red than usual in this age, thin, and highly burnished (xvi. 10).

On the other side of Adu I. are traces of mastabas, see No. 784, pl. xxx. The trench is a large sloping cutting, like those for the great mastabas; and a thick wall on the east looks as if a mastaba had been begun. But over the chamber is a tiny mastaba with two false doors, which looks as if the tomb had been thus finished prematurely.

CHAPTER II.

THE UNDATED TOMBS OF VIIth–XIth DYNASTIES.

12. Hitherto we have been following the guidance of the absolutely dated inscriptions naming the kings of the VIth Dynasty, and only noting other tombs when their position linked them with those already dated.

Now we enter on the difficult subject of this chapter, the dark age between the VIth and the XIIth Dynasty. And if in this we seem to dwell too much on small matters, it is because we have only small matters of style and sequence to help us through this period, and therefore they become as valuable as more decisive evidence is in better known ages.

There are four guides in classifying the mass of material from Dendereh: 1st, the style of sculpture; 2nd, the form of the tomb; 3rd, the position of the tomb; 4th, the contents of the tomb. These are here placed in their relative value for practical use, in the present state of the material, though not the order of value were the information complete in every direction. We have already noticed two styles of mastabas, and we begin here with these, and then go through the succeeding styles. Each group will afterward be noticed in detail.

Dyn.	Class.	Style of Work.	Form of Tomb.	Names.
III.-IV.	A	Severe.	Mastaba, square pit.	Suten·en·abu.
VI.	B	Good, early.	Mastaba, N.-S. pit or tunnel.	Mena, Adu, Zauta, Senna.
VII.-VIII.?	C	Corrupt VIth Dyn.	Mastaba, N.-S. pit.	Hotepsa, Una, Beba, Uhaa, Ptahmera, Shensetha, Merra, Beb, Sennezsu.
IX.-X.?	D	Crowded inscriptions.	Mastaba, small or absent, E.-W. pit, N. door to chamber.	Merer, Shensetha, Kathena, Beba, Nekhtu.
XI.?	E	Widespread, coarse inscriptions.	Larger mastabas, trench passage resumed.	Beba, Antef, Antefa, Antefaqer, Mera, Sebeknekhta, Mentuhotep.
XI.?	F	Rude and simple.	No mastabas, E.-W. pits.	Demza, Nemy, Nubheq, Sentekha, Sentekhneba, Hotepa, Henna, Sebekhotepa.
XI.?	G	Laboured work. Simple inscriptions. Puffy faces.	No mastabas, E.-W. pits.	Bauhotepa, Beba, Hat-hotep, Nefertkau, Menhotepa.
XI.	H	Double lines. Finer work.	Large mastabas, or E.-W. pits.	Hennu, Bet, Beba, Redukau, Antef, Antefaqer, Mentuhotep, Khnumerdu.

It is unsatisfactory to have class E, with such names as Antef and Mentuhotep, separated by F and G from class H, in which the names of the XIth Dynasty rule again. It would be far happier if E could be placed between G and H. But there are such difficulties in style that I hesitate to do so. The classes F, G, and H, are so homogeneous, and so clearly lead into each other, that it seems impossible to place such tombs of class E as Antefa, Antefaqer, and the tablet of Antef and Ay, between F and H; while, on the other hand, those three tombs are closely connected with classes C and D. It seems, therefore, that we must grant that the lowest degradation of the Old Kingdom style was not reached until the names of the XIth Dynasty had fairly started; and that the revival in style did not take place until the rise of power in the XIth Dynasty. If we then assign classes E, F, to the first century of the XIth Dynasty, when the names Antef and Mentuhotep were known, but no revival had yet arisen; class G to the rise of power and unity under the XIth Dynasty; and class H to the flourishing age of refined work under Antef V. and Sankhkara, we seem to obtain the most satisfactory arrangement. The comparative dearth of inscriptions in the VIIth to Xth Dynasties is not unlikely, in view of the scarcity of any records of that age.

13. CLASS C. VIth–VIIIth (?) Dynasties. *Minor Tombs.*

HOTEPSA. This panel (pl. x.) is so closely in the style of Senna, that it must be of the same age, or very shortly after. It was found in a N.-S. pit, 511.

UNA. This fragment of cornice (xi.c) is like that of the next tomb.

FOUR NAME MASTABA, 770. Shensetha, Enabu-suten, Beba, Imhotepa (pl. xxx.). The carvings of this are given on pls. xi., xi.A., Beba and Hentsen; xi.A, Abu-suten; xiii., Imhotepa; and other fragments of cornice, a piece of inscription, and a piece of panel naming Sebekem........., all from this tomb, are on pl. xiii., below Imhotepa. The general style is good, but a little laboured; it is larger and bolder than Senna, and can hardly be placed as late as the end of the VIth Dynasty. Perhaps later is a fragment with the names of Beb and Ankhsen (xiv., top), also from this tomb No. 770. As a guide we may note here the various styles of cornices, in their order of connection.

Class.				Plate.
B	Mena.	Fine work;	border lines.	ii.A.
B	Adu I.	Nearly as fine;	no border.	vi.
B	Adu II.	Smaller;	no border.	vi.
B	Senna.	Much smaller;	no border.	vii.A.
C	Ptahmera A.	Small, wiry;	border lines.	x.A.
C	Shensetha P.	Larger, clumsy;	border lines.	xi.A.
C	Merra.	Larger still, clumsier;	wide borders.	viii.C.
C	Sennezsu.	Wider and clumsier signs;	wide borders.	x.A.
E	Mera.	} Coarsest, widest, and clumsiest;	borders.	xi.C.
E	Antefa.			xi.C.
E	Mentuhotep.		(by Beba)	x.A.

This appears to be a sound series; following a deterioration in size down to Senna, and then as style became poorer the size of the signs increasing until the worst work, Mera, is the largest in size. The good width, and absence of border lines, of Beba and Hentsen seem to point to that being about the age of Adu I. or II. The mastaba is very peculiar in having four chambers about equal, and four or five names occurring in its sculptures: doubtless they are all of one family, but such compound tombs are rarely found. The sepulchre was reached by a long sloping passage or tunnel, of which the trench remains; but the chamber was filled with burials of about the Persian age.

UHAA. This panel (pl. x.) has the dress treated as that of Senna. The style is like that of Ptahmera A., but from the position it is probably older than Shensetha P. and Ptahmera. The plan (xxxi.) is like that of Merra, and agrees to this age.

PTAHMERA A. The sculpture is shown in x., x.A, and the cornice in x.A, where the fragments are placed in order, as found fallen along the foot of the east front. The style is coarser than anything seen so far; the relief work is clumsy, and the signs attract by their bold and mechanical cutting to make up for their bad forms. The only fragment of scenes in the whole cemetery is the piece with a goatherd, donkeys, and ploughing, pl. x. The plan of the mastaba is in xxxii.

SHENSETHA P. This mastaba is, from its position, later than Ptahmera, as it advances forward, and so eclipses the other. There is only the cornice from this tomb, pl. xi.A, and a fragment naming the daughter ......erdutsa, Bebaurt, and Khetpera is copied at the top of pl. xiv. Another tomb of the same name has, however, been mixed with this in the plate, the small double altar on the right belonging to Shensetha T. The mastaba plan is on pl. xxxii.

BEBA C. This tomb seems to be later in position than the previous. The work shows a new departure in a greater elaboration, particularly in the hair (see Beba III., pls. xi. and xi.B); but the style of the signs is much like that of Ptahmera. The plan (xxxii.) is like that of the preceding tombs. The name of the son Azaua is copied at the top of pl. xiv.

SHENSETHA AND BEBA-UR. This is probably by the same artist as the preceding carving (see pl. xi.). It is an interesting attempt to revive art by care and detail, much like the Constantine revival, but just as powerless as that to really turn the tide.

14. MERRA. This is the most important of the mastabas after the VIth Dynasty. The plan (pl. xxxi.) shows a later stage than that of Adu II. and III. The east front is much like those earlier mastabas, the number of portals is the same as in Adu I., four and nine. But the structure shows the horizontal roofed tunnel, which was brought in by Adu III.; and a further application of this by doming over a large well. The entrance leads to a small open court, from which a stairway winds round to the roof, apparently imitated from Merra. On the west this court leads to two chambers, by a low arched door; but these seem to be merely construction chambers filled in with gravel, and it is probable that others exist in the rest of the mass. The real entrance to the sepulchre begins with a well, which probably gives access to the horizontal roofed tunnel passage, but the bottom was not cleared to search for the door. There is a narrow slit window which lights the tunnel from the well. The tunnel ends by a great cross wall in which a series of relieving arches, one below another, span the upper part, and at the bottom is a doorway leading to the second well, which is small and square. This in the upper part is all one with the third well or "domed well," which is separated from the second well by a wall with arched doorway. The "domed well" was covered by a dome of brickwork; this was partly broken when found, and had to be removed in order to clear the well safely. The doming was made by placing a brick across the corner, then two over that with a rise in the middle, four over that again, and thus gradually bringing forward the

corners so that a ring of bricks could run round the well. The section of the dome showed the bricks slightly slanting inward, but mainly standing by resting on those below. There is some amount of thrust necessarily in closing over the space; but as far as possible the principle of stepping forward was used. This of Merra is the oldest dome known, as Adu I. made the oldest arched tunnel known. It was made simply to save material, the principle of leaving large hollows having been eagerly grasped for the sake of economy. Through the domed well was the entrance to the sarcophagus chamber, cut in the gravel; there standing to the left hand, or east side, with just space to pass along the side of it, was the massive stone coffin, with plain lid, all rough-faced and uninscribed. In the chamber was some pottery, as the tall ring-stand, xvi. 28, large bowl, xvii. 41, and some dozens of jars as xvii. 40 and 42. There was no trace of the interment.

Of sculpture there is an unusual quantity from this mastaba. The long inscription in relief (pl. viii.) was over the eastern entrance. One slab is lost from the beginning; then three slabs remain, though broken; the fifth is lost; of the sixth there is the lower half; the seventh, with the daughter Duduerdutsa, is complete; and the eighth and last, with the master to whom all is addressed, is also almost perfect. The whole inscription when complete must have been about 14 feet in length, and contained about 60 feet run of inscription. As the breadth of the recess of the doorway is 217 inches, these slabs, covering 164 inches, would well go into that space. Possibly there were slabs with cattle, also before the figure of Merra, as the block with a bull led by two men (pl. viii.) was found near the door. Of the portals on each side many of the panels and drums were found lying fallen below. Of these panels we have five in relief and three incised (pls. viii., viii.B). There are also two pieces of panels with the family in relief, and a band of titles in relief (viii.B). The eight drums from the portals at the base of pl. viii.B are in the order in which they were set up; the first of the left-hand column being the southernmost, and the last of the right hand the northernmost. Besides these naming Merra a ruder inscription of a *semer ua* Hotepa (pl. xiii.) was found on another drum in the second portal south of the entrance. The cornice was marked on every piece as found lying at the foot of the east face, and the pieces are placed here in their order, beginning with the right-hand column at the right end of the front.

Inside the chamber the great stone portal was found standing in position. It is given in pl. viii.A; the work is evidently by the same hand as the panels, and it shows the style of great portals after the VIth Dynasty,—rather erratic in the order and position of the inscriptions, but still keeping up the old style very fairly. The family of Merra is shown by several pieces. His wife Seheta is shown in viii.; another wife of the same rank—also royal companion and priestess of Hathor—was named Beba, see viii.B. There were two sons, as we see on a fragment in viii.B; on the same is a daughter, Beba, and another daughter, Dudu·er·-dutsa, on viii. Also another lady, Theta, who was a royal companion, has a stele made for her by a high official, probably Merra (see base of viii.B). The breakages of the slabs, and the disappearance of others, are due to quarrying here in Roman times. But for the length of the inscriptions, the quantity of sculpture, and the interesting period to which this can be assigned, this is perhaps the finest tomb in the cemetery.

15. SEN·NEZ·SU. We find close to Merra, a little behind it, another tomb, which though smaller yielded much sculpture. It seems to be very shortly after Merra, as it is rather poorer in work, but of much the same style. It might even be contemporary, as Merra was *ha*

prince, which Sennezsu never claims to be. The plan of the mastaba is simple, with only four portals and one chamber, see xxxi. top. The large stone portal, larger than that of Merra, is shown on pl. ix. It is much worse in arrangement than Merra's, and of poorer work. Three blocks fairly complete were found, and fragments of several others; some from panels over portals, others from over the entrance, ix., x., x.A. Also some blocks with a long inscription of some interest, x. And several pieces of a cornice, like that of Merra, but rather coarser, were found in the corridor. From these we have the name of the wife Iu-uta (ix., x.); the sons Merra, Sebeknekhta, Sennezsua (ix.) and Khua (xiii.); and the daughters Hotepa and and Beba (x.). We notice here the beginning of the irregular, closely-packed inscriptions which characterise the next stage D.; see particularly the lower line of the long inscription on pl. x. Unfortunately the stone was poor, for though it kept its edges well, yet it so readily broke up into fragments that it was impossible even to lift it whole in many cases. Hence the shattered state of many of these pieces.

16. Beb. This great mastaba next to Merra is the latest of the princely tombs of Dendereh. It had unhappily been used for dwellings in Roman times at the southern end, and no trace of the stonework was left in either the corridor or the stele chamber. Were it not for the inscribed sarcophagus the name of the owner could not have been recovered. The plan (pl. xxxi.) proves clearly its late date. The level roofed tunnel shows that it is of the later period, that of Adu III. and Merra; and the suppression of the well after the tunnel places it at the opposite extreme from Adu I. and II., in which that well is the only one. The series of formation runs thus:—

Adu I.	Passage,	slope roof	tunnel,	large	well,	slope passage,	chamber.
Adu II.	„	steeper	„	„	„	doorway	„
Adu III.	„	level roof	„	„	„	level passage	„
Merra.	Well,	„	„	„	„	doorway	„
Beb.	„	„	„	no well		„	„

This differs from the other mastabas in being built almost entirely of black brick with hardly any gravel fillings. The joints which run through the building are marked by white lines in the plan and section. This mastaba had been largely attacked by dealers, who had cut it about and removed parts of the structure: they had reached the tunnel, but found it so full of rubbish that they did not try to open the chamber. Of the east face we need say nothing, as it is sufficiently clear from the plan. The southern—left hand—end was so destroyed in Roman times, and denuded since, that we did not trace it out, and it should be shown with broken outlines in the plan, and not as a straight edge; it really extended farther to the south.

The entrance in the north end was blocked with brick; the thick outer wall had been built first, with a steep batter on the inner face; then brickwork had been built inside it, apparently filling a small court like that of Merra. Later, the filling of the passage having been partly removed, the filling of the court overhangs the passage. From this court a doorway led into the only well, from which another door opened into the tunnel. The floor of this well and tunnel was not cleared, as all the stuff from the inside had to be carried up to the top of the well, so that every ton of rubbish was a serious matter. After two or three weeks of clearing we reached the chamber, and there found the inscribed sarcophagus. The most important part is shown in pl. xxxvii., and the rest of the minute inscription which covers it is in the additional plates, xxxvii.A to K. The chamber was so damp that the limestone had been largely dissolved all through the grain of it; hence it was in a putty-like state in which it could be moulded by the fingers, and it could not be lifted without the hands sinking into the stone. If dried quickly it would have split and crumbled hopelessly; so each block as it was brought up was at once covered with three or four inches of sand at the back of our huts, and left to dry slowly through that coating. After two or three weeks it was safe to uncover it: the evaporation through the sand having been slower than the spread of the moisture in the stone, it had thus kept equally moist throughout, and when bared again the surface was uninjured, though very porous and soft. My wife and I then spent much of our time for some weeks lying on the ground copying all the thousands of signs. They had been carelessly written in rather cursive hieroglyphs, and then entrusted to varying skill for the cutting. Some parts are fairly done, others are so rough as to be unintelligible. A raw hand seems to have been put on it, whose only idea was to destroy the ink writing by some shape of a hole, regardless of the intended sign. When this hash became too disastrous a better hand took it up, and we have again a legible inscription. Corrupt as the text is, and grossly as it has been engraved, it is yet a first-class monument, giving chapters of the Book of the Dead hitherto only known two thousand years later; also a description of sixteen roads of the soul, and a long list of titles of Hathor, the great goddess of the city. It is by far the most important monument found here, and was of course kept at the Cairo Museum.

17. The minor inscriptions belonging to this period C need little notice. The inscription of Merru and Qebdat from the north of Adu II., and that of Rehuia A., are given in the group at the base of pl. vii.A. The stone portal of Rehuia B. is probably of this age, on xi.c. And the panel of Merer at the base of xii. seems to be so much like a coarser version of Ptahmera that we ought perhaps to class it in C.

Of the plans of mastabas which seem to belong to this age there are, besides those already described, the following:—Pl. xxxii. The mastaba by Beba T.; the real tomb of Beba T., which belongs to the next period D, being the small mastaba with double portal built into the chamber of the older mastaba. The mastaba re-used in the XVIIIth Dynasty: this is complex in form, perhaps being two tombs conjoined: below it is a great rambling cavern formed by the falling in of sepulchral chambers; this is marked in dotted outline. The large mastaba re-used in the XXXth Dynasty: the entrance is by the pit with steps, which leads to the dotted outline cavern; in that were two stone sarcophagi, marked here in full outline, each containing a body with fine amulets of the Persian period, and another body with amulets lying bare on the top of each lid. The mastabas of Merra C. and Hotepa: that of Merra C. had a lintel of a Beba in the chamber, and the doorway to the chamber has been cut away and a very small later mastaba with portal built in the space. The colonnade court is built in front of a mastaba of good type, somewhat like the courts before some of the mastabas of Saqqara, such as that of Thy: nothing was found in it, and the back of the mastaba was wrecked for Ptolemaic cave tombs.

Pl. xxxiv. Of the C period we may class the following:—No. 780 is a great mastaba, which from its simplicity in front might perhaps belong to the B period of the VIth Dynasty or earlier: the tunnel slope has been cut with a stairway sunk between two ramps; on it were two badly painted Ptolemaic steles, and several bodies were in the chambers. No. 337, Sebekhotepa was named in the eastern chamber; the western mastaba had no name. Nos. 781, 782, 271 have no further details. No. 331

had a slab of which the name is lost, copied on the right side of pl. xiii. No. 329 belonged to a man Hotepa.

18. Class D. IXth–Xth (?) Dynasties. The characteristics of this age are the crowded state of the inscriptions, the sepulchral pit being turned with its length E.-W., and frequently a northern door to the chamber of offering, which is cut off entirely from the corridor and fender on the east face. There are no large and important tombs of this age, and the general poverty and ignorance is obvious. The following are the inscriptions that we may class together here:—Hotepa and Adua, xi.B; the lintel inscriptions of a Shensetha and Hotepa (xi.B); the part of a figure in the same group is much later, of the fine work of the XIth Dynasty: the lintel of Kathena in the group at the base of vii.A. The stele of an unknown man and his wife Beba, top of pl. xi., shows the beginning of placing a small figure of a servant offering a cup to the master, and the account of the cattle in the inscription. The finely cut slab of Nekhtu (base of xi.), with his wife Hapu, three sons all called Sebekhotep, one Antef and one Beba-ā, a daughter Ansa, and a servant Ada, has also a list of cattle and property: it is by far the best example of this period of work, and the first instance of the name Antef.

The mastabas that we may assign to this age are all small and with pit E.-W.; and often a mere pit E.-W. is used without any building over it, in which case the stele is put in the pit at the mouth of the chamber. Probably to this period may belong the tombs on pl. xxxii., Shensetha G., Merra D., Hornekhta, Nekhta (the outside of which is merely uncertain, and not recessed), Zauta E., Pekhy-beb (see the small altar on right hand, pl. xv.). On pl. xxxiv., No. 326 yielded three fragments, copied at the base of pl. xiii., Shensetha T., 335, Nefuu (see right side xiii.), Henny, Anhur-nekht, Shensetha H., and the mastaba by Bauhotepa, whose pit behind it is later. And on pl. xxxv. the mastabas of Hennua, Kathena, 775, 776, Zauta D., 777, 778, 779 and 313. These all have the pit E.-W., and therefore must come after class C; the difference in size between these and the smaller mastabas of pl. xxxiv. may well be one of class and not of period; and the larger mastabas link on so to the Antefa mastaba (xxxv.) of the next class that there is no need to assign them to an earlier date. The classification by the position of the well is more reliable than distinctions that may be merely those of wealth.

19. Class E. Early XIth (?) Dynasty. We here meet with widespread coarse inscriptions, and some larger mastabas. The most important tomb is that of Antef-a, pl. xii., pl. xxxv. This is on the old style of the VIth Dynasty, with a row of internal chambers like Adu I. (xxix.), the four-name mastaba (xxx.), and Shenseta P. (xxxii.). But it is separated from those by the pit being E.-W.; and the same long line of chambers is certainly also of the XIth Dynasty, as in the tomb of Mentuhotep (xxxiii.). The long line of false doors also agrees with that tomb, and with that of Antefaqer A. (xxxiii.). We must therefore conclude that the form of the earlier mastabas continued to be followed down to the revival in the XIth Dynasty. The style of the carving is very rude and degraded, but yet full of the ideas of the VIth Dynasty. Compare the collar and the striping of the waist-cloth (xii. 1) with that of Mena or Senna; see the work of the relief inscription (xii. 2-5), beside that of Merra (viii.) or Ptah-mera (x.A), especially in the elaboration of feathers and hair on the signs. The intermediate link is seen in the relief work of "*x*, wife of Beba" (xi.), where the long cattle inscription marks it as of class D, while the relief of the children is almost as coarse as that of Antef-a (xii. 5). The breadth of the door recess is 157 inches, or the half 78 inches; the length of the slabs running toward left hand on pl. xii. is 27 inches from the midline, 9 inches block at the end of the group, and 30 inches scene of children, or 66 inches + lost parts, agreeing well to the half width of 78 inches. The cornice is shown on pl. xi.C, with the cornice of Mera, which is probably of the same age. The whole of the mastaba is denuded down to about a foot high, and the blocks of carving have thus lain with hardly any sand over them; they are therefore extremely rotted, and flake up so much that many of them could not be lifted. Many rude pots were found in the chamber, of the form xvii. 128.

20. Having shown the best example of this class, we now turn to minor pieces which link together more closely to the previous class. At the end of class D we noted "*x* and wife Beba" (xi.); to this follows Beba G. (lower part of xi.B), which shows the beginning of the style of simple rude inscriptions; and like this is "*x* and Beba" top xi.C, and "Antef and Ay" (xi.C); while still later is Beba T. and son Sebeknekhta, at base of x.A, with name Mentuhotep on a piece of lintel at the right hand (and see base xv.); and following that Demza and Hepu (base xi.C, inscrip. see xv.). With these probably go "*x* with son Pepy" (base of xiii.), and Antefaqer (xi.C), compare the *amakh* sign with that of Beba T.; and the style of this tomb shows as rude a reminiscence as the tomb of Antefa does of the VIth Dynasty style. The mastaba plan, Antefaqer A., xxxiii., shows the early type with a long trench for a tunnel running down from the north. A burial of Ptolemaic age here was remarkable for having a dog in a small stone coffin at the north end of the main coffin. To early XIth Dynasty we may probably attribute, on pl. xxxiii., No. 772, E. of Beb; and very probably the smallest and most degenerate mastabas on xxxiv., Nos. 324, 326, 314, 353, 352.

21. Class F. XIth Dynasty. This differs from the previous work in the extreme rudeness and simplicity of it, and the absence of all mastabas, the burials being only in pits, with the stele laid at the door of the chamber in the pit. We see this style beginning in Beba T. (x.A) and Demza (xi.C). But a sort of elemental rudeness, without much link to the feeling of the Old Kingdom, as it were beginning again *de novo*, is seen in this work, as in Nemy (next to Beba and Hathotep, xi.), Nubheq (top xi.C), Sentekhneba (xi.C), Sentekha (base xi.B), the three slabs from Hotepa (xi.B), and Henna (xi.).

Observe how the sign of two hills (*du*) begins to draw in at the sides in Beba G. (xi.B), and Antef and Ay (xi.C) in class E; while in class F this sloping sided figure is the rule—see Sentekhneba, Sentekha, and Hotepa.

22. Class G. XIth Dynasty. Here a distinct revival is seen, the beginning of the fine work of the XIth and XIIth Dynasties. The style is laboured and detailed, the forms clumsy but carefully finished, the faces full and even puffy. The inscriptions still very short and simple, but more carefully done. The burial still in mere pit chambers without any mastaba. The intermediate example is that of Bauhotepa (xi.B), where the *du* sign is very sloping, and the row of sons is closely like that of Hotepa in the line above. Very similar is Beba and Hathotep (xi.); with which go also the outlined figure (base of xi.) and the nameless figure *x* (base xi.B). Following these comes Nefert-kau (xi.), in which the signs have begun to pass from the earlier and ruder stage toward that of the later XIth Dynasty.

23. Class H. End of XIth Dynasty. This is marked off by the really good work which was evolved from the previous class, and by the use of broad bands or double lines to divide the inscriptions. The earliest perhaps is Hennu and Bet (xi.), which is much like the earlier slab of Beba and Hathotep next over it, and in which the signs are similar to those of Nefer·kau close by it. This was found in the entrance to the Mentuhotep mastaba, probably connected with it. Of the same style is the inscription of Beba B. (vii.A). Also the

Antefaqer II. lintel, and the large stele of Antef and wife Anebu (xii.), link on to this style, but are more advanced. While in Khnumerdu (xv.) we see a fully developed manner like the great steles of the XIIth Dynasty. This large stele, five feet high, was however not placed in the offering chamber, like those of the VIth Dynasty, but lay in the trench well, at some distance from the chamber (see the piece of plan xxxiii.); thus showing its descent from the steles of classes F and G, which were buried in the pits of the tombs. All of these have the broad bands or double lines, as on the decree of Antef V. at Koptos.

Probably of the same age is the piece of Redukau (pl. x.), judging by the figure of the servant giving drink; and the drum with name Beba from the gallery of Antefaqer II. (xii.) must go along with these. The name of King Mentuhotep (xii.) on a rather rude fragment seems to belong to this rise of finer work; it was from a mastaba to the east of Merra (see map). And the brilliant carved fragments also with a cartouche of Mentuhotep (base, right, xii.), must be but very little removed from the fine low reliefs of Amenemhat I. at Koptos. In this tomb was the pair of seated figures of Mentuhotep and wife shown in pl. xxi., see section 30. The plan of this Mentuhotep tomb is given on pl. xxxiii., and it shows that the early style of mastaba lasted on to the close of the XIth Dynasty. Of the same age probably is the mastaba of Atsa, immediately joining this to the south, the plan of which is over it (773) on pl. xxxiii.

The gallery of Antefaqer II. is unique in this cemetery, probably imitated from the rock-cut tombs of Thebes (see base xxxiii.). There is a long court in front of it, gradually deepening its way into a rise of hard gravel. The southern side is thus high enough to give space for a colonnade of four pillars and two pilasters. By the recess at the west end of the colonnade was the slab of Antef and wife; by the next recess, in the south face, was the lintel of Antefaqer II.; and by the passage in the middle of the colonnade was the drum of Beba, all shown together in pl. xii. This passage led to a small chamber with a pillar on either hand, in the west side of which are three pits. Beyond that it continued, narrowed at doorway, turned to the east and sloped down into a chamber. The whole of this we cleared out, but did not find any objects left in the tombs. The only discovery here, beside the tablets named above, was that of the late bronze vessels, evidently stolen and hidden in the sand of the corridor, near the roof. These will be described further on.

Adjoining this colonnade on the east is a peculiar chamber (see map and pl. xxxiii.), which we named the Hotep altar, as it contained a mass of brickwork of the form of an altar, which almost filled it; in short, it is a large altar fenced around by walls close to it. As we could not find any tomb or tomb-pit in connection with it, it seems possible that it was intended for offerings to the family of the colonnade tomb, after the colonnade and court had been filled up for better protection.

24. We have now passed through all the stages between the fine severe work of the IIIrd Dynasty and the revival of a somewhat neat and cold style in the close of the XIth Dynasty; and we can for the first time trace a continuous chain of examples, each of which is linked to the rest, all through the dark ages. We have seen that there was continuous degradation from the VIth to the XIth Dynasty; and the first conscious change toward a revival was a deliberate simplicity in class F, belonging to the earlier half of the XIth Dynasty. It was therefore the foundation of fresh power and organization under the Antefs which gave the spirit of a true revival. We see it growing in class G, and full-grown in class H, leading readily into the very fine work of Amenemhat I. We learn thus that new power and prosperity

precedes new art, as it likewise did in the XVIIIth Dynasty, which opened on the almost unaltered style of the XIIth. That such a change should take place entirely within one short dynasty is in accord with the great difference in work between the coffins of the earlier and later Antefs.

Before leaving the early tombs we should name a peculiar burial. Some way to the west of the Antefa mastaba was a heap of flints piled loosely together, perhaps twenty feet across and five feet high. We cut through it, but found nothing down to the undisturbed soil. A cross cut showed nothing; but seeing a hollow just at one edge of our cutting I traced it, and found a long grave quite out of the centre. In it had been a coffin, with the body of a young woman full length, head west, face north, hands at sides. Outside the coffin, at the head, were two vases of XIIth Dynasty, one white, one red. On the feet was a small mirror (pl. xx.), under the chin a kohl-pot, on the left wrist a string of small garnet and silver beads, and a thread of silver beads linking on a small scarab in a silver mounting. A spiral of silver and two beads were at the left ear. The scarabs, and a little jasper shell, are shown in pl. xx. The interest of this grave is that it shows how burials are to be looked for under flint tumuli, and at what age such were made. The great flint tumuli at Naqada, which I fruitlessly cut through, may probably yet conceal some such burial, which could hardly be found without removing the whole mass.

CHAPTER III.

THE POTTERY.

25. The pottery found in the tombs is classified roughly in three heads: that of the Old Kingdom (pl. xvi.), that between the Old and Middle Kingdom (pl. xvii.), and that of the Middle Kingdom (pl. xviii.). In order to save references the whole is continuously numbered through from 1 to 195, at the top right of each figure. Where a name is well known for a tomb it is placed below the pot; otherwise the number of the tomb is placed below at the right hand, and sometimes references to several tombs.

The plates are arranged mainly by the forms within each plate. Since arranging the plates letters A to H of the successive classes of tombs have been assigned from the references that we have already discussed in the last chapter. Anyone wishing to study these plates in detail is recommended to add in red pencil the following class letters on the drawings. Class A, figures 1, 14, 15, 21, 26, 29. Class B, figures 2, 3, 4, 5, 6, 7, 8, 10, 18, 19, 20, 23, 24, 25, 27, 30, 31, 32 to 37. Class C, figures 28, 40, 41, 42, 43, 46, 51, 76, 77, 83, 84, 102, 114, 187. Class D, figures 97, 179, 187. Class E, figures 48, 49, 50, 83, 105, 119, 120 to 126, 128, 134, 166, 167, 170, 172. Class F, figures 45, 49, 50, 54, 71, 144. Class G, figures 61, 83, 84, 98. Class H, figures 85, 87, 97, 98, 189. The other drawings may be many of them safely classed by their connection with the above-named; but these are all assigned by the style of the sculpture or form of the tomb.

26. The pottery of the IVth Dynasty is of well-known types. The large ring-stand 1 is rare so early as that. The offering bowls of very coarse brown ware (14, 15) are very usual at Medum, early IVth, and last till Deshasheh, late Vth Dynasty. The jars 21, 26 are closely like the type Medum xxx. 11; and fig. 29 is as Medum xxxi. 27. This is satisfactory, as showing how the same types were made nearly two hundred miles apart at the same time. The un-Egyptian form in pl. xxi. 1 is already described in sect. 4.

Of the Vth Dynasty we have the same spread of types in fig. 25, which is identical with the Deshasheh type 15.

In the VIth Dynasty we see the development of the long rough offering jar. In the early IVth at Medum it is pointed or irregularly tubular (*Medum*, xxxi. 15, 19); in the Vth at Deshasheh it has a rounded brim (22); in the VIth at Dendereh the brim has grown into an upright lip, see (8).

The ring-stands are of trumpet-shaped curves here in the IVth (see 1); less curved in the Vth at Deshasheh (7); more tubular in the VIth here (37), and VIIth-VIIIth (46); and vary from the curved to the quite tubular in the early XIth (48, 49, 50, 121). The type 153 is quite undated by the tomb, and is perhaps of the Old Kingdom. Low flat ring-stands appear in the early XIth Dynasty (120, 125). The tall pierced stands seem to be quite a different class. At Medum they are in pottery (*Medum*, xxx. 21), imitated in stone (xxix. 7). Here they appear with holes around the base in the VIIth Dynasty (fig. 28), and more elaborate in an undated one (38). Another of about the same time has only four rough holes (51). These pottery stands seem to be copied from stands made of crossing reeds bound together, and plastered with mud, thus leaving the triangular holes which were here copied.

Of the bowls there is little to notice. The curves seem to be identical in the IVth Dynasty at Medum (*M.*, xxxi. 4), in the Vth at Deshasheh (*D.*, xxxiii. 1), and in the VIth here (4). The quality is also much alike, a rather soft brown pottery faced with red haematite. The more pointed bowls are likewise found at Medum (xxx. 4, 12), Deshasheh (xxxiii. 18), and here (3). The Zauta type (10) has also its precedent at Medum (xxx. 36).

The conical cups, such as 16 and 32, were found at Medum (xxxi. 28), but may be there of the same age as these. The large well-rounded jars, 18, 19, 20, seem to have begun in the VIth Dynasty, the only earlier one being clumsily made (*Deshasheh*, xxxiii. 20). This type with the wider curve upward gave way in the VIIth to the drop form, with wide curve down, as 40: and this passed on to the XIIth Dynasty in types 61 and 189. The large jars 180-183 and 194-5 are probably all of XIth-XIIth Dynasty. The drop form in smaller jars is also a change due to the VIIth Dynasty (42, 43, 44).

The upright vases with flat bottoms do not seem to be known in the IVth Dynasty; in the Vth are clumsy forms (*Deshasheh*, xxxiii. 12, 13); but in the VIth they are fully developed, as in 5, 7, 11, 22, and wider in 12, 13. They became very rude by the early XIth, as in 124.

The date of the rise of the whitey-drab pottery (marked W on pl. xviii.) and scrabbled lines often made with a comb, is here shown to be earlier than the XIIth Dynasty, with which they are generally associated. The whitey-drab appears in the classes C and D (187), or about the VIIth to Xth Dynasties; and the scrabble combing appears at E (134), or the earliest XIth Dynasty. And the entire absence of any names of the XIIth Dynasty in the cemetery shows that the considerable variety of these types of pottery on pl. xviii. must be attributed to the XIth Dynasty. The little badly-formed flaskets of drab pottery are here seen to belong to classes D (179) and E (166, 167, 170, 172), or the Xth and XIth Dynasties.

Of the XVIIIth Dynasty a small quantity of pottery was found in tombs which were re-used in that age; all of it was of familiar types, except the bowl shown in xxv. 1. This has a tall peg of pottery in the middle, with three oxen walking round it; and a similar peg of pottery on the edge, where also remain some other figures of oxen. The animals may be connected with the Hathor worship, and the style of the bowl reminds us of the vases of Tahutmes III. with oxen, from the foundation deposits of Koptos. Several marks were found, mostly on pottery of the XIth Dynasty, and cut in after baking as owner's marks. These are copied on pl. xx.A. Very similar cuts are made in the present day, as evidences of ownership, on the large water-jars of the fellahin.

CHAPTER IV.

FUNEREAL FURNITURE.

27. We have already noticed, in describing the tombs of Mena and Meru, the groups of copper models, of which the better is shown at the top of pl. xxii. This group was found scattered on the floor of the tomb. In the middle is a *hotep* altar, raised on legs connected by a cross rail, and four cups which were placed one in the other; above these are a model axe and adze, and a large curved blade which might be a full-sized razor. A similar blade, with elaborate open work of wire in it, was found the following year at Abadiyeh, also of the VIth Dynasty. The beads around the group are dark and light, and have been probably black and green, before rotting in the damp; the crossing ones between the threads are in the form of flies.

28. Of beads a great quantity was found, but the dating of them is difficult, as they were hardly ever associated with any inscriptions. Only five examples of beads dated by the other remains are before us. The beads of Meru are short plain tubes, originally black and green, between the flies in the photograph; these are VIth Dynasty. Of class D, about IXth-Xth Dynasty, is a string from tomb 316 of tubular and disc beads of dull blue-green glaze, the tubes are about ·6 inch long, ·15 diameter. Of class E is a string from the double mastaba, 778 (pl. xxxv.), of blue glazed globular beads, barrel-shaped of carnelian and amethyst, and a small snake head. Of class F are two beads from a pit in the same group with that of Nemy, one barrel-shaped blue-green glaze, the other a clear carnelian disc with rounded edge. Of class H are the beads from the Antefaqer gallery tomb, shown on pl. xxii.; a long string of clear carnelian barrel-shaped and disc beads. This is but little result from so many hundred tombs; but beads come commonly into use about the end of the XIth Dynasty, while stone sculpture is most usual in the VIIth-VIIIth Dynasties, and is scarce in proportion to the tombs in the XIth Dynasty.

Of the XIIth Dynasty but one tomb was found dated, of which the contents are at the base of pl. xx. There we find all that commonly belongs to the XIIth Dynasty: globular carnelian and amethyst, barrel amethyst, round garnet, barrel and long glazed, and blue glazed with black spiral. The absence of globular carnelian and amethyst, of garnet, and of spiral patterns on the beads that we date before the XIIth, and also generally in the mass of beads from the cemetery, strongly points to these having been introduced in the XIIth Dynasty.

29. Mirrors were not often found; all the examples are outlined on pl. xx. There are three of the VIth Dynasty, one of the XIth, and one of the XIIth. The only apparent difference is that the tang diminishes in the later times; the outline seems invariable.

The alabaster vases are not very common, all that were found being three outlined on pl. xx., the group found together of the VIth Dynasty, pl. xxi., and the group of the Antefaqer tomb, pl. xxii.

It will be seen that none of the forms of the VIth Dynasty, on pl. xxi., recur in the drawn forms pl. xxi., except the large alabaster, 524, which is known to belong to the VIth Dynasty. This shows that there is a great break between the stone vases of the VIth Dynasty and the majority here, which are of the XIth. The only vases from N.-S. pits, presumably before the VIIIth Dynasty, are those from tombs 524, 242, 274, and 32. Those from E.-W. pits, presumably after the IXth Dynasty, are Nos. 495, 473, 515, 508 and 480. Of the late XIth Dynasty are the three of Antefaqer, pl. xxii. And those which are probably of the XIIth Dynasty are Nos. 488, 431 and 700. We now have better material than ever before for dating the forms of the alabaster vases. But we shall not draw conclusions here, as a large number, and many dated examples, have been found at Hu, and will appear in the volume on Diospolis.

We may notice, however, that the thin slips of slate do not occur before Antefaqer at the end of the XIth Dynasty (xxii.), and the only other examples are along with blue marble kohl pots which seem to belong solely to the XIIth Dynasty. The only blue marble kohl pot which we can date here is in the solitary tomb with a XIIth Dynasty name, No. 700 (base of xx.). In that tomb also is the solitary example of a paint slab and rubber. It seems, therefore, that paint slabs, slate slips and blue marble may all be dated definitely to the XIIth Dynasty.

30. The rude trays of offerings of pottery, pl. xix., have not been precisely dated before. Most of these were found in indistinguishable pit tombs without any sculpture. Some few are, however, dated. The earliest is 15, of class D, or about the IXth-Xth Dynasty. The next is No. 3, that of Mera, which is of class E, or the earliest XIth Dynasty. The next is No. 13, which is of Hotepa, class F, or middle XIth Dynasty. It seems, therefore, that they began as simple tanks just before the XIth Dynasty, and the models of food were added later. The complex forms with shelters, staircases, and upper storeys, probably belong to the XIIth Dynasty. Unfortunately the most elaborate have lately been forged very successfully, so that no fine specimens can be trusted unless found on good authority.

31. Very few statuettes were found in the tombs. The seated figure of Adu II. (pl. vii.), and the two rotted wooden figures in a minor burial in front of Adu II., have already been noted. These were the only figures belonging to the Old Kingdom; and though we searched carefully for *serdab* chambers, such as those of the Saqqara mastabas, not a single instance could be found; nor in those tombs nearly denuded away were any chips of statues ever seen about the surface. The figure of Adu II. was in the filling of the main well, about half-way up. We were therefore forced to the conclusion that statuary was very rare in Upper Egypt, and the *serdab* system unknown, in the Old Kingdom; hence the army of *ka* statues found in the tombs of Saqqara and Deshasheh seem to be peculiar to Middle Egypt.

The best figures were those of Mentuhotep and Nefermesut, misnamed Mestu (pl. xxi., the painted side inscription pl. xv. base). The man's head is lost, but that of his wife is of excellent work; slightly more formal and liney than that of the Old Kingdom, but yet admirable in the power of expression. The surfaces are finely smoothed and coloured. It was found in the N.-E. corner of the inner chamber. From the very fine work of the sculpture of this tomb, with the name of King Mentuhotep (last group, pl. xii.), this belongs to the close of the XIth Dynasty.

Another figure is that of Atsa (pl. xxi.), found in the mastaba next south of Mentuhotep. This was in its original hiding, and shows that no *serdab* was built in the plan. It was placed in a niche in the N.-W. corner of the sepulchral chamber cut in the clay deposit, and plastered over, so that it was only suspected by accident. Three copper axes of the type on pl. xx. were in the chamber. This tomb, from its position, must also be about the end of the XIth Dynasty. Besides these statuettes were two figures, one a woman seated alone, the other a woman nursing a child. These are shown on pl. xxi. Two quaint figures of mourners were found in a tomb, one tearing the hair, the other weeping. They are made from jars turned on the wheel, and then pinched into features, and arms added (see the base of pl. xxi.).

CHAPTER V.

THE CATACOMBS OF SACRED ANIMALS.

32. Next in time, we come to the catacombs for the sacred animals, which were begun in the XVIIIth Dynasty, and were added to until Roman times. When we first settled at Dendereh I observed a great bank of coarse gravel close to our huts, rising some ten feet higher than the plain. We began by cutting trenches through this; but reached nothing, until, after passing the gravel bank, the men found the brick roofs of tunnels. Gradually we discovered and cleared these, in every tunnel moving out some yards length of rubbish at once, and so baring the floor in sections. Where there were burnt bones on the floor they were left to be cleared by my friends or myself, so that nothing should be overlooked. It was a considerable piece of work, the length of the passages being about 1900 feet, or over a third of a mile, and about 6000 or 7000 tons of stuff to be moved. It was thoroughly done, and the floors sounded all over for any buried deposits.

The oldest part appears to be a long row of chambers side by side, entered from a narrow passage running past the doors, marked XVIII. Dyn. on the plan, pl. xxxvi. These and all the other chambers were constructed by digging out a mass of gravel, building a brick vault in the hollow, and then replacing stuff over it: the great bank of gravel that we first found being the surplus due to the cavity of the chambers. In one of the chambers in the middle of the row there were some scraps of carved ivory under the burnt bones; among them two sistrum handles, on one of which could be read the inscription of a priestess of Hathor named Bukau (pl. xxiii.A). From the work this is probably of the XVIIIth Dynasty. More certain, however, were the pieces of blue glazed ware, shown on pl. xxiii. These were found broken up and cast aside, amid the burnt bones, and are clearly pieces of old temple furniture of Tahutmes III. and Amenhotep II., the same kings who made so much blue glazed furniture for Nubt, including the great *uas* sceptre. They were nearly all in the west end of the narrow passage, and a few in the west chambers. The great *ankh* (7) is exactly like those from Nubt. The pieces of wands (2, 3) show the bend as on the dancers' wands figured in *Deshasheh*, pl. xii. There were several pieces of bowls and vases, mostly defaced by the fire, but some showing patterns as in figs. 6, 14. The hollow balls painted in stripes, figs. 8, 9, are common in this period; there were fragments of dozens of such, and it seems that they were used in decoration, possibly representing pendant fruit like the violet glazed bunches of grapes for attaching to the rafters. The entirely novel objects are the papyrus stems fitting into cross bases, figs. 10, 11, 12. Some fragments of such may have been found before, but their nature and design has not been apparent. Their use in a temple is not obvious; but as the Hathor cow is often represented walking in the midst of marsh plants, it is possible that a grove of these papyri was placed beneath and around a statue of the sacred cow in the temple. The band of glazed ware (19) shows traces of hieroglyphs, although the whole surface is burnt. Lastly, the little figures of Taurt (15, 17), and Hathor (16), and the beads (18), are just what were common in the XIIth Dynasty, and lasted on in the early XVIIIth Dynasty, until the changes produced by the wars of Tahutmes III. The clearing of the temple of Deir el Bahri has taught us this continuance of style. All of this glazed ware has been badly burnt, so that not much of the blue survives; most of the surface is reduced to metallic copper by the action of the muffled fire. Some fragments of ivory were also found, of which the best is the king's head for inlaying, at base of pl. xxii.

What was the cause of this burning? At first we thought it might have been intentional, but there is no reason to suppose so. Rather, it seems, the chambers had been filled with animal mummies, wrapped in cloth with resins to preserve them; such mummies had been also stacked in the narrow passage until it was filled, and mingled with them were pieces of broken furniture from the temple. Then by some accident the mass caught fire; so fiercely did it burn, that the whole inside of the passage and chamber is vitrified, and the slag has run down the walls. This reduced the bulk to a layer of merely calcined bones and the indestructible glazed ware, a few inches deep on the floor. The tunnels were then clear, and in Roman times they were entered, and pieces of Roman pottery left behind. Also a large quantity of broken glass cylinders of that age were thrown away in the innermost end of the passage, marked on the plan: these will be described in the next chapter. Such seems to have been the history of the earliest catacombs here; and we cannot suppose such fragile glazed ware to have been in use for more than one or two generations, so that its ejection from the temple would be very likely under the new magnificence of Amenhotep III., which abounded in glazed ware. The use of these catacombs belongs then to the earlier half of the XVIIIth Dynasty. There is no evidence as to when the burning took place, except that it was before Roman times.

33. The extension of the catacombs by a new passage from N. to S. at right angles to the previous, seems to have been early; probably before the burial of these glazed objects. It will be seen that after the N.-S. passage was begun, and its chambers, an additional chamber has been added to the north of the old E.-W. passage. The old passage cannot then have been choked by burials; though perhaps the end of it already was, as the doorway is made as near the east as possible. So it appears as if by the time of Tahutmes III. the extension to the north was begun. There are no proofs of its age, except that the first half of it was finished, up to the first doorway, before the XXVIth Dynasty; as bronze situlae (xxiv. 10, 11, 12, 13) were found buried in a trench in the floor along the east side, as marked on the plan. Probably then these tunnels may be due to the XXIInd or XXIIIrd Dynasty.

Beyond that a change of direction took place, and six more chambers were added up to a new doorway, while yet further four more chambers were added to a final doorway at the north end. These may belong to the XXVIth-XXXth Dynasties. A slight cornice to a doorway here agrees well to this late date. The fire did not extend beyond the second or third chamber on the west side of the N.-S. passage, and did not touch the chambers of hawks on the east side. Many of the tunnels were empty of all remains. Some contained bird mummies, hawks, ibises, and various smaller birds. In the burnt mass were bones of gazelles, cats, ichneumons, birds, and snakes. But in no part of the whole catacombs were there any burials of kine; and it seems as if the sacred cows were always buried singly in the open cemetery, except where a great mass of bones occurred in the pit of the tomb of Abu-suten. The whole of the selected specimens of the animal mummies and bones have been handed to the Natural History Museum at South Kensington, where they are being elaborately studied in connection with Dr. Anderson's work on the Egyptian fauna.

34. The old catacombs having been carried on as far as the ground was suitable, a new block was laid out in later times, probably Ptolemaic. These were to the south of the old ones, with a passage entered by steps from the north. The axis of the passage was just in the line of the older passage. The space was all excavated deep enough to hold the chambers, and the surplus gravel was thrown out on the west. It will be seen that all the walls are double, and not only the passage walls as in the older catacombs. This means that every chamber was independently built, without any connection with the others; whereas in the older part only the passage was an independent tunnel, with doorways which opened through the chamber ends, and the chamber sides served to carry two arches each.

Very little was found in these late catacombs, most of which were filled with blown sand. The earliest group was that of "bronzes and hawks" in the first west chamber. Here many embalmed hawks were buried, some with gilt stucco heads, but all were destroyed by burning. Over one was a hollow bronze case (xxiv. 19); and with it were the bronze Horus (18), Ra seated (20), and Hawk (21). These belonged to the regular use of the catacombs, and from the bronzes we may fairly date these buildings to the Ptolemaic time. In the end of the same chamber was a jar of mosaic glass, which we shall notice in the next chapter.

At the end of the passage were a few pieces of Roman bronze work, including the pan top from a tripod table. The two long chambers to the east were full of dogs, some dried whole (see base, pl. xxv.), some loose bones. This abundant burial of dogs in Roman times may perhaps give the age of a burial of dogs' bones in the offering chamber of mastaba 779, shown at the base of pl. xxxv.

CHAPTER VI.

THE LATER BURIALS.

35. Very few tombs of any importance were found of later date than the XIth Dynasty, though the number of burials of the Ptolemaic and Roman ages is prodigious. In a pit in the small mastaba of Adu IV. (pl. xxxv.) was a burial of a singer of the temple of Hathor, named Mutardus, daughter of Nes·hor·akhti·mer and Ruru, whose tablet (pl. xxv.) was made by her daughter Res·ankh·rent·es. She is shown holding the sistrum and adoring Horakhti; a proof that Horus was worshipped here in connection with Isis by the time of the XXVth Dynasty.

Two other steles were found of rather later date, see pl. xxv. One is of Horsiast adoring Osiris, Isis and Horus; the other of Pedu·hor·-sam·taui adoring Atmu (?), Osiris, Horus and Ptah.

The next burials of importance were in a re-used mastaba (pl. xxxii.). The stairway of large steps ended at a blank face of gravel, and a narrow doorway opened on the east into a chamber. In this lay two limestone sarcophagi intact. On each of the bodies was a fine set of amulets, the scarab with wings and four genii, elaborately worked in blue paste. Upon the flat top of each sarcophagus was another body with amulets, but not so fine as those in the inside. The period is probably the XXXth Dynasty. Of about the same time is a rudely-cut sarcophagus in sandstone, with inscriptions along one side (pl. xxiii.A), which we sawed away. They refer to Nesi-Hor going in Duat under the protection of Shu and Tefnut, Anpu, Isis, Horus, Selk, and minor deities.

36. The great mass of Ptolemaic tombs were to the east, north and west of the catacombs. They were scattered without any system, as closely as might be, often breaking through below, over ground which had already been occupied with some long pit tombs of the early ages.

The entrance to each tomb is by a very narrow and steep stairway, descending about five feet, just large enough to squeeze into. Coarse pottery of offerings is found in these stair pits. In the east and west groups large peg-bottomed amphorae, one or more, are found in the pits, showing that this system came down to Roman times. At the bottom of the pit a little doorway in the end leads into a small square chamber, only about four feet high, the floor of which is below the door-sill, the roof level with the door lintel. This doorway was occasionally blocked by a stone slab, but usually built up with brick.

The chamber inside was about five or six feet square and about four feet high. Opposite the door, and usually also on each side, the upper half of the wall was cut into a recess, about five or six feet front to back. And on these platforms the mummies were stacked together, close side by side, with their heads at the edge along the chamber side. Thus each chamber contained a large number of bodies, sometimes only one or two, usually about a dozen, or even as many as thirty, laid one on the other. Sandstone steles (pl. xxv.A) were placed in the tomb; when in position they stood against the chamber wall beneath the mummy recess, just below the head of the mummy to which each belonged.

The mummies when best prepared were in wrappings of coarse cloth, thickly swathed around into large unwieldy masses. On the heads were masks of painted or gilt stucco, and cartonnage pectorals and foot cases on the body. Or sometimes a continuous cartonnage or painted cloth covered the whole. On the outside of the wrappings were attached the amulets of blue glazed pottery (pl. xxvi.) or of stamped wax, in a more or less regular distribution: even when they had not been disturbed or fallen out of place they did not seem to have been accurately placed. The bodies with large numbers of amulets had also name labels of limestone (pl. xxvi.A, B), usually written on with ink, tied on to the throat; the labels when of wood had nearly all perished. Some of the richer class had shrouds of bead-work in patterns, showing the scarab and wings, the four genii, &c. These were but coarsely done and of poor colours. Such examples as were in good condition Mr. Davies preserved by covering the outside with a coat of melted bees-wax, as I had done long ago at Illahun.

The poorer mummies were swathed and coated with bitumen; the head had been removed, and was reattached by a palm stick through the spine. Sometimes eyes of glass or coloured paste were set on.

37. The amulets (pl. xxvi.) are mostly made of a coarse blue glazed ware, moulded, and sometimes painted with detail in black. As this is the most complete series known of this age all the varieties are here published in photograph. They may be classified as follows:—

Osiris standing, mummified.
Isis winged, standing.
Nebhat, „ „
Isis „ kneeling.
Nebhat „ „
Isis seated.
Osiris, Isis and Nebhat seated, triad plaque
Min.
Bes.
Taurt.
The four genii, each separately.
„ „ „ together, one plaque.
Anubis and Ptah, plaque.
Anubis laying out deceased on bier.

Deceased on bier.
Uza eye.
Uza eye, winged, on legs.
Heart.
Breast.
Two fingers.
Ba bird.
Kneeling man holding palm branches.

Ape.
Lion, human-headed, walking.
Lion couchant.
Cat.
Bull couchant.
Sheep.
Ram's head.
Jackal seated.
Jackal on tomb, two forms.
Ichneumon.

Vulture.
Hawk crowned.
„ sideways.
„ facing.
„ *akhom.*
„ „ with sistrum.
„ „ with hawk on stand.
Ibis.

Uraeus.
Uraeus with folded body.
Uraei and sun.
Scarab.
Scarab with wings, straight.
„ „ „ curved.

Uaz, papyrus plant.
Reed, *a*.
Frame of garlands for the breast.

Deep collar, hawk's head ends.
Pectoral, Osiris and hawk.
Star.
Carpenter's square.
" plummet stand.
" stand with plummet.
Head-rest.
Double seal.
Ankh.
Girdle tie.
Dad.
Dad crowned.

This gives sixty-five varieties, beside two or three small forms which are so rough as to be unintelligible.

38. The position of these amulets is variable, and they seem to have been put on with only a rough regard to symmetry. Some, however, are tolerably constant in position. The mourning Isis and Nebhat are on the shoulders; below them the four genii, two on either side. An *uza* eye is also on each shoulder. The jackal is generally on the hips; the hawk on the shoulders or hips. The winged scarab is usually on the breast-bone. The star is twice on the neck, once on the navel. The *dad* is usually on the navel. Of course these amulets are by no means always present in a group, but these are the general positions when they do occur. The whole question of the position of amulets needs to be studied together; but, unhappily, there is scarcely any information on it except what I have observed at Nebesheh and Hawara. Broadly, the positions mostly remain the same in each of these groups. The carpenter's square and plummet, for instance, occur each but once at Dendereh, but in the same position—on the left breast—in which they are found at both Nebesheh and Hawara. The *dad* is almost always on the stomach at each place. It is much to be wished that of the thousands of these small amulets discovered by plunderers a few hundreds might be reserved for careful and exact record.

An interesting formula occurs on the cartonnage of two bodies (base pl. xv.), which seems to be new to us. It runs, "A royal offering, and bread, for the Osirian Pahequ, son of Pashemhor; he went to Osiris at the 19th year," or similarly for Pashemhor, son of Pedu·hor·sam·taui, "he went to Osiris at the 44th year." This phrase of going to Osiris seems as if it might have passed into early Christian phraseology.

Of the sandstone steles (pl. XXV.A) and the labels (pls. XXVI.A, B) the inscriptions are all that need notice, and these are dealt with by Mr. Griffith in his chapter.

A few late tombstones are given at the end of pl. XXV. The upper one seems to have a line of some unknown writing sideways on it, possibly in some Syrian alphabet. Below is a stone of one Titianos, and an inscription partly Coptic.

A few miles back in the desert we noticed a great number of stone heaps. These proved to cover shallow late Roman burials without any objects.

CHAPTER VII.

BRONZES, GLASS, &c.

39. Two groups of bronzes were discovered, apparently of the same date, and therefore perhaps hidden for the same cause. As the date of manufacture comes down to the XIXth Dynasty, they may have been rightfully hidden in the troubles of the end of the XIXth or of those of the XXIst Dynasty. But as the hiding places were rather far from the temples, to one of which these doubtless belonged, it seems more likely that they are the proceeds of a robbery.

The first group found was in the chamber of a small mastaba, No. 340, in the S.-E. corner of the cemetery (see map, pl. xxvii.); it consisted of ten objects (see pl. xxiv.), as follow :—

Fig. 1. Cooking pot with swing handle, blackened outside.
2. Long-necked vase, fluted body.
3. Jug with fluted body.
5. Large pan with two handles.
7. Bowl with loop handle.
8. Dish.
10. Libation situla, dedicated to the ram of Amen.
15. Adze.
16, 17. Axes.

The second group was in the sand filling of the colonnade in front of the gallery tomb of Antefaqer (pl. xxxiii.); it consisted of three objects (pl. xxiv.), as follow :—

4. Libation vase.
6. Similar, with dedication by Ramessu II.
9. Incense burner.

The main interest of these is in the fluted vases (2, 3), which have not been found before, although they are well known on the monuments of the XVIIIth Dynasty. No. 2 has a chased garland round the neck, of the style of Amenhotep III. and onward. No. 3 has a handle soldered on at the top, but never attached below. The soldering in these is autogenous soldering, or melting on some of the same metal; it is well seen in the bottom of the dish, fig. 8, which has broken through and been mended. The inscription on fig. 6 is the two cartouches and titles of Ramessu II. "beloved of Amen-Ra, lord of the thrones of both lands, lord of heaven." That on fig. 10 shows the head of the ram, with a table of offerings before it and a line of dedication, rather difficult to read; as it was unexpectedly kept at the Cairo Museum, I am sorry not to be able to give a copy.

40. Other bronzes found are the situlae, figs. 11 to 14, found with two little worn alabastra in a trench in the floor of the animal catacombs. The large one with figures has two lines of inscription, hard to read, as such things usually are (see top pl. xxiii.A); it is the dedication "To Amen-Ra, lord of the thrones of both lands, (may he) give life, strength, health, uplifting, and a good old age to Therkes, (his) mother, the lady of the house, Hathor." The age of these is probably the XXIIIrd-XXVth Dynasty. Therkes is a foreign name, possibly of a Karian soldier, Tharkos, or some such name.

The group of Roman bronzes from the catacombs has been described in section 33.

Of these bronzes much more than half the value was kept in Cairo: the vase No. 2, large dish 5, inscribed libation vase 6, incense burner 9, inscribed situla 10, and adze 15.

41. Two discoveries of glass, apparently of Roman age, were made in the animal catacombs.

In the first were the pieces of about forty cylinders of glass, each about one inch across and an inch and a half long, with square holes through the axis. Their colours were brilliant, imitating lazuli, jasper, and turquoise. They had probably been broken in order to remove them from the square metal rods on which they had been fixed, perhaps for the stems of candelabra.

The history of their destruction had been that they were scrupulously preserved even when broken from the rod; most minute chips were kept together; then a cloth containing the fragments was shaken out in the farthest end of the narrow passage of the catacombs (marked glass cylinders, pl. xxxvi.). That they were not broken up there is shown by the small chips lying mostly close together, as if shaken from a cloth; if broken in the passage the chips would have flown wide.

42. The other discovery, similar in its nature, was a jar of about the age of Constantine, standing in a corner of the later catacomb, marked "Mosaic glass" in pl. xxxvi. This was filled with pieces of glass inlay and mosaic, mostly squares of about an inch and a half. All had been set on a backing, and many had certainly been retained by metal strips which had been soldered on a metal back plate. It seems probable, from the similarity of the patterns to those of the Ptolemaic cartonnages representing deep collars, that all of these had been part of a great collar adorning the statue of Isis, or from a sacred bark. The pieces had been stripped away evidently in order to re-use the metal backing, as many of the soldered metal strips were cast aside with the glass. This is just like the breaking up of the cylinders, in order to remove the metal rods. This heartless utilitarian smashing of disused material is in curious contrast to the careful hiding away of the waste stuff as sacred property in the catacombs. That dedicated property should be so much respected as late as Constantine, and trouble taken to bury it reverently, is not what might have been expected.

As this glass has been divided between different museums (half to Cairo, the rest to the British Museum, Boston, Philadelphia and Chicago), it may be well to give a catalogue of it here.

Inlaid glass, with a setting of bronze strip around each piece of inlay.

- Blue square; rosette in it white on yellow 4, on red 3; red on white 2, on yellow 3; yellow on white 2, on red 2, on green 2.
- White square; rosette red on blue 6; blue on red 5; yellow on blue 3, on red 2; blue on yellow 2.
- Yellow square; blue on red 3, on white 2; green on blue 1; white on blue 1.
- Green square; red on white 2.
- Red square; blue on yellow 6; white on blue 2; yellow on blue 1.
- Blue octagon; rosette in it white on yellow 6, on red 2; yellow on red 2, on green 1; green on red 1.
- White octagon; blue on red 2; yellow on blue 3, on green 1; blue on yellow 6.
- Green octagon; yellow on blue 1, on white 2; white on yellow 2, on red 3.
- Red octagon; yellow on blue 1, on green 1; white on yellow 2.

Squares with raised boss in centre: blue on white 3; red on blue 1; green on red 1.

Discs in octagons; green in red 1; red in green 1; white in blue 1; blue in white 2.

Striped squares, red, white, and blue stripes, 16.

Fused glass mosaics:

- *Uza* eye; on red ground 2.
- Ankh; in green 2, in blue 2.
- Flowers; yellow on white 1, white on blue 1.
- Lotus flower; red, blue centre 8; white, red and blue centre 8; red calyx, striped 5; orange calyx, striped 3.
- Papyrus; orange calyx 3; white calyx 5.

Triangles; for zig-zag pattern borders; red 34, white 63, green-blue 51, dark blue 9.

Drop pendants; green-blue 9; dark blue 16; red 7. White settings for these 29.

Besides these there was a great quantity of plain strips for borders. The whole covered about six or eight square feet, and so must have come from a large object. There were 158 patterned pieces (or parts of such), and 218 plain pieces, beside strips. With these were some scraps of inlay of wings of fused mosaic; and similar pieces from hawk figures, and two glass heads of hawks, were found in a small jar also hidden in the catacombs. We have not attempted to illustrate these, as to do so suitably would need costly coloured plates.

43. Three finds of coins were made. One lot of 242 tinned bronze *folles* of the Diocletian age was buried in rouleaux between the bricks of the floor of a Roman house at the back of the temple. The numbers of each emperor were—

		Mint Marks.
Diocletianus,	14	ALE·ANT·AQS·B·NTE·RP·SIS·SP
Licinius,	11	ALE·ANT·MKV
Valeria,	11	ALE·ANT·RP
Maximin, Caes.,	38	ALE·MKV·NTA, B, Δ·SMNB·
" Imp.,	72	ALE·MKV·MKVA·NTB·SMNA
Maximian, Caes.,	11	ALE·KB·N·NT·PT·ST·TR·TS·
" Imp.,	71	ALE·ANT·AQS·AS·KΔ·MKV·NKV·PT·SIS·SMKA·SMNΔ·SMTS·T·TT·
Constantius, Caes.,	6	ALE·KB·ST·T·TR·
" Imp.,	1	SISA
Constantinus, Aug.,	7	ALE·

The proportion of the various places of mintage is Alexandria 171, Kyzicus (and Karthage?) 17, Antioch 15, Thessalonika 13, Nicomedia 9, Rome 5, Treves 5, Siscia 4, Aquileia 3.

Two other lots of later coins were found in small jars. They were all washed and classified as far as could be while I was at Dendereh. There were of—

Carthage	1	..
Constantine I., deified	1	8
Constantine II.	..	4
Constans	1	27
Constantius II.	4	71
Constantine family (illegible)	3	71
Helena	..	1
Magnus Maximus	..	1
Julian	2	25
Jovian	1	1
Valentinian I.	28 (with Valens)	102
Valens		119
Gratian	1	20
Valentinian II.	25	152
Theodosius I.	24	257
Flaccilla	1	5
Honorius	7	19
Arcadius	28	217
Theodosius II.	9	..
Valentinian III.	1	..
Legible	137	1100
Barbaric	62	..
Illegible	172	978
Total	371	2078

44. These samples of coinage may be assumed to be a tolerable average of what was in circulation when they were buried. They suggest some interesting inquiries, to which we may give some answers, taking them in connection with four other deposits of the fifth century A.D. found at Hawara, and published in "Hawara," p. 13.

The proportion of coins of any past reign is the resultant of two variable quantities, the rate of coinage in that reign, and the waste of the coinage ever since it was struck. Now that waste will probably go on at about the same rate under similar conditions of civilization, and may be assumed to be at an average during the century or so which we have to deal with. That the waste was considerable is clear from the almost entire disappearance of the copious coinage of the Constantine family within a century and a half.

To treat the statistics that we have of finds of coins they must be placed on a uniform basis. This is best done by reducing or increasing the numbers of each reign so as to produce for each find a total of 1000 for the period that we are dealing with; thus all the finds are comparable together.

The next step is to divide the amount of the coinage of each reign by the number of years of the reign, so that we have long and short reigns on an equality, and the numbers show the amount surviving of each year's coinage.

The third step is to estimate the year of burial. This may be reached fairly by assuming that the last reign which is represented coined at the same rate as the previous reign; thus if Leo coined at the rate of 20 per annum, and there are 40 of Zeno, probably the burial was after two years of Zeno.

The fourth step is then to place the years elapsed from coinage to burial against the number surviving of each year's coinage.

As an illustration we may take the working out of the first find just catalogued above. As we touch the reign of Valentinian III. we cannot put the burial before 426 A.D., though the scanty coinage of Theodosius II. would lead us to a rather earlier date.

	A.D.	Actual Numbers.	Per 1000.	Per Year.	Years before Burial.
Constantine family	337—351	9	66	4·7	82
Julian	360—363	2	15	5·0	64
Jovian, 7 mos.	363—364	1	7	12·0	62
Valentinian I. and Valens	364—376	28	206	17·2	56
Gratian	376—381	1	7	1·4	47
Valentinian II.	383—392	25	184	20·5	38
Theodosius I.	379—395	25	184	11·5	39
Honorius	395—423	7	52	1·8	17
Arcadius	395—408	28	206	15·9	25
Theodosius II.	408—450	9	66	3·7	9
Valentinian III.	425—455	1	7	7·0	1
		136	1000		

It need hardly be remarked that separate emperors of East and West must have the rates per year added together for the rate of coinage of the whole empire, to be comparable with the coinage of sole emperors. Thus Honorius and Arcadius are together 17·7 per annum. As many coins of Arcadius went west as those of Honorius came eastward, in all probability.

The fifth step is to combine these results from different finds so as to discover the rate of waste. If, for instance, we have of Valentinian II. 20 coins *per annum* of the reign surviving after 38 years, as above, and in another find 5 coins *per annum* surviving after 92 years, we have definite information as to the waste of coinage.

From comparing the rate of waste in the six finds above named, there appears to be a loss of a tenth of the coinage in every five years. The rate from different instances varies somewhat, a tenth being lost in 2·9, 4·6, 4·9, 5·3, 5·7 and 10·0 years. Taking a loss of a tenth in each five years, it implies that 1 in 48 coins was lost every year. If we suppose four dozen of these little *minimi* to have been usually carried about in the pocket of each man, and that he lost one a year, it will certainly seem but a moderate allowance for accident and carelessness. It will be convenient for reference to state what the scale of waste is at the rate of a tenth in five years; the waste of any quantity in any number of years can readily be taken from this table. Of 100 coins struck there will be left at the end of—

Years.	Coins.	Years.	Coins.	Years.	Coins.
1	97·9	17	69·9	33	49·9
2	95·8	18	68·4	34	48·8
3	93·9	19	67·0	35	47·8
4	91·9	20	65·6	36	46·8
5	90·0	21	64·2	37	45·8
6	88·1	22	62·9	38	44·9
7	86·3	23	61·6	39	44·0
8	84·5	24	60·3	40	43·0
9	82·7	25	59·1	41	42·1
10	81·0	26	57·8	42	41·3
11	79·3	27	56·6	43	40·4
12	77·7	28	55·4	44	39·6
13	76·0	29	54·3	45	38·7
14	74·5	30	53·1	46	37·9
15	72·9	31	52·0	47	37·1
16	71·4	32	50·9	48	36·4

Years.	Coins.	Years.	Coins.	Years.	Coins.
49	35·6	84	17·0	118	8·3
50	34·9	86	16·3	120	8·0
52	33·4	88	15·7	122	7·6
54	32·1	90	15·0	124	7·3
56	30·7	92	14·4	126	7·0
58	29·5	94	13·8	128	6·7
60	28·2	96	13·2	130	6·5
62	27·1	98	12·7	132	6·2
64	26·0	100	12·2	134	5·9
66	24·9	102	11·7	136	5·7
68	23·9	104	11·2	138	5·5
70	22·9	106	10·7	140	5·2
72	21·9	108	10·3	142	5·0
74	21·0	110	9·8	144	4·8
76	20·2	112	9·4	146	4·6
78	19·3	114	9·0	148	4·4
80	18·5	116	8·7	150	4·2
82	17·8				

Beyond this limit there begins to enter another consideration, of stray coins being rediscovered and reused. For all practical purposes such a table suffices. To show the use of it we may say that in a find of coins (proportioned throughout to a total of 1000, so as to be comparable with other finds), if there be 5 per annum of a reign whose middle was 33 years before, that will mean that there were 10 per annum struck for every 1000 coins then in use, inasmuch as 50 coins is the residue surviving of 100 after 33 years. Or, instead of proportioning, we can use any part of the table; as for instance in this case, we can look for 5 coins in the table, which is at 142 years, and then at 33 years before that (i.e. at 109 years) we find 10 coins. Thus for the given rate of waste which seems to hold good among *minimi* in the Vth century A.D.—namely a tenth every five years—this table shows what the waste of any number is in any number of years up to 150.

Now from this it is clear that, given the number of coins of any reign *per annum* of the reign, and the years elapsed, we can say pretty certainly how many they were at any earlier time, and therefore at the time when they were struck. Thus we can say what addition to the currency each emperor made per year of his reign. From the material we have named already we can thus deduce that for a thousand coins in circulation at the time of the following reigns—

	Coined Yearly.
Constantine family	31
Julian	19
Jovian	47
Valentinian I. / Valens	47
Gratian	5
Valentinian II. / Theodosius I.	58
Honorius / Arcadius	33
Theodosius II.	10
Marcian	59
Leo I.	21
Zeno	over 7

Thus it is possible to work out the actual rate of coinage during each reign; and though these numbers may easily vary a little owing to the accidents of the deposits, yet they show very clearly how the activity of the mint was started afresh by Jovian, Theodosius, and Marcian, and ran gradually downhill after each fresh start. These results only apply of course to part of the Eastern Empire; in the west the proportions of the coins of eastern and western emperors is naturally different.

We have here a new source of interest in the exact records of finds of coins, and a fresh light on the economic study of the empire.

CHAPTER VIII.

THE INSCRIPTIONS.

By F. Ll. Griffith, M.A., F.S.A.

45. The inscriptions from the cemetery of Dendereh fall into two distinct groups of quite different dates—the great collection of mastaba inscriptions from the VIth Dynasty to the XIth (pls. i.-xv.), and the inscriptions of the Ptolemaic and Roman period (pls. xxiii.-xxvi.B); it is a singular fact that hardly any are to be placed outside these groups. The first group represents a fine amount of material, most of which has come down to us in an extremely fragmentary state. Professor Petrie and his assistants gathered up every fragment of inscribed stone they could find. From many tombs only a few chips were recovered, yet sometimes even these have preserved names of the owner or of some of his family. After careful examination of all the fragments some had to be set aside as useless; but all that is of interest is shown in the plates. Though names and titles and funerary formulae constitute the bulk, the stela of Chnemerdu, scraps of biographical inscriptions and cartouches of Mentuhetep show that historical matter of importance was not wanting among the monuments of the cemetery. If these had come down to us intact, undoubtedly they would have thrown a comparatively clear light on the dark period between the Old and Middle Kingdoms. Even as it is a long and interesting series of documents is now added to the scanty collections of material for this time; and the strange absence of monuments of any other Pharaonic period itself raises questions of great importance.

In this chapter on the inscriptions the aim in view is not so much to bring out their historical value as to translate examples of them literally or give summaries of their meaning. Before dealing with the contents of the plates in detail, it will be well to explain, as far as may be, the funerary formulae which so constantly recur in Egyptian tombs.

46. Though this is not the place to enter into a discussion of the ideas of the Egyptians as to the future of their dead, a very brief statement may be permitted of what seem to have been the main considerations kept in view by the priests with regard to burial.

Obviously there was in the first place the corpse itself to be considered. This the Egyptians called *chat*. In course of time they contrived to preserve it in a very complete state, deranging only the internal organs and the brain, and embalming some portions separately. But in earlier days the best mode of treatment they could devise was either to let the flesh decay naturally in the ground, or else to quicken the operation, and bury only the well-cleaned framework of bones upon which the body had been built, and on which it might again be reconstituted by the help of spells. For this remnant of the material body an outfit of clothing, unguents, &c., was provided, such as had been needed in the life-time. This equipment may be called the permanent outfit, and the burial with its accompaniments of coffin and permanent outfit was termed by the

Egyptians *qrest*, a word which may possibly in origin mean something like "the treatment of the skeleton," as W. Max Müller has pointed out.

Secondly, there was the immaterial life, consisting of sundry activities, perhaps in early times designated as the *kas*, the "workers," which set the body in motion, the chief of these being the true *ka*, or life and "energy," and the *ba*, or "soul" and will. The life was of far greater importance than the corpse, which was only as it were a habitation occasionally required for the life, and which might be replaced by a statue or other counterfeit representations. Without the life the body lay inert; nevertheless the life apart from the body required daily nourishment, and could enjoy the luxuries of existence. No doubt the Egyptians reasoned that the "life" was not material, and therefore its feeding would not be material: the *ka* of the man would feed on the provisions or their counterfeit presentiments, and yet not consume them. The bringing of offerings on feast days was duly arranged for, but the matter was also placed beyond the reach of human shortcomings by the dogma that the gods themselves provided supplies. The ever recurring expression *pert-kheru* is probably to be translated "coming forth of a voice" or "summons," denoting the divine call to the dead to partake of sacrifices; the offerings themselves also were often called *pert-kheru*. The Egyptians were not, perhaps, ever persuaded of the truth of any one set of doctrines, and they were willing to take any measures that might help to attain a success which must have seemed at times somewhat problematic. Later their beliefs and practices became exceedingly complex and contradictory. We seem to discern that in the early days their views were simpler, but evidently they thought their preparations for launching the dead into futurity of little avail if spells were not pronounced, of which the gist is the assumption that all *is* right. State a thing to be—in proper form—and by the supernatural force of the statement it actually *is*. Such appears to be a leading principle of magic in all countries.

47. In the Old Kingdom the normal type of the common magic formula to be pronounced for the dead is: "Favour accorded by the king and Anubis, a good *qrest* (or burial equipment) and long endurance to (name and titles)," or "Favour accorded by the king and Anubis, the coming forth of a summons, bread and beer, oxen and fowl, &c., to (name and titles)." The formula reads like a joint decree of the king of Egypt and the god of burial. That the god of burial should be invoked was natural; it was also fitting to invoke the favour of the king in whose dominion the deceased had lived his life, and in which lay both his tomb and the property which endowed it. In some extremely early cases (*Mastabas*, 74-7 (?), and *Medum*, pl. xiii.) the decree is in the sole name of Anubis; sometimes in the IVth Dynasty it is in that of the king alone; but generally it is their joint decree, the king always taking the precedence, and the formula was actually entitled by the Egyptians, "Favour accorded by the king." Perhaps he was looked upon as the donor or sanctioner of the material offerings which the god enabled the dead to profit by, or, as Prof. Petrie thinks, the king himself as high priest was supposed to make the offering for the deceased (Mar., *Abydos*, ii., pl. 48). It is hardly necessary to say that the king is designated merely by his official title, and is never any specific Pharaoh. At a somewhat later date another decree, parallel to and following the one in the names of the king and Anubis, was inscribed in the names of the king and of Osiris, king of the dead, into whose realm the deceased passed. Subsequently we find invoked Geb, the god of the earth, in whose bosom the tomb was excavated; then—as presiding over the locality in which the man had lived, died and was buried—the local god of the nome,

Eventually the gods decreeing favour to the dead became very numerous, and were often summed up as "all the gods." In the XIIth Dynasty the formula on the tomb-stones changed considerably. Its type then is, "Favour accorded by the king and Osiris, &c.; may he (Osiris) give *pert-kheru* to the *ka* of N."; but of this the mastaba inscriptions from Dendereh, which are all of the Old Kingdom form, furnish no examples, though it is not without a parallel in the Pyramid texts of the VIth Dynasty.

48. Pl. I. This plate must be studied in connection with the other inscriptions from the tomb of Mena reproduced on pls. ii., iii. The earliest inscription, however, in the whole series from Dendereh, is shown on pl. ii., and is that of Seten-n-abu. As is clear from the later spelling of the name on pls. viii. and xi.A, Seten-n-abu, not Abu-seten, is the correct reading. As meaning "king of hearts," this name may be compared with the common *Khenti-kau*, "first of *kas*." Seten-n-abu was *rekh seten, hen neter Hether*, "royal acquaintance and priest of Hathor"; any other titles he may have held are lost, but no doubt he was the chief man of his day at Dendereh.

We now reach one of the most important series of inscriptions, those from the tomb of Mena, who lived in the reign of Pepy II. of the VIth Dynasty, and probably also under the preceding kings, Pepy I. and Merenra: he was certainly sheikh of the pyramid cities of all three kings. From one of the slabs (pl. ii.) we see that he was also called Men-ankh Pepy, a name compounded with that of the pyramid of Pepy II., and probably received in old age: for a similar compound compare the name Mennefer Pepy on pls. vii., xiii. Mena is one of the very few Egyptians known named after Menes, the founder of the first historical dynasty of Egypt. The occurrence of this name at Dendereh is not without weight in connection with the theory that the king whose tomb was lately found at Naqada is Menes himself. As at Kahun, not far from the two pyramids of Senefru, the name Senefru was common during the XIIth Dynasty, so it may well have been that the name Mena was used during the VIth Dynasty at Dendereh, owing to the proximity of Menes' tomb. Naqada is but twenty miles south in the adjoining nome; Abydos, the supposed capital of the first two dynasties, is fifty miles west, and separated from Dendereh by the VIIth nome of Upper Egypt. More examples of the name should be looked for north and south of Naqada, and around the entrances of the Qusêr road from the Red Sea.

The stela (pl. i.) shows a folding door with bolts, decorated with two sacred eyes, indicating protection or watchfulness; on the lintel are inscribed the titles and name of Mena, implying that he is the owner of the house. There are four representations of the figure of Mena approaching this door, each of them accompanied by an inscription giving his name and titles; above is the announcement, "Favour given by the king and Anubis, *pert-kheru* to the *ha*-prince, &c., Mena, who is deserving well of Osiris." The underlying idea seems to be that the house contains a banquet for Mena. A similar inscription runs along the cornice of the stela, and below it is a picture of Mena sitting at his banquet in a chamber or court of the house. He wears a leopard-skin, and before him is a table spread apparently with palm-branches or reed-stems; behind and below it are numerous trays of offerings. In the earliest representations of this scene the table is covered with halved or quartered loaves of bread, but these became more and more conventionalized, until towards the end of the Old Kingdom the meaning was lost and the shapes became unintelligible; so they continued to be drawn throughout the Middle Kingdom, after which the conventional half loaf form was for a time resumed. At Dendereh constantly, and occasionally elsewhere at the end of the Old Kingdom and during the Saite revival, the objects are clearly intended for reeds or palm-branches, and bear out Borchardt's explanation of them as such (*A. Z.*, 1893, p. 1). It is of course extremely probable that leaves were actually used as a pleasant table-cover on which to place the food: halved loaves were a more barbarous and utilitarian substratum. The inscription immediately above this scene reads: "Favour accorded by the king and Osiris; a thousand of bread, a thousand of beer, a thousand of oxen, of oryx, of *re*-goose, *terp*-goose, of pin-tailed duck, of widgeon, of pigeons, a thousand of cloth and of thread, a thousand of all good vegetables and of all good things to the *ha*-prince, Mena."

Mena is entitled *ha*, chancellor of the King of Lower Egypt, governor of a fortified town, confidential friend of the king and *sekhem* of the *bat*. With the exception of the last title, which is new, these are the ordinary titles of great people of the time. The reading *sekhem* instead of *kherp* seems proved by the variant on the lintel (pl. ii.); otherwise we might have read *kherp mebat*, "constructor," or "organizer of a *mebat*." *bat*, determined by the figure of a boat, is a new word; it may designate the sacred bark of Hathor at Dendereh, but as this bears a quite different name in the Ptolemaic Edfu list (Brugsch, *Dict. Géog.*, 1362), we must wait for further instances before translating the title.

Pl. II. The five rectangular blocks with raised inscriptions shown in pls. ii., ii.a, are the remaining specimens from a number of slabs engraved with the ordinary formulae, which were placed over recesses in the exterior wall of the mastaba. The first inscription reads: "Favour that the king accordeth and Anubis, a summons, food and drink to the chancellor, the confidential friend of the king, deserving before Hathor lady of Dendereh, Men-ankh Pepy, whose good name is Mena." The second reads: "Favour that the king and Osiris accord, his good burial in the goodly West"—titles and name. (Two of the stone lintels from the tops of the recesses, inscribed simply "the *ha*, Mena," are shown on pl. ii.a.) The fragmentary block with incised inscription, showing a man and his wife, was found on the east side of the tomb of Mena. The inscription in front of the man was evidently of a type well represented from other tombs at Dendereh; over the woman is inscribed, "his wife whom he loves, the royal favourite Nebt-at-ef."

Pl. II.a. Restored line of inscription on the stone cornice:

"[Favour granted by the king, and Osiris lord of Busiris and] Khent-Amentiu lord of Abydos in all their places, [funeral offerings to the *ha*, Mena: he saith, I judged brothers] to their reconciling, I heard the word [of him whose throat was contracted (with fear?), I cured] the wandering of the oppressed, I saved the weak from the hand of him that was stronger than he, I held forth justice to the just, of [the desire of long life] upon earth. I was noble .... I am one to whom a summons and food shall issue (*pert-kheru*) in Dendereh amongst the devoted: the lector, [the superintendent of] Pharaoh's [garden, the *sekhem*] of the *bat* ...., the superintendent of the Black Land, lord of the Red Land, lord ...., priest choosing the guard (?) of this temple, devoted [to] Hathor, [mistress of Dendereh, Mena.]"

For the two forms of Osiris, as god respectively of Busiris and Abydos, see *P.S.B.A.*, November, 1899.

The passage referring to *pert-kheru* is of great importance if it refers to privileges enjoyed by Mena during his life-time, i.e. if the *pert-kheru* were supplies of provisions from the temple or palace; perhaps, however, it is safer to understand it as referring in the future tense to post-mortem prerogatives.

On the same plate there is shown a defaced but important fragment of a stone on which two inscriptions had been symmetrically engraved side by side, each reading from the centre outwards. On pl. xxvi.c will be found my transcription from the original as checked by an earlier copy of Professor Petrie's, and also by the photograph. The inscription on the left:—

"Favour granted by the king and Osiris ....
[*pert-kheru*]
in the Uag festival and the Hermopolite festival.........
the *ha*, Mena. He saith, 'O ye ....
.... as ye love [the king ....]
say ye, thousands of bread and beer, thousands ....
[to the superintendent]
of all 'earth-hair' of the Nome, the devoted [Mena
..............."

The inscription on the right:—

"Favour granted by the king and Anubis, [a good burial]
in the Western Hill ....
as one truly devoted ....
the lector, the superintendent of Pharaoh's garden ......
of southern barley, spelt, oxen ....
of Hathor, mistress of Dendereh ...."

The title "superintendent of all earth-hair (*shen ta*) of the nome" occurs again in the inscription shown on the right-hand top corner of pl. iii. *shen ta*, whatever it may be, is a substance commonly prescribed in the medical papyri; but it is by no means certain that the *shen ta* of the title is the same thing. In these texts *sepat*, "Nome," is constantly used without qualification for the nome of Dendereh.

The inscription on the rectangular block shown on the lower left-hand corner of the plate runs: "Favour granted by the king, and Anubis upon his hill, and Ami-Ut lord of the Sacred Land, the coming of a summons, food to .... Mena. O ye who live and are upon earth, who love life and hate death, as ye .... as ye desire to be followers of the god of your city on earth, [so say ye thousands of] all good things to the chancellor, &c., &c., Mena."

Pl. III. The inscriptions, &c., represented on this plate were painted on the walls of the doorless burial chamber of Mena: the roof was merely painted to imitate granite. The body no doubt lay in one or more coffins with its head to the north. The north wall consisted of two equal slabs, grained to imitate wood, which represented folding doors, on either leaf of which was painted a sacred eye. Compare the false door in pl. i. On each slab a short horizontal line and two vertical columns of inscriptions record the name and dignities of Mena. On the unmutilated slab we read that he was *ha*, chancellor of the King of Lower Egypt, confidential friend (of the king), lector, *sekhem bat*, governor of Men-nefer (Memphis), the pyramid city of Mery Ra (Pepy I.), and of *Kha-nefer*, the pyramid city of Merenra, superintendent of [all] fowling and hunting (*mer uha nu neb*) of the nome, superintendent of all "earth-hair" (vegetation, trees?—see above) of the nome, also that he was "deserving before Osiris, lord of Dadu, in all his places." The mutilated inscription on the other half of the wall doubtless testified that he was deserving before Anubis; here, as on the long walls of the chamber, it will be seen that the inscriptions on the east refer to Osiris, and those on the west to Anubis.

On the east wall the horizontal inscription runs: "Favour that the king grants and Osiris, lord of Busiris, chief of Western people, lord of Abydos; *pert-kheru* to him in the Uag festival, the Hermopolite festival, the festival of the beginning of the year, the festival of New Year's day ...... every good festival, according to what belongs to the day each day, the *ha* prince, the governor of a fortress, the confidential councillor (of the king), the well deserving, Mena." Below this inscription at the north end of the wall is the grand false door; then, corresponding to the section devoted to sacred oils on the west wall, is a tabulated list of offerings forming the daily menus of the deceased; lastly, there are pictured, in five rows, piles of food, sometimes decorated with flowers—bread, flesh, fowl, wine, beer, vegetables, fruit, placed on stands or mats, or in fine dishes and bowls.

The west wall is divided into compartments corresponding to those on the east wall, and above them the horizontal inscription reads: "Favour granted by the king and by Anubis, who is on his hill, and by Ami-Ut, the lord of the Sacred Land; that he be buried well in the West, the Western Mountain, in his chamber of the necropolis—the chancellor of the King of Lower Egypt, the governor, the confidential friend (of the king), deserving before Hathor, mistress of Dendereh, Mena." Below this inscription at the north end of the wall is the grand false door, from which bolt and eyes are nearly obliterated. The middle division is concerned with ten (?) sacred oils (or rather seven, tabulated in ten compartments) used in embalmment and various ceremonies, two vertical columns of inscription announcing: "Giving all pure oils...... [to Mena]." Beneath the names and pictures of the oils in their several well-sealed vessels are short speeches addressed to Mena by the embalmers, such as recur with variants in the Pyramid texts (*Neferkara*, ll. 308-317), and seem to be almost meaningless plays on the names of the oils. The southern end of the wall, below the horizontal inscription, is divided into five rows of offerings in boxes and on stands with names and numbers, connected with the toilet of the dead. The first two rows show boxes of linen; the first is of *hatiu*-linen, and of this there are enumerated: 100,000 pieces or lengths of the six-thread quality, 110,000 pieces five-thread quality, 110,000 four-thread quality, 100,000 two-thread quality, 120,000 one-thread quality. Next comes an inventory of the contents of the box holding the [*p*]*eqt* linen, so with the box of "fine royal," that of "fine royal *dau*," that of "leading," and that of "large"—six chests of linen in all. Of each kind of linen, except the *dau*, different degrees of fineness appear to be indicated by the number of threads in a given space of the cloth; but it is curious that though six-, five-, four-, two-, and one-thread cloth are mentioned, there is no three-thread quality. Row 3 shows one coffer containing balls of incense 21,000, another containing the same number of vases of *seth* oil, and another with 10,110 (?) jars of *heknu* oil. In the fourth row are necklaces, pendants, bracelets, &c., of gold and choice stones, "gold, carnelian, lapis-lazuli," &c.; and in the fifth row is a couch or stand laden with jars, head-rests (of "alabaster"), cloth, &c. The rest of this row is effaced.

The south wall, at the foot of the coffin, seems to have been painted with much the same kinds of stores as the west wall; but most of this has disappeared.

Pl. IV. The tabulated list of offerings from the east wall of Mena's sarcophagus chamber (see pl. iii.) on a larger scale. Throughout the Old and Middle Kingdoms this list varies scarcely at all from tomb to tomb; it included everything required for the daily personal needs of an Egyptian noble—unguents, eye-paint, &c., as well as food.

49. Pl. V. A wall of the upper chamber of Adu I., copied by Mr. Davies, with restorations made from Professor Petrie's earlier copy. It gives the titles of Adu as chancellor, privy councillor, lector, and governor of Men-ankh, the pyramid city of Nefer-ka-ra (Pepy II.), and of Men-nefer, the pyramid city of Pepy I. Adu is here represented "harpooning fishes," accompanied by "his son whom he loves, the governor of a fortress, chancellor of the King of Lower Egypt, privy councillor, the lector Zau (?)," by another "son whom he loves, the lector, the scribe of *amu*-boats, Adu," by a daughter, "royal relative, priestess of Hathor......," and by "his wife whom he loves, the unique royal ornament (?), deserving before the king, Beba."

Pl. V.a. The inscriptions from the sepulchral chamber of Adu I. The walls were painted with offerings, somewhat in the style of the closed chamber in the tomb of Mena; the room itself, however, was T-shaped, not merely oblong. See plan in corner of plate. The entrance is at A, E. A band of pictured offerings, with an inscription below, runs round the transepts half-way up the walls. From A-D the inscription reads: "Bringing choice meats, the pick of the table, to the chancellor, &c., [Adu, well-deserving before Osiris]. (B-C) May he be followed by his noble *kas* ...... may he pass along the sacred ways of Ament (C-D) on which the rewarded are met; he joins the earth, he crosses the sky, the Western Mountain gives her hands to him, in peace, in peace, before the great god as one rewarded." E-H: "Bringing choice meats, all good vegetables, and all good things to him who is rewarded before the great god, (F-G) lord of Ament, the chancellor of the King of Lower Egypt, the governor of a fortress, the privy councillor, lector, great prince of the Nome, who is over the secrets of every secret communication brought (G-H) to the Nome, rewarded by Osiris, lord of Busiris, rewarded by the great god, Adu." The coffin was placed, head to the north, in the long limb of the cross H-D, on the three walls of which a line of inscriptions ran under the cornice, the offerings being represented below. On the east wall (H-I) was a false door with "Favour of the king and Anubis, *pert-kheru*, &c.," and beyond it an inscription proceeded: "Favour of the king and of Anubis on his hill and of Ami-Ut, lord of the Sacred Land; he hath a good burial in his chamber of *kher-neter*, the Western Mountain; a very good rank (or old age ?) as rewarded by the great god lord of Ament, the *ha* superintendent of the South Country [in very truth] (*n bu maa*, cf. inscription on I-K and the common expression *n un maa*), the chancellor of the King of Lower Egypt, privy councillor, lector, great chief of the Nome, Adu." Below this inscription were tabulated offerings, &c., as on pl. iii. On the west wall (D-K) the inscription is in much the same words as on H-I, the grant being made to Adu by favour of the king and "Anubis in the Divine Hall" of "burial and good old age (?); he joins the earth and crosses the sky, the West gives him her two hands in peace, in peace (i.e. with welcome) before the great god." Above the granaries on K-I, at the foot of the coffin, nothing but the name and titles of Adu were inscribed.

In these inscriptions the cerastes hieroglyph is always drawn as decapitated, though the head is not omitted, and the hieroglyphs representing human figures are drawn without the lower limbs.

Pl. VI. Cornice fragments from the same tomb, that of Adu I. "[I satisfied the poor ?] with bread and beer," and—connecting the second and fourth fragments from the top right-hand corner of plate—"never was [the like] done [by] others to whom had fallen this office (*aat*) of chancellor of the King of Lower Egypt."

Stela of Sekhet·hetep (?): Favour granted by the king and Anubis, *pert-kheru* for the "royal acquaintance, priestess of Hathor, lady of Dendereh, well-deserving before Osiris, lord of Busiris, well-deserving before the great god ...... Sekhet·hetep (?)."

Cornice fragments from the tomb of Adu II.: "Favour accorded by the king and Hathor, lady of Dendereh," &c. ...... "[I judged brothers] to their reconciliation, I loved what was good before the great god, I heard the word of him whose throat was contracted, I cured the fault of the weak (?) with the intent ...... [those who saw] my workmanship therein (in my tomb ?), they praised god ...." The fragments of stelae below the cornice fragments are also from the tomb of Adu II.; the first fragment should be joined to the third from the left. In translation they are of no interest, but they contain curious forms and variants.

The three fragments at the bottom of the

plate, found near the tomb of Adu II., show nothing remarkable except the spelling of the name Degat on the central one. Degat rather than "Qebdat" is the reading. The same fragment is clearer on pl. vii.A, "Various." On the left-hand fragment is, "I was beloved of my father, praised of my mother, I was beloved of [my brethren]," &c.

50. Pls. VII., VII.A. Below further fragments from the tomb of Adu II., on pl. vii., are others from the tomb of Pepy-Seshem·nefer (not "Pepy-Ta-Snefer"), whose good name was Senna. He held the usual titles of "royal chancellor," "confidential councillor," also those of "superintendent of writing," "superintendent of the houses of corn-storage," and a hitherto unknown title, "making the voyage of Hathor, lady of Dendereh." On pl. vii.A he is also entitled "lector, chief of the secrets of divine speech, chief of the secrets of the divine chancellor." On the fragments of the cornice (pl. vii.A) there is mention of various trees, *keselt*, *ahu* (?), and [*ses*]-*nezem*: the last is the carob tree. Evidently he was an enthusiastic planter of trees, and his *sma*-land—probably the borderland between the alluvial soil and the desert—was "filled with oxen, goats, and asses." On one of the fragments there is a reference to a "[keeper] of *thentet*-oxen, great chief of the Nome Shensetha." Perhaps this was the personage who "sent" Pepy·Seshem·Nefer on some mission. Shensetha is a name that occurs again on pls. xi.A and xi.B.

The broken stela in the middle of pl. vii. is copied on pl. xiii.; it mentions a man named Mennu·nefer·Pepy, whose good name was Senbat. Doubtless the man was called after Men-nefer, the pyramid of Pepy I.

The fragments at the bottom of pl. vii. are from the tomb of Zauta, whose good name was Resa. He was "governor of a fortress, privy councillor, lector, superintendent of the garden of Pharaoh, great prince of the Nome"; his wife was "royal acquaintance, priestess of Hathor, lady of Dendereh, Mererta." Vide pl. xxvi.C.

The broken tablet of Beba (II.) on pl. vii.A reads: "Sa·aa (?), royal acquaintance, by his name, owner of offices in his city...... I made its door of acacia, I brought to it...... I castrated (?), I caused it to be great and mistress of the lands (?)...... I made a dockyard (?) upon the border (?) within one year ......" The small fragments to the right belong to another tomb, No. 324, and are drawn in connection on the top of pl. xv., where they form the words *n hay* "unto the naked."

Among the "Various" on pl. vii.A there is a block mentioning a "scribe of the *smayt* land Rehuia"; a block naming Degat, already printed on pl. vi.; a block with the inscription "O ye who live and are on earth, who love their city-god, say ye thousands of bread, beer, &c., to the owner of this tomb, Katha"; lastly, a fragment with a curious name of a boat (?) *mecha* or *cha*, which name occurs also on another insignificant fragment not published in the plates.

51. Pls. VIII.-VIII.C. Sculptured blocks from tomb of Merra. The barbarous yet detailed style of relief sculpture employed in this tomb is very remarkable.

Pl. VIII. Five horizontal lines of inscription in relief.

l. 1. Favour that the king granteth and Anubis (?) .... *pert-kheru* to] the keeper of the *thentet*-cattle, Merra; his burial in his chamber which is in the necropolis [the Western Mountain], a very [good] old age (?) as a favour that the king granteth and Osiris lord of Busiris and Khent-Amentiu [.................. that he be followed by his *kas* to the places *l.* 2. .... deserving] before the great god, *pert-kheru* to him in his chamber that is in *kher·neter*...... in the Uag, the Hermopolite feasts (&c.) ......, according to what belongeth to the day each day, the *ha*, the superintendent *l.* 3. of the priesthood, Merra; he saith I ....] little ones, I gave bread to the hungry, clothes to the naked; I saved the oppressed from the hand of him that was stronger than he; I judged brothers to [their] reconcilement........... of the desire *l.* 4. .... privy councillor, great chief of the Nome, lector, chief of the transport (of Hathor), superintendent of the divine service, keeper of the *thentet*-cattle, Seten·en·abu, whose good name was [B]ebaqer. I filled with northern barley and spelt, cattle, goats .... that is in .... I caused a man to *l.* 5. .... his lord, as is done unto a good heir; I overthrew his enemies in very truth, that is not ...... said in ...... his house with ...... I made sweet its odours with .... [I filled] its granary with northern barley and spelt, as was done by Seten·en·abu Beba."

Evidently Seten·en·abu Beba was a predecessor of Merra.

The titles of Merra, as recorded in pls. viii., viii.B., are "*ha*, superintendent of divine service, keeper of the *thentet*-cattle, over the secrets of the divine treasure, over the secrets of divine words, over the secrets of the morning house (place of the king's toilet?), chief of the transport of Hathor lady of Dendereh." (This "transport of Hathor" was no doubt some ceremonial voyage or crossing of the Nile.) One of the stelae on pl. viii. describes him as "strong in mouth, stout of heart, finding the knot in its entanglement, speaking according to his voice (?); the people were silent on the day of mourning (?)." The *thentet*-cattle are not known apart from these inscriptions; probably they were the sacred kine of Hathor.

Pl. VIII.A. The inscriptions of this curious false door present only the funerary formulae with the titles and name of Merra. It is from blocks shown on pl. viii. that we learn the name of "his wife whom he loves, the confidential royal favourite, priestess of Hathor lady of Dendereh, Seheta," and of "his daughter whom he loves, Aui·rdet·sa (?). In the lower right-hand corner of pl. viii.B we have the titles of a woman, "familiar royal favourite (?), priestess of Hathor lady of Dendereh, Theta."

Pl. VIII.B contains nothing of special interest.

Pl. VIII.C. It is distressing that the fragments from the cornice should be so incomplete. A good deal of rearrangement is required to place them in something like their original order, and even when that seems to have been found the translation is in places very difficult. Including at the beginning two small fragments not shown on the plate, we obtain:—

"[Favour of the king, Anubis on his rock and Ami-Ut, lord of the Sacred Land, to the *ha*, chancellor of the King of Lower Egypt, confidential royal friend, lector [Merra; he saith, I laboured] for Dendereh in [its entirety, I ....] its little ones more than (?) its no|bles (?) I .... the farmers of Dendereh, when | there were harvesters (?) therein. I | was one that desired to eat (?) what he saw, that is, I was not | one who ate bound (?). I was beloved of | Dendereh in | its entirety, praised of his city and beloved of it, and of travellers | and negroes of the foreign land. | I was one who hated evil things, | I loved not to command conspiracy (?) | .... it was my abomination to s|lay men .... | but I did good | for Dendereh in its entirety. I was a haven (?) for this land in its entirety."

The rest is too fragmentary to be intelligible. The hieroglyphs are curious, not to say incorrect; the strangest of them is perhaps the ten-legged crab (from the Red Sea?) substituted for the scarab; probably the only examples of the kind in Egyptian sculpture are found here and on pl. x.

52. Pls. IX.-X.A. Sculptured blocks and fragments from the tomb of Sen-n(?)·nezsu, whose name means "brother of the little," i.e. of the poor. He was royal chancellor and steward.

Pl. IX. Above the cornice of the false door: "Favour accorded by the king and Anubis, *pert-kheru* to," &c. Below the cornice, the same from Osiris. On one side, "pure bread that cometh from Dendereh"; on the other, "...... from the temple." Over the door are titles, lists of offerings, &c., and "the steward Sen-nezsu, he saith: 'I came out of my house, I entered my (tomb?)-chamber, I said what the great loved, what the little praised, with the desire of offering justice unto the great god lord of heaven (Ra).' "

From these inscriptions and those on the other two blocks given in the plate we learn the names of " his wife whom he loveth, confidential favourite of the king, priestess of Hathor mistress of Dendereh, Auuta," of " his eldest son whom he loveth, the royal chancellor, steward of the house of war, the deserving, Merra," of "his son whom he loveth, the royal chancellor, steward of the house of the stores and of war, Sebeknekht," and of "his son whom he loveth, the royal chancellor, the steward of the house of war, Sennetsua." Above his sons, in small characters: "...... I conciliated them with bread, beer, northern barley, spelt ...... clothing, oil, honey: then may my name remain (even) in the necropolis."

Pl. X. Here we see some of his daughters: "[his daughters whom he loves], confidential favourite of the king, priestess of Hathor lady of Dendereh, the deserving, Hotepa," and " the confidential favourite of the king, the deserving, Beba."

The fragments of biographical inscriptions on this plate are very tantalizing. "...... which my father, who loved his house, [built ?] for me; I found it as enclosures of bricks, I [renewed it with stones? I supported ?] it with standing posts of wood of every sort; of eleven (cubits) in height, furnished with doors of *u*[*an*-wood ?] ...... gardeners (determined by a man carrying pots of water by means of a yoke) were making vegetables (compare the picture in *El Bersheh*, I., pl. xxvi., *B. H.*, I., pl. xxix. right), pond-keepers were planting trees, the little man was owner of his bow (or yoke), every man was owner of his own work: I did this throughout, throughout in very truth. This is not as said .... my father, Merra." It seems as if this belonged to Merra, son of Sen·nezsu.

Another fragment gives two lines following on a funerary inscription: "...... that grew in it, of men, northern barley, spelt, gold, copper (or pottery ?), cloth, oil .... in its length, 88½ cubits in its breadth, 300 trees in it ...." The rest is not comprehensible to me.

Another fragment gives: "[of] goats, ships, of everything."

Of inscriptions on this plate which do not belong to Merra, we have one of a " confidential royal favourite, priestess of Hathor of Dendereh" named Hetepsa. Another fragment shows a man seated with his wife, who holds out the baby for him to dandle; she is "his wife whom he loves, the royal acquaintance, Redu·ahu (?) " (i.e. " Feet-of-kine," not " Uaru·kau "). On one fragment, "Adu, whose good name is Uhaa," has much the same titles as Merra on pl. viii., viz.: "*repa ha*, royal chancellor, confidential associate of the king, superintendent of divine service, keeper of the *thentet*-cattle." Ptah·mera, (in the lower left-hand corner), was "royal chancellor, superintendent of the audience chamber."

Pl. X.a. Belonging to Sen·n(?)·nezsu there are here several bits of funerary formulae, e.g. "[O ye who love life] and hate death, as ye love [the king say 'favour accorded by the king']." Three or four other bits may probably be connected thus: "[the steward] Sen n(?)·nezsu, he saith, 'It was that my master sent me on a peaceful commission, which I did ...... [I took tribute of ?] their people, their trees, their fields .... cattle. I returned in [peace.' "

Of the fragments from the tomb of Ptah-mera (cf. pl. x.) those from the cornice give minute portions from the benevolent formulae so commonly met with at Dendereh, while the small stela says: " I came forth from my house, I entered my chamber, I said what the great loved, what the little praised."

On the fragments belonging to Beba and his son Sebek·nekht there is the phrase, "I made (i.e. cultivated) men, cattle, asses, goats."

53. Pl. XI. Inscription of Beba and his wife Henutsen: " Favour that the king accords and Anubis upon his hill, and Ami-ut lord of the Sacred Land, *pert-kheru* to the chancellor,

the governor of a city, the confidential friend, the lector, the superintendent of divine service, who is over the secrets of weighing words (trials), who is deserving to his lord, the great chief of the Nome, who is over the secrets of every secret word brought to the Nome, the well-deserving of Osiris, he whose good name is Beba." "His wife whom he loves, priestess of Hathor lady of Dendereh, Henutsen." The shorter inscription, to the right, gives the title "first after the king" for Beba, and "confidential royal favourite" for Henutsen. On a block in pl. xi.A. an inscription for the same man states: "I ......] all things over which I had control. Moreover, I gave bread to the hungry, clothes to the naked; I took over the river him who had no ferry boat"; and on fragments of his cornice inscription (also on pl. xi.A) there are other common charitable formulae.

The third block at the top of the plate represents a "confidential friend (of the king), a superintendent of horned and hoofed animals(?)." His name, ending in *a*, is lost; beside him sits "his wife whom he loves, Beba." He says: "I made men, cattle, goats, asses, barley, and durra, clothes ...... a boat on the water, trees in the garden (?) and the field ...... that which I had done by my own strong arm."

The first block in the second row shows "the chancellor and superintendent of the Audience Hall, Shensetha," standing: approaching him with a vase of "sweet ointment of the house thou lovest, for the excellent *kas* ......" is "his wife, loved by and loving him in very truth," with "his beloved daughter, Bebasher."

On the second block in the same row are a man's son, Shensetha, and his daughters, Hatherhetep and Senta, bringing offerings.

On the third block the barbarous hieroglyphs give the names Henua, Nekhta, Beba, Nekhta, Beba ...... and Beba. The wife's name, Bet, is given by the middle block in the fourth row.

In the third row the first block shows a man named Uhemy, seated with his wife; the second shows a "confidential friend, Beba," standing with his beloved wife, Hatherhetepa" (see the copy in pl. xiv.); and the third a woman named Nefert·kau or Nefert·ahu.

The first block in the fourth row gives a long inscription: "Favour granted by the king and Osiris, lord of Busiris, *pert-kheru* of bread and beer, oxen and ducks to him, that he prosper in his chamber of *Kher-neter*, the well-deserving one, Nekhtu, who saith: "I made 31 head of people, 33 oxen, 13 asses, 100 goats, 4 *amu*-boats, 5 *dept* boats. I built my house increased beyond my father's, land, enclosures (?), groves in the field; I was deserving before the great god, lord of heaven, the priest Nekhtu, true of voice." With him is "the well-deserving one, his wife whom he loves, Hep, true of voice," and "his daughter, Naa." Of the figures approaching him, those in the top row are each called "his son Sebekhetep"; in the lower row are his sons Antef and Beba, and his daughter Naa. Both names and formulae show this inscription to be of the XIth Dynasty.

Pl. XI.A (see also under Pl. XI.). In the middle of the plate are two blocks belonging to a man named Seten·n·abu and holding the titles "*ha*, ruler of a fortress, confidential friend, superintendent of divine service, over the secrets of the divine treasury," also "lector." He is said to have been "watchful of head to the command of the nobles."

The rest of the plate contains inscriptions from the mastaba of Shensetha. No titles are there, but the blocks of the cornice give fragments as follows: "[I gave clothes to the] naked, I conveyed over (the river) him who was without ferry boat, I ploughed [for him who had no yoke of oxen]. [I did no evil (?) in] all this land, but I did this as a task that accomplished the set standard of work (?), and did what my master was well pleased with." "I judged between comrades to unite their heart." "...... festivals; I satisfied them with bread, beer, northern barley, durra ......"

Pl. XI.b. On the top of the plate are further fragments of inscriptions relating to the same man: "...... in Dendereh to its entirety; I gave Dendereh landed rights (?) in it, giving unto him who was loved as to him that was hated. I made *mekha* (?) boats." "Moreover I satisfied all artificers that did work for me in this tomb with bread and beer, barley and spelt, clothing, ointment, honey, and all good things: of the desire......" "I gave bread to the hungry, clothes to the naked, I regarded the word of him whose throat was contracted. I gave...... to the poor, I caused not evil conspiracy." On a fragment drawn on pl. xxv.b, Shensetha is entitled "captain of the host," and is accompanied by "his attendant, Antefa."

Below the inscriptions of Shensetha is one of Hetepa, a "confidential friend." He says: "I was beloved of all my people, I gave bread to the hungry, clothes to the naked, I was one beloved of his brethren throughout Dendereh." The block on the left (marked "Beba III.") shows Hetepa seated with his wife Ankh·senna; behind them stands "his friend of the place of his heart, Per-Aru," while the sons, Azau and Adu, are approaching with offerings (for hand copy of Azau's name, see pl. xiv.).

On this plate there are also blocks from the tomb of a "keeper of the *thentet*-oxen, Adua," and from the tomb of Hetepa with fragments of one of the benevolent formulae, &c., &c.

Pl. XI.c. Certain phrases from the cornice of Mera are conspicuous. "I was beloved of my father, praised of my mother," "I gave cattle (?) to] him who was without a yoke of oxen (*ḥeter*), I gave seed corn to him who begged [for it."

Antefa, or Antefa·aqer, is entitled "first after the king," and—on a door drum—"treasurer and confidential friend." On his cornice we are told that he "transported him who was without a ferry-boat, [gave cattle (?) to him who had no] yoke of oxen, and ploughed......" On pl. xiv. there is a hand copy of the names of his wife and children from one of these blocks: "His wife whom he loved, I......, his son, Antef," &c.

54. Pl. XII. Here we have further fragments belonging to the same Antefa. On the block, which shows him seated by his wife and approached by his children, he is styled "chancellor, confidential friend, keeper of the corn-store." The large slab inscribed in wondrous relief-hieroglyphs records the favour of the king and Anubis on the right-hand inscription, and on the left hand the favour of the king and Osiris, with the usual appeal to those who are "living on earth, who love life and hate death," and some obscure statements of his excellence.

The slab of Antef·aqer II. has the epithet "true of voice," which seems to be the certain indication of a date not earlier than the XIth Dynasty.

The cartouches of Mentuhetep are interesting; in the one to the left the large and detailed hieroglyphs are of almost unsurpassable excellence.

Pl. XIII. Here are hand copies of a number of curious fragments, but the most translatable is of "Adua (tomb 331)," which gives a name Rehury (?). He says: "...... stall (?) of goats, stall (?) of asses...... trees, a boat in the water, crew...... I drew from my store, I ploughed for ......[I was] one beloved of his father, praised of his mother." Another, from tomb 326, seems to read, "I made 5000 cubits of land, 20 asses, 200 goats,......, clothes, and I gave...... to my city. Verily, I did this with my own strong arm."

Pl. XIV. Hand copies of numerous names, &c.

55. Pl. XV. The great stela of Chnemerdu is perhaps the most important single object that was found in the cemetery. It is in bad condition, and Mr. Davies, who copied it first at Dendereh, revised his copy for this publication a year later at Gizeh, examining specially many difficult points. We learn from the inscription that Chnemerdu was the steward of a queen

who had inherited in the South great rights apart from her husband, whom we may imagine to have been, nominally, king of all Egypt.

(1) Grace accorded by the king and Osiris Lord of Busiris and Khent-Amentiu, Lord of Abydos in [all their places: *pert-kheru* bread and beer, oxen and fowl, clothing] (2) and thread, thousands of all good things

to the chancellor, the privy councillor, him that is in the heart of his great mistress, persistent in coming as cooling .... (3) knowing his postures (?), firm of seal, good in opposition (?), excellent in dealing (lit. place of hand) in every going; lord of reverence, great of hand, successful .... (4) white of raiment, noble of body, divine to look upon; knowing the method of accomplishment, fine (polished, well-trained) of heart, a collection (embodiment ?) of nobles, comprehending the heart, (5) controlling what is in the belly, gracious (?) of countenance to the petitioner until he saith what is in his heart. entering the heart of his mistress, belonging to the place of her heart, given to her as it were a council that is great in (6) precept, one well-beloved in the mouth of men, eminent of seat in the Great House, the steward, the deserving, Chnemerdu:

(he) saith, 'I was one beloved of my mistress, (7) praised by her in what belonged to the day each day: I spent a long period in years before my mistress, the royal favourite Neferu-kayt, her that was great (8) in her *kas*, eminent in her positions, great of fathers, eminent of mothers, support of this heaven for her noble fathers, most eminent of this land, (9) heiress from amongst the South country. Behold she was daughter of a king, wife of a king whom he loved; she inherited from her mother Nebt ...... (the name must have been of the form 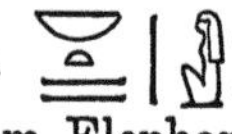), (10) chief of the people beginning from Elephantine, ending at the Aphroditopolite (Xth) nome, of women connected with (?) governors of cities, and nobles of the whole land. I became under the household of my mistress (?) (or of her handmaid) .... (11) the littleness of my origin (?); for she knew the excellence of my handiwork, how I forwarded the way of the nobles. Then she placed me in Dendereh, in the great treasure (?) (12) of her mother, great of writing, eminent of sciences, great council-chamber of the South. I made extensions (?) thereof, piles of wealth, riches for it (?): not failed (?) anything (13) thereof, of the greatness of my knowledge of things. I organized it, I made fair its conduct with beauty more than aforetime, I made strong what I found decayed, I tied what I found loose, (14) I fulfilled what I found inchoate. I neglected not all the feasts that I found done in this estatė, the sacrifice established in every daily service, every festival done in its seasons (?)—*yr r nw-f* (?)—for the health of my mistress Neferu-kayt, (15) for ever and ever. I organized my house on a goodly plan, I enlarged every court of it, I gave provision to him who begged it, herbs to him whom I knew not as to him I knew, of the desire that (16) my name might be good in the mouth of those on earth. I was indeed a noble great in his heart, a plant sweet of desire, I was not drunken, my heart did not forget, I fainted not [in what was given into my hand (?)] (17) It was my heart made my place eminent, it was my nature caused me to continue at the front. I did, yea I did all these things. Behold I was one in the heart of his mistress, I was keen, I established my surroundings, (18) I learnt every business, the estate was organized therewith, and I sent support to what I found fallen, saying 'Behold it is exceeding good that a man do the best things of his heart for his mistress, the most eminent of (19) his memorials.' I made for her a great treasure of all precious things, done in excess of what I found. I displayed every aptitude (*aun*) in this situation: I outran all my compeers: if there was a thing undertaken in this estate I was he that understood it. (20) Most eminent of men, a noble tree made by God, he caused me to excel by his plan, greatly noble by the work of his hand (?) My mistress was as Lady of the South country, as great foundation of this land (?). Long endure her *ka* (21) upon the great throne! may she make millions of years in life like Ra eternally!

pert-kheru unto the deserving Chnemerdu in the Uag-feast, the Thoth-feast, in the .... feast, in the feast of Sokaris (?), in the feast of the heat, in the beginning of the year, in the great feast, in the great going forth, in all feasts. Let the hand be put forth to him with offerings that appear before Hathor, may the eminent ones of Per-wr make him divine, and the priests of the noble staircase: may he travel the roads that he will in peace, in peace, the deserving, Chnemerdu."

(he) saith, "I was one who fulfilled his duty, and was beloved of mankind in what belonged to the day of every day.

The scene below shows a servant, Antef, pouring unguent from a vase before the great man, under whose chair sits a hound. The inscription reads, "Opening unguents before the face, unto the *ka* of the deserving one, Chnemerdu." Behind the servant are three figures, "his friend Adedu, Apuy and Tha-nub." Over the table are the usual unguents in seven jars, with their names above.

56. The hieroglyphs of the earlier Dendereh inscriptions are interesting in a quite peculiar way. Often they are rather well formed, though with a certain barbaric tendency; but on close examination it will be observed that individual signs, while bearing a general resemblance to the ordinary types, are in fact very different. Thus, in pls. viii.c and x. the crab is substituted for the scarabaeus, in pl. x. the handled basket—usually *k*—for the plain basket *neb*; and those who have made any special study of the forms and pictorial meanings of hieroglyphs will recognize how often the engraver has departed from the usual traditions, the substitutions being in some cases reasonable, in others quite meaningless. One might be disposed to attribute this state of things to a fundamental difference in the writing such as would be implied by a South Egyptian system of writing differing in origin from that of Northern Egypt. But it will be observed that the differences are sporadic and the types very irregular on the Dendereh monuments. The art of engraving monumental inscriptions had deteriorated greatly as early as the VIth Dynasty all over Egypt, even in the centres of civilization. The scribes wrote freely in a cursive hand, and owing to the practice of clearer spelling they no longer needed carefully to observe the distinctions between the signs. A scribe of the period of our inscriptions who could easily write hieratic, would find it difficult to instruct the decorator how to render his hieratic into well-formed hieroglyphs; from the VIth to the XIth Dynasty the barbaric stelae present many extraordinary attempts to render the half-forgotten signs in detail. With the monumental revival at the end of the XIth Dynasty the knowledge of hieroglyphs revived throughout the country, but the great break in tradition—though never perhaps complete, since some men of hieroglyphic learning doubtless were always to be found—left its mark on the XIIth Dynasty renascence. How conventions changed, probably through ignorance, can be seen by the history of the table of offerings as shown in the scenes (cf. pp. 42-43). In the IVth Dynasty this is represented garnished with halves or quarters of tall loaves of bread. Abundance of bread as basis for a meal is seen at modern marriage feasts in Egypt, &c., but this primitive sort of table-cloth, suggestive of nothing but food, was probably soon improved upon. Late in the Vth Dynasty the meaning of the representation was already obscured, and the bread had assumed impossible forms, even on the walls of the tomb of Ptahhetep. In the period between the Old and Middle Kingdoms, by a slight deviation in outline and the addition of some detail, it appears sometimes as a garnishing of palm leaves, a pleasant device that may well have been in actual use. In the XIIth Dynasty the uncertain forms of the Vth Dynasty were again in vogue; in the XVIIIth Dynasty the table was generally piled with various offerings, and the convention was almost abandoned, to be fully revived, however, in the XXVIth Dynasty.

57. A few inscriptions lie between the XIth Dynasty and the Ptolemaic age.

Pl. XXIII.a. Inscription from the handle of of a sistrum: "Favour granted by the king and Hathor Nebhetep; she giveth good life to the *ka* of ...... Bukau." The sistrum was sacred to Hathor, and the head of the handle is usually carved with her mask.

Inscription from a situla: "Amen-Ra, lord of the thrones of the two lands, gives life, prosperity and health, a long duration, a good old age to Therkes, whose mother was mistress of a house, Hather ......"

A sandstone sarcophagus is inscribed with name of Nesi·her, to whose aid come the different deities and demons sculptured upon it.

Pl. XXV. The first of the three stelae shows "the lady of the house, Mutardus," holding a sistrum and worshipping "Ra-Harmakhis the great god lord of heaven." Mutardus, whose name is repeated with curious variations, was a musician in the House of Hathor. She was daughter of Nesi·tamer and Ruru; and the tablet was set up by "her son who makes her name to live, Par, son of Artau."

On the middle stela the "Satisfier of her Majesty, Horsiesi," offers to Osiris, Isis, and Horus. Favour is granted by Osiris, Ptah-sokar, "Hathor lady of Dendereh, Horus Samtaui and the gods and goddesses in Dendereh, they give *pert-kheru*, &c., &c., and all things that appear on the altar before Hathor lady of Dendereh, to the Satisfier of her Majesty Horsiesi, son of the Satisfier of her Majesty Petismataui, born of the lady of the house, the musician of Hathor, Ant-ha." "Satisfier of her Majesty" is the title of the high priest of Hathor at Dendereh in the Edfu list, Br., *Dict. Géog.*, p. 1361; apparently "Musician of Hathor" was the title of the chief priestess.

The third stela shows a man worshipping Ra-Harmakhis and Ptah on the one side and Tum and Osiris on the other—the pairs corresponding as living and dead forms respectively of the same two gods. The deceased is "the Osiris Netem-ankh, son of the Satisfier of her Majesty, &c., PeduHorsamtaui, born of the lady of the house Ṇer(?)-nut." The titles of PeduHorsamtaui are put forth very fully, but are obscure. They seem to be "servant of Horus Maks, satisfier of the heart of a thousand, first priest, second priest, scribe of the temple of Hathor, lady of *Shen* (?), scribe of his treasure, priest of the gods, the plough of the arm (?), fourth class, priest of Horus, the scribe of the ...... Hathor, lady of Dendereh, fourth class."

58. Pl. XXV.A. Demotic inscriptions, &c., Ptolemaic and Roman.

I. *tʾ ḥ·t n Pʾ-šre-wp sʾ Gmt, pʾ ḫʿq* (?)

"The tomb of Psheiapi son of Gemt, the barber (?)."

Professor Petrie is inclined to see in the crossed circle and object resembling a four-pronged fork the Buddhist symbols of the wheel of life and the trisul. The inscription gives no support to this view, and Mr. E. J. Rapson, who has seen a copy of the symbols and a transcript of the legend, thinks the form of the symbols unlikely. Can they be intended for a cake and a flesh-hook? or are they symbols of a trade? The meaning and reading of the last sign are quite uncertain.

II. Quite illegible on the squeeze, and mostly so in the photograph.

III. (1) *tʾ h·t Ysyr* (2) *Pʾ-te-Hr-smʾ-tʾ·wi sʾ Pʾ-šre-Yḥy* (3) *nt smne ḥr pʾ tw n* (4) *pʾ pr n ḥtp n Yn·t*

"The grave of Osiris Petesomtus son of Psenais (?), who is placed on the hill of the resting-place of Tentyra."

IV. *ḥtp tns* (sic) *Ysyr ḫnt Ymnt* ....
n pr-ḫrw t ḥnq yḥ ʾpt
ḥtp·w tf yḫy nb nfr ....
Ysyr ḫnt Ymnt n Ys wr mw·t ntr
Nb·t-ḥe sne ntr (?) *n Ysyr Pʾ-te-Ḥr sm tʾ·wi*
zty n-f pʾ .... *sʾ pʾ šre-Yḥy*

"Grace royally accorded (?) by Osiris Khentamenti
of *pert-kheru*, bread, beer, oxen, fowl,
offerings, fatlings, all good things ....
Osiris Khentamenti, to Isis the great, the mother of a god,
Nephthys sister of a god (?), to the Osiris Petuhorsamtaui
who is called the .... [son of] Pasherenahy"

V. *mbʾḥ Ysyr Wnfr pʾ ntr ʿʾ ḥr yb*
Yn, Ys wr·t mw·t-ntr Ynp
ḫnt syḥ-ntr ....

"Before Osiris Onophris the great god in
Denderah, Isis the great, divine mother: Anubis
in the divine house ...."

VI. Worship of Osiris, Isis and "Harmakhis the great god" by Nespehy (?).

VII.	*t' ḥ·t* .... *s'* *p' ʿḫm* (?) *p' šre Tḥwt p'*	
VIII.	*t' ḥ·t n* .... *nwy s' Qrms* (?)	"The grave of .... son of ...."

IX. Illegible on squeeze and photograph. The design is apparently a coffin on a bier between two bunches of flowers for offerings. Cf. the flowers on the tables of offering, Nos. 17-20.

X.	*t' ḥ·t p' ʿt p' bk* *Ḥr my p' qlʿ t'* ...... *qt*	"the grave of .... Pabekhis
XI.	*T'i-wp mt t' gš* (?) *t' ḫry Ysyr*	
XII.	*ʿnḫ p' by n p' Gplws* (?) .... *n yft n rnp·t* LIX.	"lives the soul of .... 59 years (of age)"
XIV.	*mb'ḥ Ysyr Wnfr p' ntr ʿ'* *p'-bk s' p'i-* .... *n p' ʿnt p' q* ... (?) *p' Ḥr*	"Before Osiris Onophris the great god Pabekhis son of .... of the frankincense the steward (?) of Pa-Her."
XV.	*Ysyr p' ʿt ʿlʿl* (*s'*) *p' te Ḥr sm' t'·wi*	
XVI.	*te·t htp stn n Ysyr Ḥr Ys Tḥwt Ynp* *te-w pr-ḫrw n t' ḥnq yḥ·w* *'pt·w htp·w tf·w yḫ·w nb nfr wʿb* *n Ysyr p' šre* .... *s' P'i-ḫ, mw-f T'i-ḫ.* *te-w n-f* ...... (?) *qse nfr·t pr mne z·t* (?)	"The king giveth an offering (?) to Osiris Horus Isis Thoth and Anubis they give *pert-kheru* of bread, beer, oxen, fowl, offerings, fat things, all good and pure things to the Osiris Pasheren ......, son of Pakh, whose mother is Takh. They give to him ...... good burial, a house lasting for ever."

The first of the tables of offerings is inscribed for "the Osiris the divine wife of Nefer-hetep (a form of Chonsu) Ta-ast (?) true of voice."

Pl. XXV.b.

A.	*t' ḥ·t n P' šre*(*n*) *Yhy* *s' Ḥr-nfr, p' ḥme nb, ḥnʿ* *T' šre·t* (*n*) *Yhy t' p' Šy* *t'e-f ḥm·t.* *rnp* XXIX, *ybt* IV *šme hrw* XVIII.	"The grave of Psenpahy son of Her-nefer, the gold-worker, with Senahy daughter of Psais his wife. Year 29, Mesori 18."
B.	*r* (?) *t' ḥ·t P'-te-Hr-sm-t'·wi* (?) *p' ʿt* *P' šre* (*n*) *Tḥwt* *p' grg.* *rnp* VIII *ybt* IV *š'e hrw* X.	"The grave of Patehersamtaui ...... Pashenthot the hunter. Year 8, Choiak 10."

C. "Pashem son of Pabek." On a sandstone slab over the figure of a mummy.

D. Tablet. Pedupamenkhu adores Ra-Harmakhis, Osiris and Isis the Great. His parents are Pedubak and Herert.

At the bottom of Pl. XV. are two hieroglyphic inscriptions of very late date—

"Royal offering (?) to the Osiris Pehequ son of Pashem: he went to Osiris at 19 years (of age ?),"

and

"Royal offerings (?) to the Osiris Pashem true of voice, the elder, son of Peduhorsamtaui. He went to Osiris at 44 years (of age ?)."

Pls. XXVI.a., XXVI.b. These labels are often obscure, especially in the proper names, which also are of little interest. The following are perhaps the most interesting:—

No. 6. Osiris Petiamenophis .... the scribe of the House of Horus.

No. 10. Osiris Nes-Min the elder, (son of) Petesis.

No. 12. Pa-akhem son of Hor p' ......, the sheikh (?).

No. 24. TasherenPetiHorsamtaui, daughter of PetiHorsamtaui (Πετεσομτους). Osiris.

No. 25. Pa-shere-Ahy son of Pa Akhem, the gold-worker. His name remains before Osiris.

No. 28. Osiris Nes-Hor-renpy-Ta-Beyk, born of Tasherepakhem, the wife of Pakhem son of .... the steward (?).

No. 29. Osiris Tasherepakhem daughter of Pa ...., the wife of Pakhem son of .... the steward.

No. 46. Osiris .... his soul hath gone to Osiris.

No. 48. "Anpe (Anubis) in Wyt, who is at the head of the divine bower. May there be given to thee a house of refreshment (*per tekhe*, lit. 'house of intoxication'!), oxen, fowl, all good things that are good that are pure that are rich, N. son of M. who went to his fathers in the year of life 27, 6 months 21 days. Lives his soul for ever before Osiris." Here we have some curious renderings of old formulae, note especially the version of *pert-kheru* (!).

No. 53. This label, though in Greek, still entitles the deceased "Usiris."

Coffin of Beb.

59. Pls. XXXVII.–XXXVII.k. Though this monument belongs to the earlier group of the Dendereh inscriptions, the nature of the long texts inscribed upon it places it in a separate category. The coffin was composed of separate slabs of limestone, rough outside, but on the inside closely inscribed with religious texts, no doubt in order that the deceased might have the magic formulae at hand for reference in case of need. This is in fact the usual position in which they are found on early coffins of stone or wood. On the slab forming the east side of the coffin the inscriptions had been utterly destroyed, but on the opposite side, on the two ends and on the inside of the lid, much remained; all this Mr. and Mrs. Petrie laboriously traced and copied. Apart from any question of mutilation, the writing is exceedingly bad. First it was drawn with ink upon the stone in a semi-cursive style, and was then chiselled in a perfunctory manner by a mason, whose work in places reduced itself to mere chisel holes. Fortunately a good deal of the black ink remained, thus assisting the copyists in ascertaining the reading.

The texts are of special value, since they are in many cases early versions of those known from papyri of much later date as parts of the so-called Book of the Dead. The chapters of the Book of the Dead hitherto found on coffins of the Middle Kingdom, or slightly earlier, are very few in number; we have here an entirely new series for that period. The following notes can serve only as a starting-point for others, and we may look for many fresh identifications. Doubtless it would repay the student to examine anew the obscure writing of the original in the Gizeh Museum.

The name of the owner occurs only at the north end, where he is called "the *repa ha*, Beb" (pl. xxxvii.f), in somewhat barbarous hieroglyphs. The key plan (pl. xxxvii.) shows the arrangement of the existing inscriptions. Where the original starting-point was it is not easy to say: probably the inscriptions round the coffin began on the west side, that being the place of honour, while the inscription on the lid began again independently, as the first texts in each case seem to be addressed to the local goddess Hathor. The local allusions, which of course do not occur in the Book of the Dead, are of particular value and rarity.

The lid (pls. xxxvii.-xxxvii.B) is inscribed in four broad longitudinal bands of columnar writing, interrupted by occasional tabulations of texts. The upper band is the narrowest and is divided for two-thirds of its length into two half-bands of short columns. Its text is evidently addressed to Hathor, and contains a list of incidents connected probably with the feasts of Dendereh. The first half-band is headed by "I come to hear," and contains a list of 100 festal incidents. The second half-band was no doubt headed by the word "in"; it gives a list of about 100 localities in which the incidents severally took place. It is clear that the whole is addressed to the local goddess Hathor, and that Beb desires to renew after death the pious relaxations of his earthly life at Dendereh. Reading with this key to the arrangement we have in ll. 19 and 119, "I have come to hear the coming forth of the god in the desert hills of the god"; and other instances of correspondence between the entries in each half-band are clear in ll. 72 and 173, 77 and 178.

In ll. 1-5 Beb says:

"I come that I may hear the talk (?) of the feast, thy (fem., as relating to Hathor) *thentet*-oxen, thy *semut*, the dances, the flood .... (19) the coming forth of the god, the uplifting of the bark, the throwing of the stick .... the bringing of the *kas*, the joining of the *kas*, the giving of praise .... (76) the gathering of the lotuses, the music .... (90) the hounds........... (95) the laying down of bread and beer, the partaking of bread and beer, the manifestation of the god, the drink offerings, peace in life, the giving of ...." &c., &c.

The localities specified in the lower half-band (ll. 101-200) may well have been favourite places (in the neighbourhood of Dendereh?) in which Beb wished to enjoy the above-named sights and sounds. Among them are (104), "the Southern Islands, the Islands of Life, Kenset (there was a district of this name above the First Cataract), Nerau (?), the Pools of Coolness, the Divine Pool, the Divine City, the Middle Islands, the Divine Place, Taking Offerings, the Divine Hill-country, &c., &c.

ll. 201-256, in columns the full width of the band, continue with a hymn to Hathor, which ends with l. 222. Then begins an address to certain divine "lords" concerning Beb's complete knowledge of mystic roads, sixteen in number, with their names, &c., in succession. The Chapter of the Sixteen Roads continues into the second band. The next formulae (262 *et seqq.*) deal with a succession of eight nets or snares, of which the names are given; these are to be escaped by addressing them in the words prescribed.

ll. 276-292 contain the Chapter of Escaping from the Net, already known as chap. cliii. of the Book of the Dead, the table (282-290) showing the names of the component parts of the net and of its makers and users—the spindle for the thread, the netting-needle, &c., &c.

l. 294 seems to be the beginning of a chapter hitherto unknown. It concerns escape from some evil: "Osiris knoweth its name, he shall not fall into it; I know its name, I shall not fall into it."

l. 321 begins a chapter perhaps "of [bringing?] a man's magic (?) to him in *Kher-neter*"; it mentions the "Island of Flame" (323). l. 337 mentions the "locust."

ll. 354-380: "Chapter of passing through the West."

ll. 384-396: chapter of "Going out into the Broad Space."

ll. 397-400: chapter of "Being with (?) the great."

In the third band, ll. 415-416 seem to be a chapter of "Giving bread in On."

ll. 417-418: chap. xliii. of the Book of the Dead, for having the head restored and not taken away after it has been cut off—referring probably to the early practice of dismemberment, for which see especially *Deshasheh*.

l. 424: chap. xlvi. of the Book of the Dead.

Over ll. 425 *et seqq.* we read "Opening a fortress (?) in the horizon"; and beyond, "Building a fortress (?) in the horizon."

In ll. 474 *et seqq.* are certain phrases often recurring in the Book of the Dead: "'Then what dost thou live upon?' say the gods to me. I live on what ye live on .... what I hate is filth, I will not eat."

Over ll. 546 *et seqq.* are the headings "Entering the boat; the four pillars." The latter are the four pillars of heaven, identified in the vertical columns of text below the heading as follows: the Southern is Hermopolis, the Northern is Buto, the Western is Heliopolis, the Eastern is *Ān.*

In ll. 556 *et seqq.*, "I shall not die, my body shall not be taken from me, the dog shall not eat me, the falcon shall not tear me." Beyond this is a chapter of "bringing the magic of a man to him in Hades."

ll. 590 *et seqq.*: chap. xxxii. of the Book of the Dead, of driving off the crocodiles that would take a man's magic power from him.

In l. 621 there is a chapter referring to some transformation. From l. 625 to the end of the inscription on the lid (656) there is a large part of the lengthy chap. lxxviii. of the Book of the Dead, the chapter of "transformation into a sacred sparrow-hawk." Possibly this was completed on some other part of the coffin.

The sides and ends of the coffin itself were inscribed in two rows, of which the upper one is by far the better preserved. The North end (657 *et seqq.*) gives the hieroglyphic list of offerings, &c., and "Favour accorded by the king and Anubis (in his two forms)."

On the West side—the place of honour—we have texts probably connected with Hathor (cf. l. 688, and the last phrase in l. 698, which is evidently addressed to a goddess). In l. 699 begins a long chapter addressed first to Meht-wert, one form of the cow-goddess, and then to Neper, the god of corn. At l. 742 we have apparently a new text. It is difficult to discover what were the texts in the now mutilated lower row.

The inscriptions on the South end are likewise obscure.

Needless to say that the texts from this coffin which can be identified with chapters from the Book of the Dead, differ greatly from the latter as found in papyri of the New Kingdom or later.

In order to understand the Book of the Dead, we require to trace the growth of each chapter if possible to its origin, but at any rate to its earliest written form, and in any systematic collection of the early material, the texts from the coffin of Beb will certainly take an important place.

REPORT ON ANIMAL MUMMIES.

By Oldfield Thomas, F.Z.S.

60. Mr. Thomas has kindly sent me the following identifications of the animal mummies from the catacombs.

Cercopithecus pyrrhonotus, Hempr. and Ehr.

One very imperfect skull appears to be referable to this species.

Cercopithecus sabæus, Linn.

One mummied specimen, which has been determined by Dr. Anderson with the help of a Röntgen ray photograph.

Felis chaus, Güld., *Felis caligata*, Temm.

Among the considerable number of cat remains, two or three skulls evidently belong to the comparatively large *F. chaus*. The remainder are provisionally referred to *F. caligata*, but differ a good deal among themselves in size. It is difficult to say whether these differences are merely due to age and sex, indicate a difference of species, or—as seems very probable—show that the Egyptians had several races of tame cats, just as in the case of the dogs.

Herpestes ichneumon, L.

An imperfect mummy, and a large number of skulls. The ancient skulls seem to average rather smaller than do modern ones of the same species, but it is possible that the difference is due to alteration in the bones induced by incineration, and is not really natural.

Canis familiaris, L.

Five mummied specimens, and a large number of skulls and other bones. The majority of the skulls belong to a dog of about the size of a spaniel, and suggest the Pariah dog of India, or the ordinary street dogs of oriental towns. One skull and one mummy, however, belong to a much smaller form of about the size of a terrier.

Lepus, sp.

One lower jaw of a hare is in the collection. It cannot be exactly determined, but may be *L. ægyptiacus*.

Gazella dorcas, L.

Three imperfect skulls, all of females, and some fragments of horn cores. Of the three small gazelles, *G. dorcas, leptoceros*, and *isabella*, which might have been in the possession of the ancient Egyptians, these fragments appear to agree most closely with the corresponding part of *G. dorcas*, although they are too imperfect for the determination to be quite certain. Both *G. leptoceros* and *G. isabella* have decidedly more convex parietal profiles than the mummied fragments, while in *G. dorcas* there seems to be a fair agreement in this respect. *G. dorcas* is now found throughout Lower Egypt; *G. leptoceros* in the sandy deserts of Western Egypt, extending southwards into Nubia; and *G. isabella* is the common gazelle of the southern Red Sea littoral and some parts of Upper Egypt.

Bos indicus, Linn.

A number of skulls. These specimens do not appear to be separable from the common domestic oxen now found in Egypt.

Ibis, (?) *religiosa*. Two mummies.

Cerchneis tinnuncula. Two mummies.

Cerchneis naumanni. Two mummies.

Anser (?) *ægyptiacus*. One mummy.

Among the animals from Abadiyeh in 1899 there are already noted the ass and the hartebeest.

REPORT ON METALS.

By Dr. Gladstone, F.R.S.

61. Of the statue of King Pepy, Dr. Gladstone writes :—

"The pieces of metal belonging to the VIth Dynasty from Hierakonpolis consist of a thin central portion with a metallic appearance, which is covered with a thick incrustation of silicious earth and vari-coloured minerals, especially black crystals, which under the microscope have all the appearance and lustre of cuprite, and give the reactions of suboxide of copper. Portions of the undecomposed core, from which the mineral crust had been as far as possible scraped, appeared very crystalline and dark coloured under the microscope: it was almost entirely a mixture of copper and copper oxide. The general analysis of this metallic portion gave

Copper . . .	78·3	per cent.
Alumina . .	1·5	"
Carbonate of lime .	2·5	"
Insoluble residue .	0·9	"
Oxygen, &c. . .	16·8	"
	100·0	

There was but a doubtful indication of tin in the metallic core, but the presence of some black oxide of tin (cassiterite) in the surrounding crust was less doubtful. It is of course impossible to say from these data what may have been the original proportion of tin, if any, in the metallic alloy, but it was probably small.

The pieces of copper from the vase of Mera at Dendereh, of about the same period, closely resemble those just described, but the minerals on the surface were still more varied and beautiful when magnified. The central portion was so extremely thin that it could not be separated from the crust. Under the microscope it seemed to consist almost entirely of cuprite. The evidence of tin was a little stronger than in the previous specimen, but in any case it could not be determined quantitatively.

The thin sheets of copper from Tomb 431 at Dendereh, belonging to the XIIth Dynasty, showed much less oxidation or mineralised crust. A portion freed from the outside coating gave 94·8 per cent. of copper, and indications of 1·1 per cent. of tin. There was also a trace of arsenic.

Lead was not observed in any of these specimens. Such traces of iron as existed were doubtless accidental.

These analyses confirm the belief that tin was added to the copper in these early periods, though in small quantities.

As to the gold foil from the tomb of Adu I., of the VIth Dynasty. Different pieces of the foil varied a good deal in colour. I examined some of the brightest, and some of the darkest gold. The brighter portion gave the following result :—

Gold . . .	78·0	per cent.
Silver . . .	18·0	"
Sand, &c. . .	4·0	"
	100·0	

A darker piece was submitted to a more careful analysis, and gave

Gold . . .	81·7	per cent.
Silver . . .	16·1	„
Copper . . .	trace	
Insoluble residue .	0·8	„
Loss . . .	1·4	„
	100·0	

It is evident therefore that these two specimens consist almost entirely of electrum; i.e. gold with a considerable amount of silver, such as was generally obtained from the River Pactolus and other parts of Asia Minor. It is not likely it was the gold of Nubia, for that contains very little, if any, silver. The copper in the second specimen was so very small that it cannot be supposed to have been added intentionally. The microscope showed that the portion insoluble in acids was the fine sand of the desert."

DESCRIPTION OF PLATES.

Frontispiece. View in mastaba of ADU I., from the square well, looking up the tunnel. The narrowness of the well prevented this being photographed, and it is therefore reproduced from a drawing in which every joint has been put in from measurement. The great archway is the oldest example of such brickwork yet known, though small archings appear in the IVth Dynasty. The uniform grey of the lower part of the well is the natural bed of marl, in which the well and chamber are cut. The upper part is of built brickwork, level with the general body of the mastaba, the entrance being above the ground level. For plan and section, see pl. xxix. For description, see pp. 8, 9.

PL. I. False door of Prince MENA. This retains a good deal of the original colouring, but has been chipped about in later times. The work is careful, and detailed in the offerings, though inferior to that of the great steles of the IVth Dynasty. For description, see pp. 5, 42. Now in Cairo Museum, *Catalogue Scientifique*, no. 1662.

PL. II. False door of ABU-SUTEN; this name should rather be read SUTEN EN-ABU. The view of the existing lower part of the stone false door is shown at the base of the plate. For the plan of it, see pl. xxviii. Although there were some traces of drawing on the side blocks, the only sculpture was at the back of the door niche. This sculpture is shown on this plate; its characteristics are those of the earliest sculptures of Saqqara, and it probably belongs to the close of the IIIrd Dynasty. See pp. 5, 42. In Brit. Mus.

Slabs of Prince MENA. The great drum at the top was placed over the entrance of the chamber of offerings. In Brit. Mus. The square slabs were inserted over each of the niches on the eastern face. For plan, see pl. xxviii. For description, see pp. 6, 43. One each in Cairo, Brit. Mus., Boston. Slab with Nebt-at-ef at Philadelphia.

Passage of ADU I. View of north entrance to tunnel, showing jointing of brickwork, with part of the closing-wall left across the mouth of the tunnel. This is the opposite end of the same tunnel seen in the frontispiece.

PL. III. Sarcophagus of MENA; drawn by Mr. Davies. The sides of this small chamber are of limestone, and the whole of the design is painted in various colours on the surface. A great deal has therefore entirely disappeared, owing to efflorescence of salts, and it was only with close examination that the present amount could be recovered. Only the two door-slabs, top right hand, were in sufficiently good state to be removed. They are now at Chicago University. See pp. 6, 44-5.

PL. IV. Enlargement of list of offerings in pl. iii.

PL. V. Fresco in entrance-chamber of ADU I. This had been greatly destroyed in ancient times by weathering. A hand copy of the traces of the inscription was made by me when first found, and later on Mr. Davies made the full-sized tracing of the whole which is here reproduced. No part of it was removed. See pp. 8, 45.

Pl. VI. Cornice of Prince Adu I. These strips were found scattered along the eastern face, having fallen from the top of the mastaba wall. At Boston. The slab with men offering was found also on the east side. The slab of Sekhet-hotep was found in the north-east chamber. See pp. 8, 46. Both at Philadelphia.

Cornice of Prince Adu II. This was found likewise fallen before the false doors of the eastern face. At Philadelphia. The slabs below seem to have formed part of the great inscription over the doorway. At Bristol. The inscribed corner-piece at the left hand being probably part of the door-jamb. At Bristol. See pp. 9, 46.

Qebdat, &c. This name should rather be read Degat. See pp. 10, 47.

Pl. VII. Statue of Adu II., found broken, half-way down the well of the mastaba. At New York. The two slabs of Adu II. and his wife Ana were found in the chamber of offerings. One now in Cairo Mus., *Cat. Sc.*, no. 1657; the other at Manchester.

Slabs of Pepy-ta-snefer = Senna. This name should rather be read Pepy-seshem-nefer. These slabs are in perfect condition, having been stored together in the chamber, and never erected over the false door panelling. At Cairo, Brit. Mus., Manchester, Bolton, Bristol, Greenock. Of the broken pieces, see transcription at the beginning of pl. xiii. For plan, see pl. xxx.; inscriptions, pp. 11, 47. Two slabs in Cairo Mus., *Cat. Sc.*, nos. 1659, 1661.

Slabs of Zauta-resa. These were much broken up, owing to the bad quality of the stone. The mastaba is planned on pl. xxviii. See pp. 7, 47. At Melbourne, Detroit, and Bolton.

Pl. VIII. Tomb of Merra. Over the outer doorway of the mastaba was a façade of seven inscribed slabs. Of these, the first and fifth have been entirely destroyed, and the others have all been broken in their overthrow. The five slabs and cornice now at New York. The standing figure of Merra at the left end appears to have been a good deal too tall for the slabs of inscription that remain, and it seems not unlikely therefore that the slab (in Brit. Mus.) with the bull and two herdsmen formed part of a line of animals beneath the inscription. Below this are three of the stone panels which were along the eastern face. See pp. 15, 16, 47, 48. At Brit. Mus., Cairo, and Manchester.

Pl. IX. Tomb of Sen-nezsu. The large false door (now at Bolton), one panel from the east face, and part of a scene of offerings, are described on pp. 16, 48.

Pl. X. Other fragments and inscriptions of Sen-nezsu. See p. 49. Inscription of 300 trees at Chicago. Others Manchester and Bolton.

A fragment of Uaru-kau should perhaps rather read Redu-ahut. See pp. 21, 49. At Greenock.

Slab of Hotep-sa. See pp. 14, 49.

Slabs of Ptah-mera and Uhaa. See pp. 15, 49.

Pl. XI. Heading read VIth to XIth Dynasty. The seventh block, without name, is of Nemy or Uhemy, tomb 518.

Beba and Hentsen, see plan, base of pl. xxx. See pp. 14, 49.

x wife Beba, pit tomb, see p. 50. At Edinburgh.

Shensetha and Beba-ur or Beba-sher. At Philadelphia. See pp. 15, 50.

Beba III. or C. For plan of mastaba, see pl. xxxii., and pp. 15, 50.

Henna or Henua. At Liverpool. See pl. xxxv. and pp. 19, 50.

Nemy or Uhemy (blank in plate). See pp. 20, 50. At Chicago.

Beba and Hathotep. See pp. 20, 50.

Nefert-kau or Nefert-ahu. See pp. 20, 50. At Chicago.

Nekhtu. See pp. 19, 50. At Ashmolean Mus.

HENNU and BET. See p. 20. At Ashmolean.

Outline figure. See p. 20. At Univ. Coll., London.

PL. XII. Mastaba of ANTEF-A. Remarkable for the extreme rudeness of the work, showing the lowest point of degradation of the Old Kingdom style. Plan, top of pl. xxxv. See pp. 19, 51. At Chicago and Philadelphia.

ANTEF-AQER II. and BEBA. This small drum, lintel (at Brit. Mus.), and finely carved panel, now so much broken (at New York), all belong to the great gallery tomb at base of pl. xxxiii., described on p. 21..

MERER, probably before XIth Dynasty. See p. 18. At Chicago.

KING MENTUHOTEP. The first cartouche is comparatively rough, but the fragments of the second show the finest work of the Middle Kingdom. See pp. 21, 51.

PL. XIII. Most of these fragments already bear reference to the plates and descriptions. IMHOTEPA, tomb 770, comes from the great Beba and Hentsen mastaba.

PL. XIV. VIIth to XIth Dynasty. ...ERDUTSA and BEBA-URT is from the mastaba Shensetha P., pl. xxxii.

PL. XV. Great stele of KHNUM-ERDU. See position of pit, pl. xxxiii. Translation, pp. 51-2 (in Cairo Mus.).

Figures of MENTUHOTEP and NEFER-MESUT. See pl. xxi., and p. 26.

Cartonnage inscriptions. See pp. 33, 55.

PLS. XVI.–XVIII. See pp. 23, 24.

PL. XIX. See p. 26.

PL. XX.. Mirrors, p. 25. Alabaster vases, p. 25. Slate slips, p. 26. Scarabs and mirror from flint-heap, p. 22. Group at base of plate, p. 25.

PL. XXI. Piece of bowl of black incised ware, found beside the earliest mastabas, IIIrd Dynasty. See p. 5.

Stone vases, and mirror, from tomb north of Zauta B. See base of pl. xxviii. At Cairo and Manchester. Described, beginning of p. 8.

Slab with vases from ADU I.; described, p. 8. At Edinburgh.

Statuettes of MENTUHOTEP and NEFER-MESUT, XIth Dynasty. See p. 26. At Ashmolean.

Two statuettes of women, XIth Dynasty. See p. 27. At Cairo and Philadelphia.

Statuette of ATSA. See p. 26. At Cairo.

Two figures of mourners. See p. 27. At Univ. Coll., London.

PL. XXII. Copper models, and beads, of MERU. See pp. 7, 25. At Ashmolean.

Flint knife, beads, and alabaster of ANTEF-AQER. See p. 25. At Ashmolean.

Tomb 309, beads, piece of ivory wand, bone figures, crocodile, &c. At Univ. Coll., London.

Ivory, XVIIIth Dynasty, fragments from inlay work of temple furniture (?). See p. 28. At Boston.

PL. XXIII. Blue glazed pottery, XVIIIth Dynasty, thrown out from temple into animal catacombs. 1. Menat. 2, 3. Pieces of wand. 4, 5. Heads of Hathor from sistra. 6. One of many fragments of patterned bowls. 7. Great *ankh* of Tahutmes III. 8, 9. Hollow balls moulded on twists of straw, probably for suspension in ceiling decoration; fragments of many more were found. 10, 11, 12. Model papyrus stems on cruciform stands, with cartouches of Tahutmes III. and Amenhotep II. 13. Model oar. 14. Body of vase. 15, 16, 17. Rude figures of Ta-urt and Hathor, such as were made in XIIth and continued to XVIIIth Dynasty. 18. Long beads. 19. Ring-stand (?). See p. 28. All at Philadelphia.

PL. XXIV. Bronzes, fully described. See pp. 34, 29, 30. No. 1, Philadelphia; No. 3, Ashmolean; No. 4, New York; No. 7, Chicago; No. 8, Univ. Coll. London; Nos. 11-14, Ashmolean and Boston; Nos. 16, 17, Pitt-Rivers Museum and Melbourne; Nos. 18 and 21, New York; No. 19, Brit. Mus.; No. 20, Philadelphia.

PL. XXV. Pottery dish, XVIIIth Dynasty. See p. 24. At Ashmolean.

Stele of Mutardus. See pp. 31, 53. At Boston.

Stele of Horsiast. See pp. 21, 54. At Chicago.

Stele of Pedu-hor-sam-taui. See pp. 31, 54. At Cairo.

Dog mummies. See p. 30.

Funereal tablets. See p. 33. "Makhai" at Ashmolean; "Titianos" at Edinburgh.

Pl. XXVI. Glazed pottery amulets from Ptolemaic mummies, classified in list, pp. 32, 33. Distributed to fifteen museums; best set to Philadelphia, second to Univ. Coll., London.

Pl. XXVII. Plan of Dendereh cemetery. The position of the temple is approximately fixed to show its relation to the cemetery. The position and direction of each of the tombs was fixed separately. The plans are all reduced photographically from the larger plans which follow. (R) refers to tombs opened by Mr. Rosher, after the survey. See p. 4 *et seqq.* for description.

Pls. XXVIII.–XXXV. These plans of mastabas have all been fully noticed in the text, for references to which see the Index. The broken shading in the plans is used to represent loose gravel filling. The dead black is solid brickwork, and chambers intentionally left clear remain white.

Pl. XXXVI. Plan of catacombs. The white line, left in the thickness of the walls, shows the separation into two independent walls from which spring the vaultings to either side. See pp. 28-30.

Pl. XXXVII. A portion of the long inscriptions on the great sarcophagus of Prince Beb. See pp. 17, 18, 56.

DESCRIPTION OF EXTRA PLATES.

Pl. II.a. Cornice of mastaba of Prince Mena; arranged according to the sense, from the fallen blocks. See pp. 6, 43. Cairo Museum.

Two drums from over the false door on the east face. Also two panels with figures from the same. See p. 6. At Manchester and Bristol.

Strip of inscription from the side of the recess of the great stele, pl. i. See p. 6.

Slab, defaced, reading bilaterally from a middle line; probably the middle slab of the inscription over the door. See pp. 6, 43, 44. Slab (left hand, base), found outside mastaba of Mena, which might belong to that of Meru adjoining. See pp. 6, 44. Both at Chicago.

Pl. V.a. Bands of inscription around the sepulchre of Adu I. The sequence of the lines is given by the lettered plan in the corner. The whole of this, along with the other blocks of the scenes of offerings, and lists of offerings, is now in the Cairo Museum. See pp. 9, 45, 46.

Pl. VII.a. Slabs and cornice of Senna; order not known. See pp. 11, 47. At Chicago.

Various pieces of cornice, and lintels. In middle, the top one is of Merru, N. of Adu II. Below is a lintel of Degat (at Manchester), (pp. 10, 47); and a lintel of Rehuia A. (pp. 18, 47). At the base is a lintel of Kathena (pp. 19, 47). At Manchester.

Beba II., or B., is of XIth Dynasty. See pp. 20, 47. The fragments near it are copied at the top of pl. xv.

Pl. VIII.a. False door of Merra. See pp. 16, 48. Now in Cairo Museum.

Pl. VIII.b. Panels and parts of family scenes of Merra. See p. 16. At Liverpool, Edinburgh, Dundee, Glasgow, and Chicago.

Pl. VIII.c. Cornice of mastaba of Merra. See pp. 16, 48. At New York.

Pl. X.a. Cornice of mastaba of Sen-nezsu, and fragments of scenes. See pp. 16, 17, 49. At Philadelphia.

Cornice of Ptahmera, in order as found lying before the E. face. Also a slab in relief. See pp. 15, 49. At Chicago.

Slab of Beba T. and Nekht, and piece of Mentuhotep at right: all found together. See pp. 20, 49.

Pl. XI.a. Slabs and cornice of Beba and Hentsen (at Detroit), and of Abu-suten or Sutenenabu. See pp. 14, 50.

Cornice of Shensetha P. (see pp. 15, 50), at Detroit; the small double altar of Shensetha T. (pp. 15, 19).

Pl. XI.b. Beba III. or C. See pp. 15, 51. Though with name of Hotepa, this came from the tomb of Beba C.

Shenseta, Hotepa (omit Kednus). The top right-hand piece is of Hotepa (pp. 19, 51). The half-length figure is not connected with any other pieces: from the style it may belong to the late XIth Dynasty.

Hotepa. At side is a lintel of Sebeknekhta and Beba T. See copy, pl. xv. (p. 20).

Hotepa and Adua. See pp. 19, 51.

Hotepa, three blocks. Another, and the latest, person of this name. See pp. 20, 51.

Beba G, tomb 490. See p. 20.

Sentekha. See p. 20.

Bauhotepa, showing the beginning of the revival of the XIth Dynasty. See p. 20.

Pl. XI.c. Rehuia B. See p. 18.

x and Beba. See p. 20.

Nubheq. See p. 20. At Boston.

Sentekhneba, or read Senta (?). p. 20.

Antefa cornice, same tomb as on pl. xii. pp. 19, 51.

Mera. See p. 20, top; p. 51. Una, p. 14.

Antef and Ay, see p. 20. Demza and Hepu, see p. 20. At Boston.

Antefaqer I. or A. For plan, see pl. xxxiii., middle. See pp. 20, 51. At Manchester.

Pl. XX.a. Marks scratched on pottery. These are mostly of the XIIth Dynasty. No. 27 is of the IVth Dynasty. Nos. 1 and 42 are written in black ink.

Pl. XXIII.a. Inscription on sistrum handle. See pp. 28, 53.

Inscription on bronze situla. See pp. 34, 53.

Marks of VIth Dynasty on building blocks.

Ivory figure of woman and child.

Sandstone coffin of Nesi-hor; hand copy, not exact facsimile. See pp. 31, 53. At Chicago.

Pl. XXV.a. Sandstone tablets of Ptolemaic age. For positions, see p. 31; translations on p. 54. At Boston, New York, Chicago, Philadelphia, and Melbourne.

Pl. XXV.b. Demotic inscriptions in pl. xxv.a, and others, demotic and hieroglyphic. See pp. 44, 47, 51, 54.

Pls. XXVI.a, b. Limestone labels placed with the mummies of Ptolemaic age, inscribed in ink; a few are incised, as Nos. 18, 24, 25, 53. See pp. 32, 55.

Pls. XXXVII.a. to k. Inscriptions of the limestone sarcophagus of Prince Beb. The plan of the sheets is given on pl. xxxvii. Every column and line is numbered, and the numbers placed to each fifth. The only place where the name occurs is at the middle of the end, pl. xxxvii.f. See pp. 17, 56. All at Cairo.

Pls. A to O. Skeleton measurements in millimetres. In these plates all the measurements were made by Mr. D. MacIver; the arrangement of the plates we discussed together; the working the material into this shape was then done by Mr. MacIver; and then his MS. was worked up into these diagrams by me, with help from Miss Orme and my wife. The figures were all printed in strips, and then cut out and stuck into their right places, after I had ruled the sheets.

Throughout the diagrams the object has been to preserve the skeleton number of each measurement, so that any unusual variety could be tracked in other tables; at the same time, by arranging the numbers in cumulative piles, to form groups, so that the distribution could be seen as by a curve. The medians or means, and usually the quartiles or mean variations also, are shown by lines of thick dots.

Pls. A, B. Skull measurements, arranged so as to compare the three periods, in both male and female, the levels of the numbers in the diagrams being the same on either side. The length and breadth being co-ordinated, the index is shown by diagonal lines, and the limits of usual classes—dolichocephalic, &c.—are marked by thick brackets.

Pls. C, D. Skull breadths, at three points, in three periods, male and female. Arranged to compare the differences between the periods.

Pls. E, F. The alveolar and facial indices. The alveolar index is the basi-nasal ÷ the basi-alveolar length. The facial index is the nasi-alveolar ÷ the basi-alveolar length, or the relative height of the face. Arranged to compare the various periods.

Pls. G, H. The nasal and orbital indices, as usual.

Pls. J, K. The absolute lengths of the arm bones. The three best dimensions are given in

J, and those which are less satisfactory in K. Arranged to show the differences between male and female, and various periods.

Pl. L. Scapula measurements, nearly all of VIth–XIIth Dynasty, with a few Ptolemaic distinguished. The index is shown as in the skull measurements, Pl. A.

Pl. M. Sacrum measurements treated as the scapula measures. Also clavicle measures.

Pls. N, O. Leg bones, male and female. The level of the numbers is the same on each side, so that comparisons can be made across the sheet.

No conclusions are drawn from this mass of material here, as it is intended to discuss all this very fully, together with an equal amount obtained in the following year at Hu by Mr. MacIver (to appear in *Diospolis* next year), and also along with the previous collections of measurements published from Medum, Deshasheh, &c.

PRINTED BY GILBERT AND RIVINGTON, LIMITED, ST. JOHN'S HOUSE, CLERKENWELL, LONDON, E.C.

INDEX.

[1] "In general I use here letters to distinguish between persons of the same name when their order is uncertain; but when the relative order is known, Roman numerals are used, as Adu I., II., III., IV.": above, p. 7.

PLATES

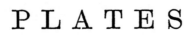

ABU-SUTEN.

PRINCE MENA.

FALSE DOOR OF ABU-SUTEN.

PASSAGE OF ADU I.

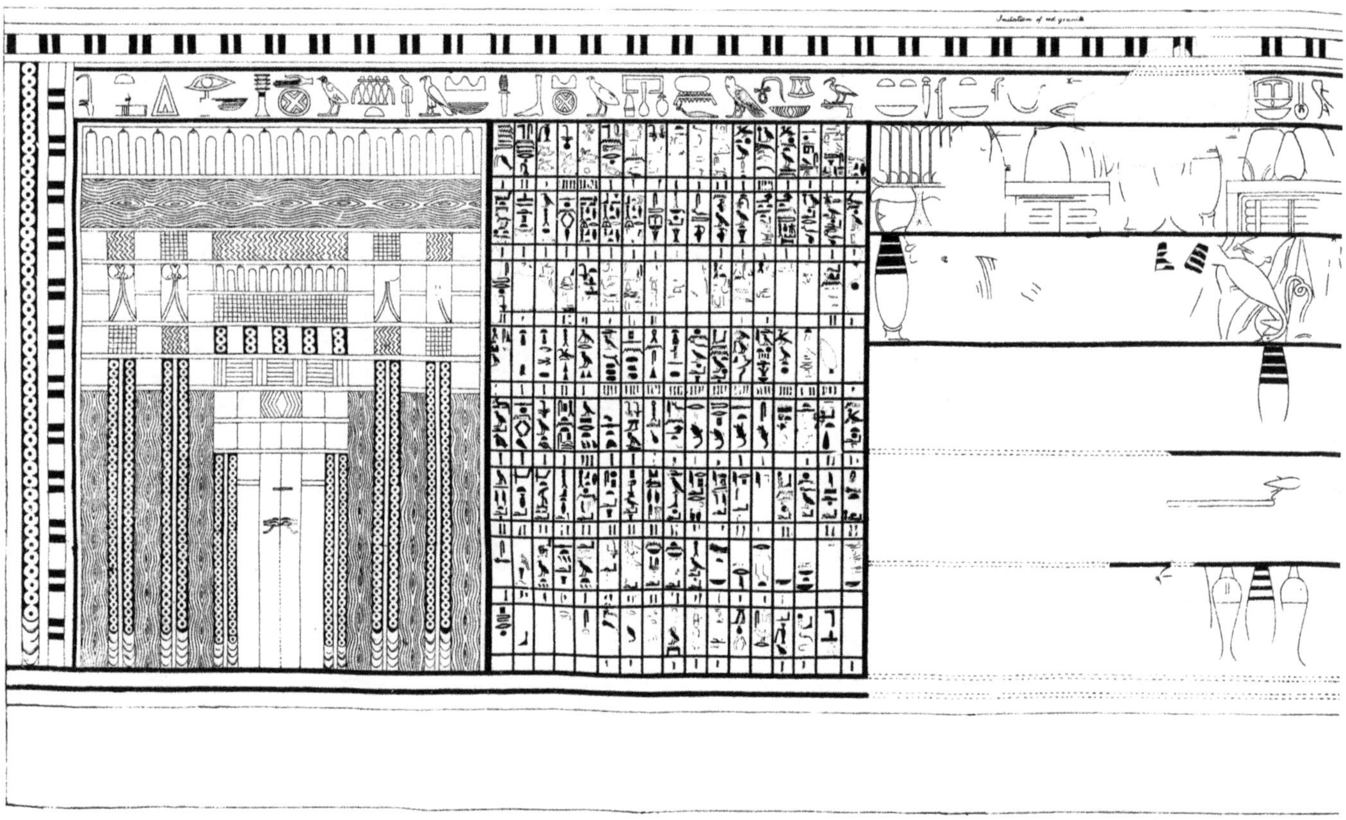
Imitation of red granite

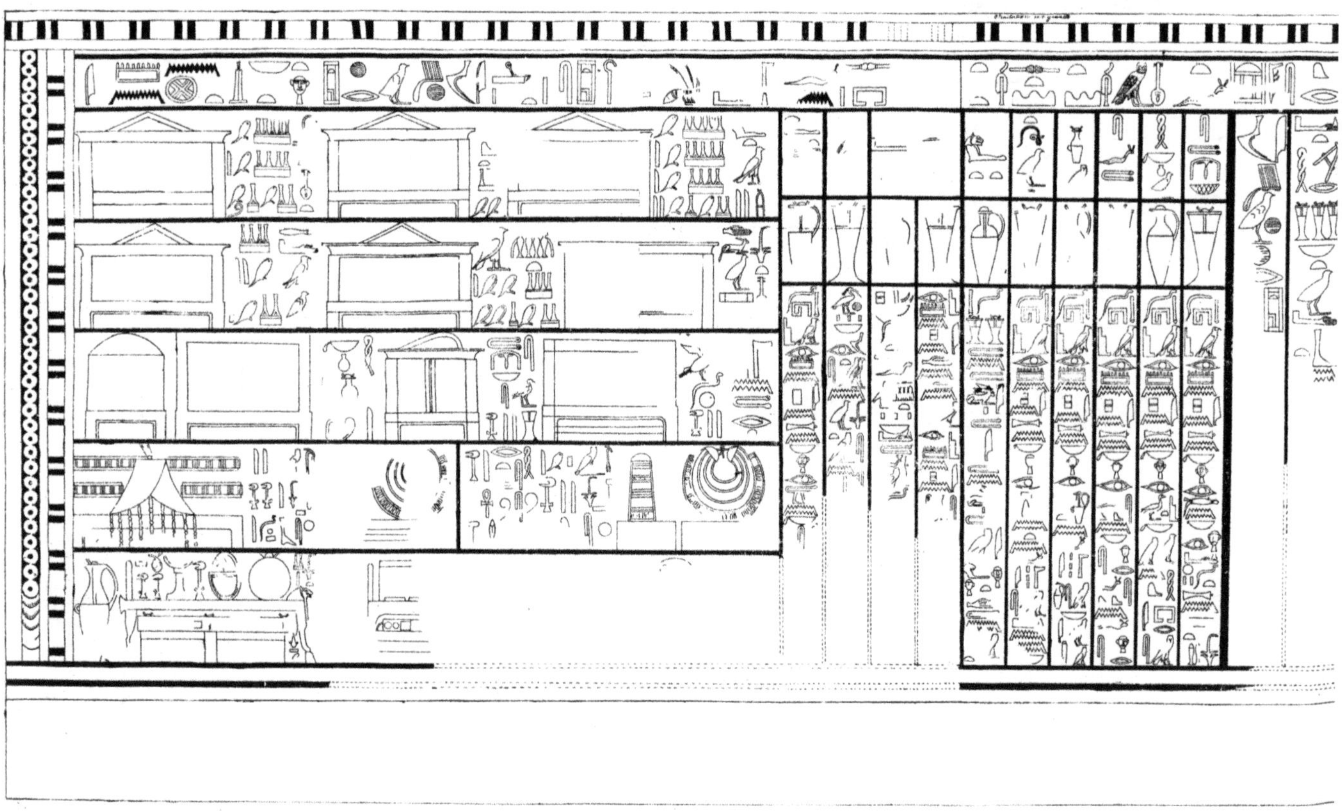
Imitation of red granite

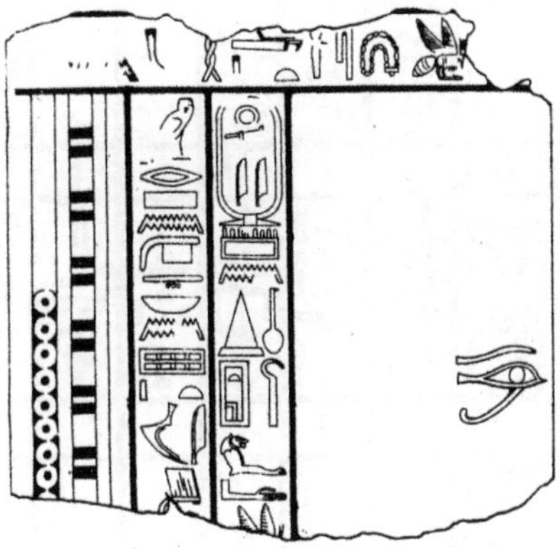

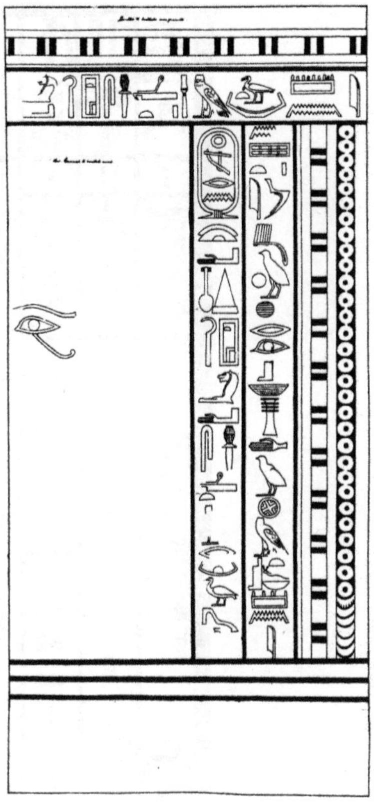

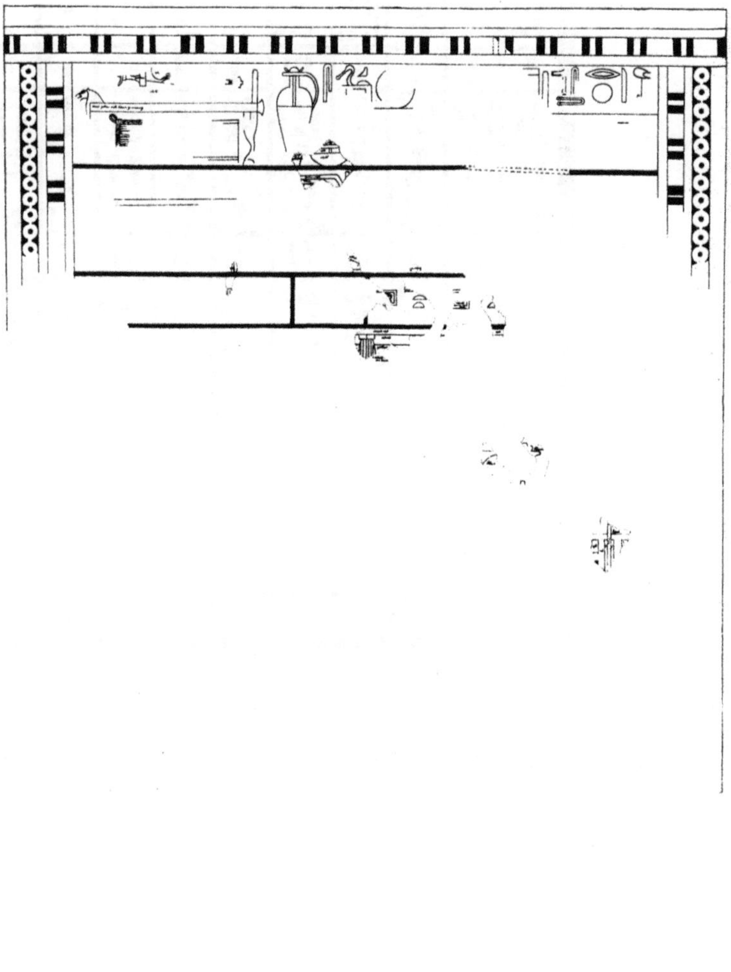

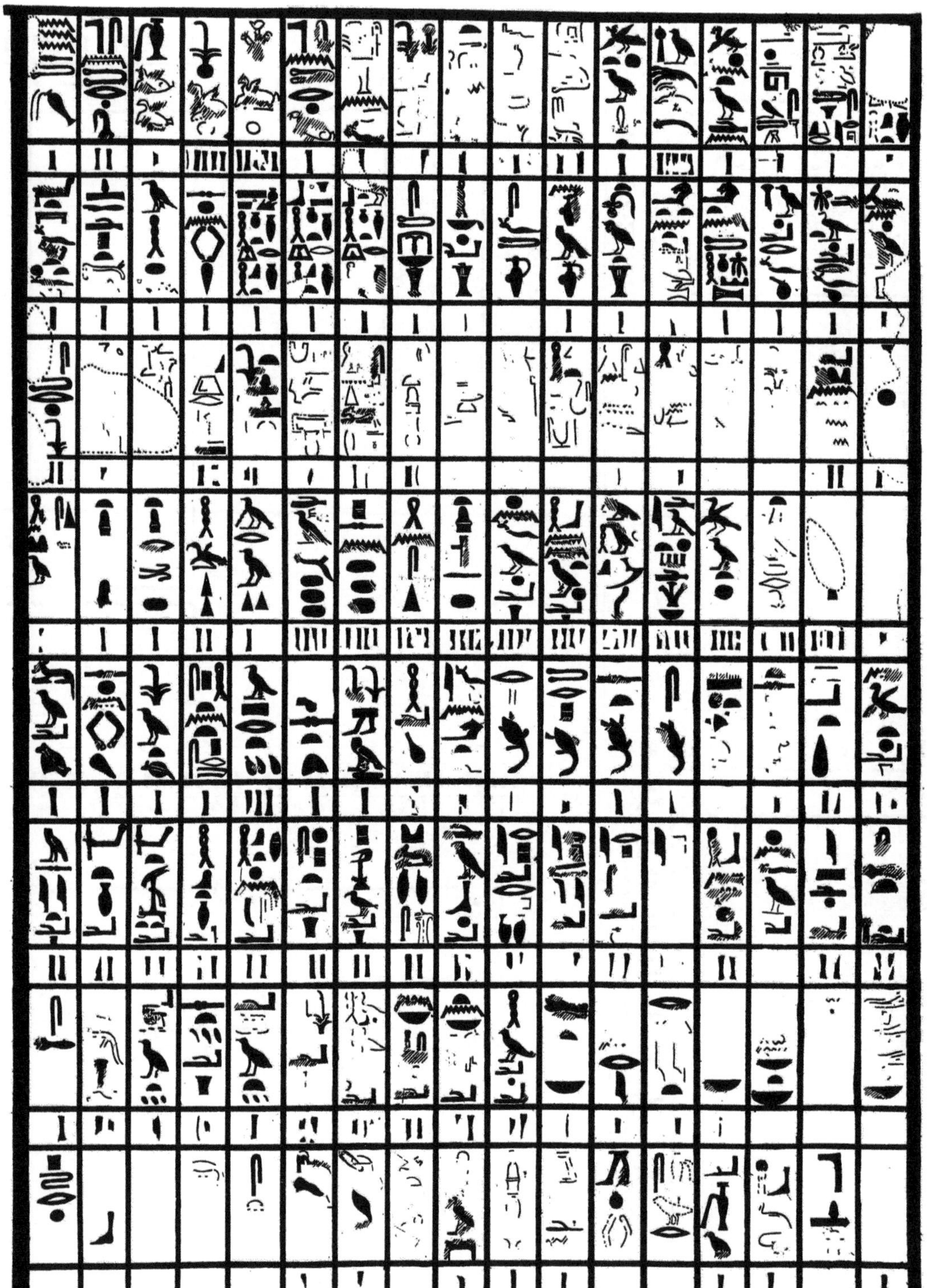

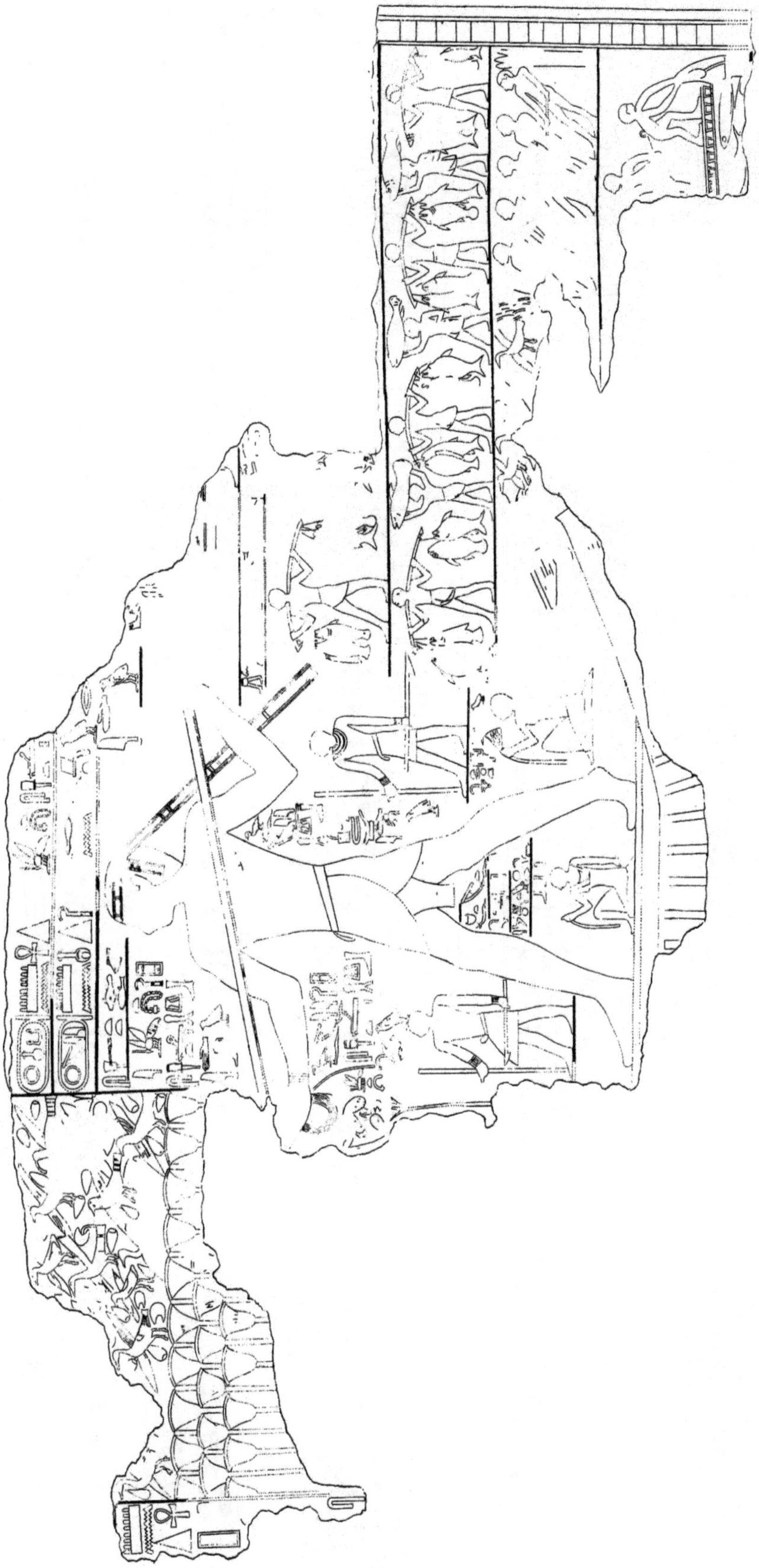

1 : 320
PLAN

PRINCE ADU I.

SEKHET-HOTEP IN ADU I.

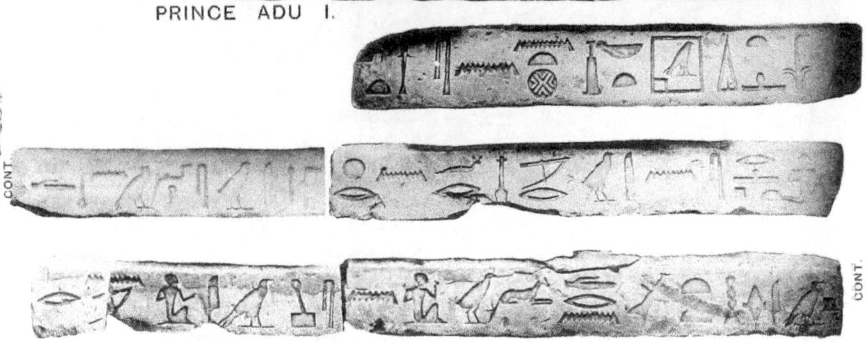

PRINCE ADU II.

QEBDAT, &c., N. OF ADU II.

ADU II.

(1 : 7)

PEPY-TA-SNEFER, = SENNA.

SENNA.

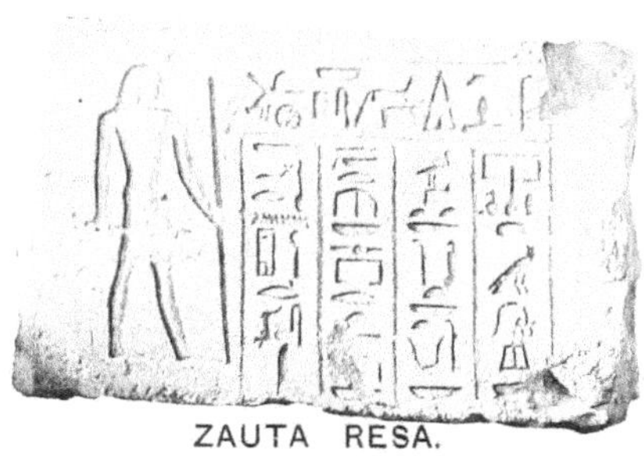

ZAUTA RESA.

ZAUTA RESA.

PEPY-TA-SNEFER—SENNA.

VARIOUS.

BEBA II.

ONE SLAB LOST.
ONE SLAB LOST.

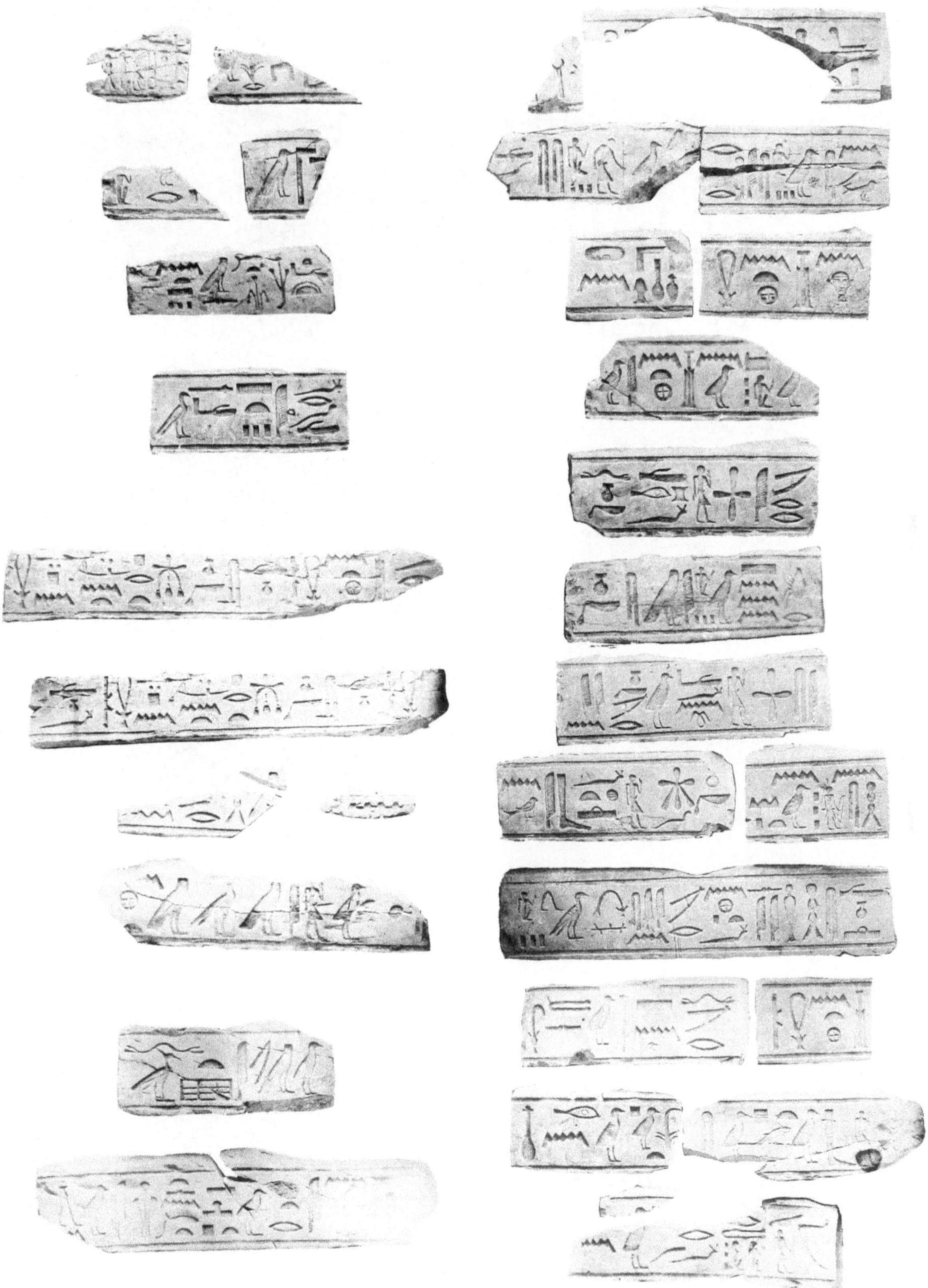

(Order as found fallen on the ground.)

1 : 8

SEN-NEZ-SU.

SEN-NEZ-SU.

UARU-KAU.

HOTEPSA.

PTAHMERA.

UHAA.

SEN-NEZ-SU.

PTAH MERA CORNICE, IN ORDER AS FOUND.

BEBA AND NEKHT.

PTAH MERA.

1 : 10 BEBA AND HENTSEN.

BEBA AND HENTSEN.

X, WIFE BEBA.

SHENSETHA AND BEBA-UR.

BEBA III.

HENNA.

BEBA AND HATHOTEP.

NEFERT KAU.

NEKHTU.

HENNU AND BET.

OUTLINED FIGURE.

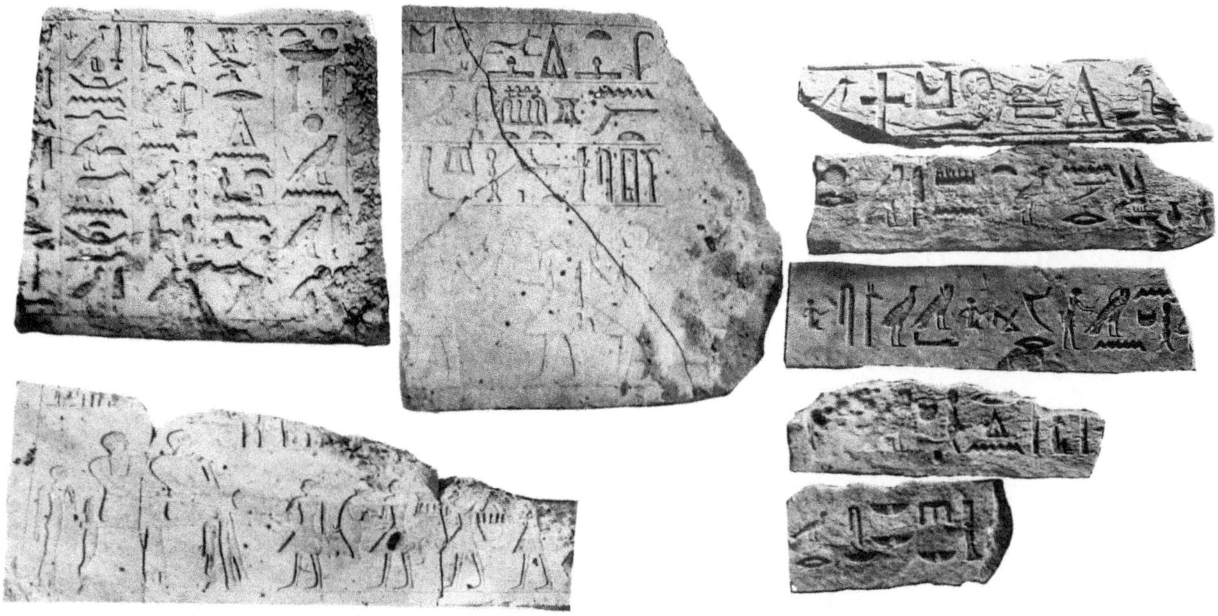

BEBA AND HENTSEN.

ABU-SUTEN.

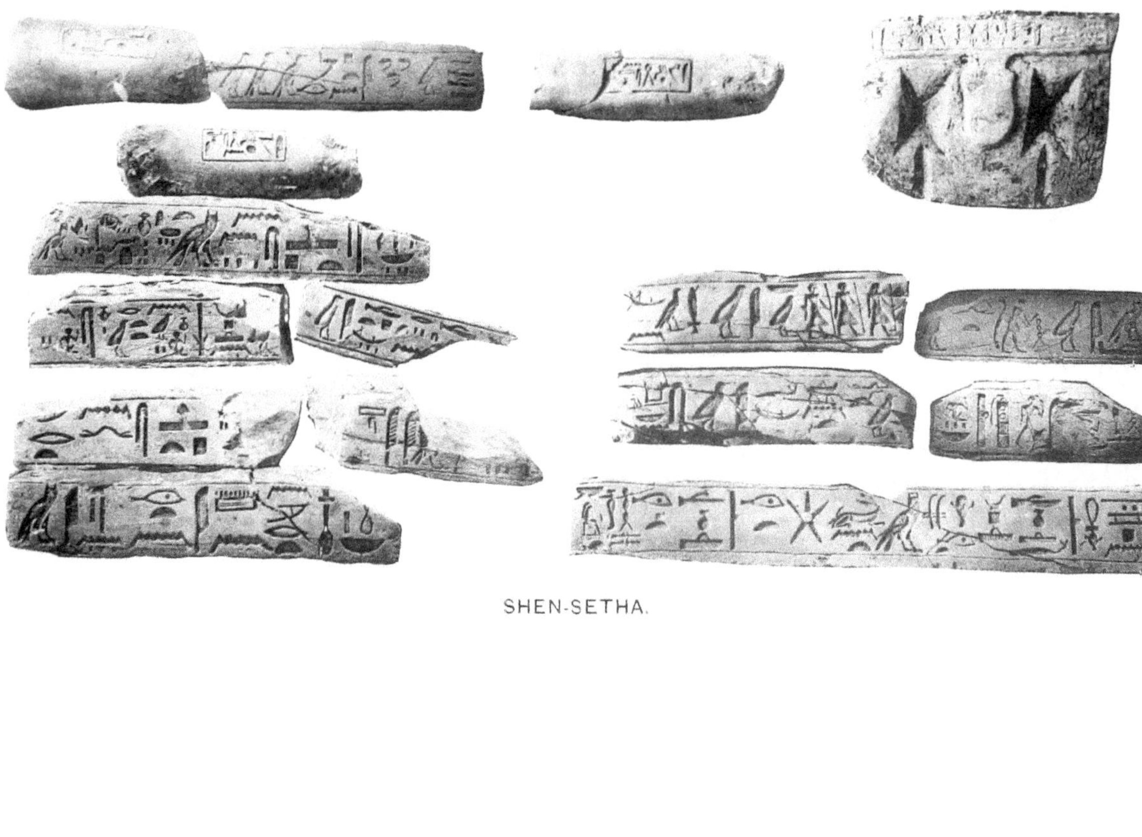

SHEN-SETHA.

BEBA III.

SHENSETA HOTEPA.

HOTEPA.

HOTEPA AND ADUA.

HOTEPA.

BEBA.

SENTEKHA.

X.

BAUHOTEPA.

REHUIA.

X AND BEBA.

NUBHEQ.

SENTEKHNEBA.

ANTEFA.

MERA (325) AND UNA.

ANTEF AND AY.

DEMZA AND HEPU.

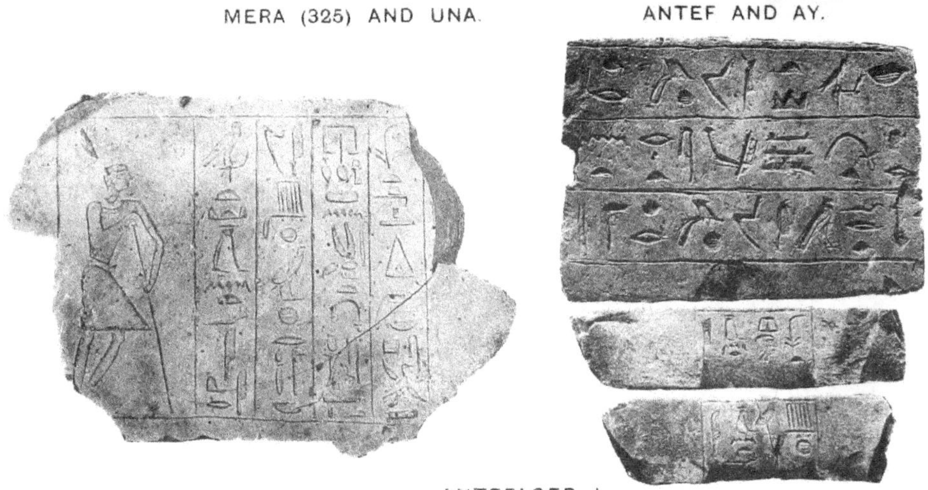

ANTEFAQER I.

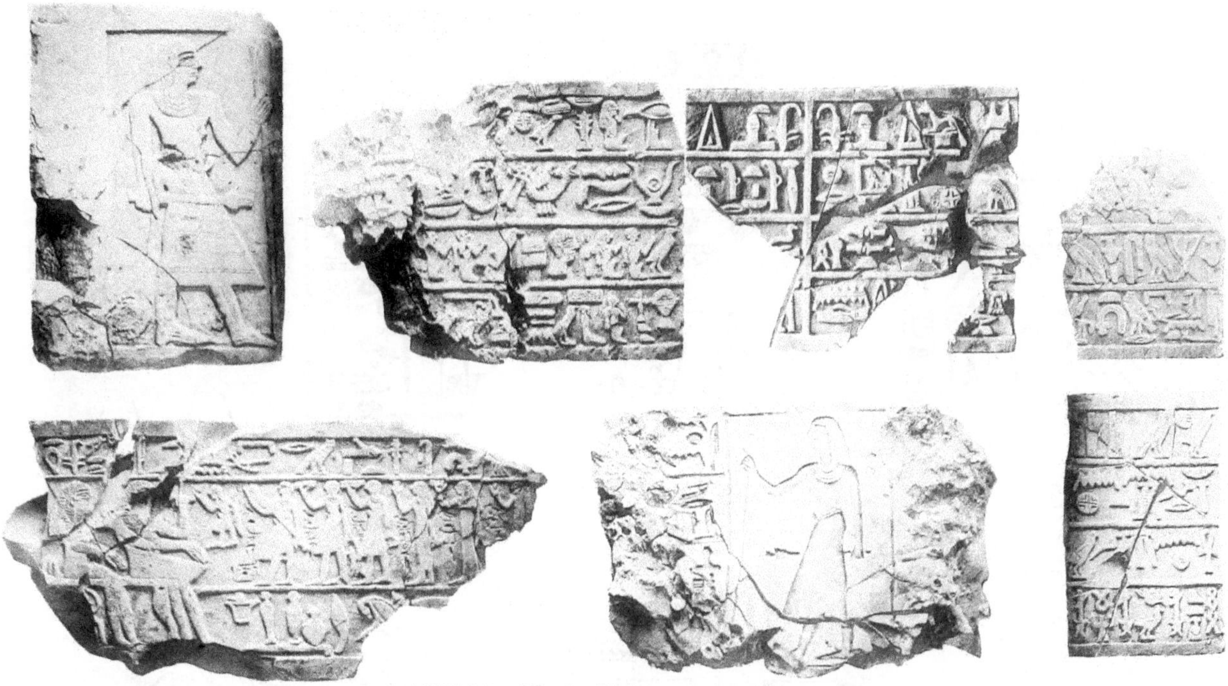

MASTABA OF ANTEF-A.

1 : 10

GALLERY OF ANTEF-AQER II. AND BEBA.

MERER.

KING MENTUHOTEP

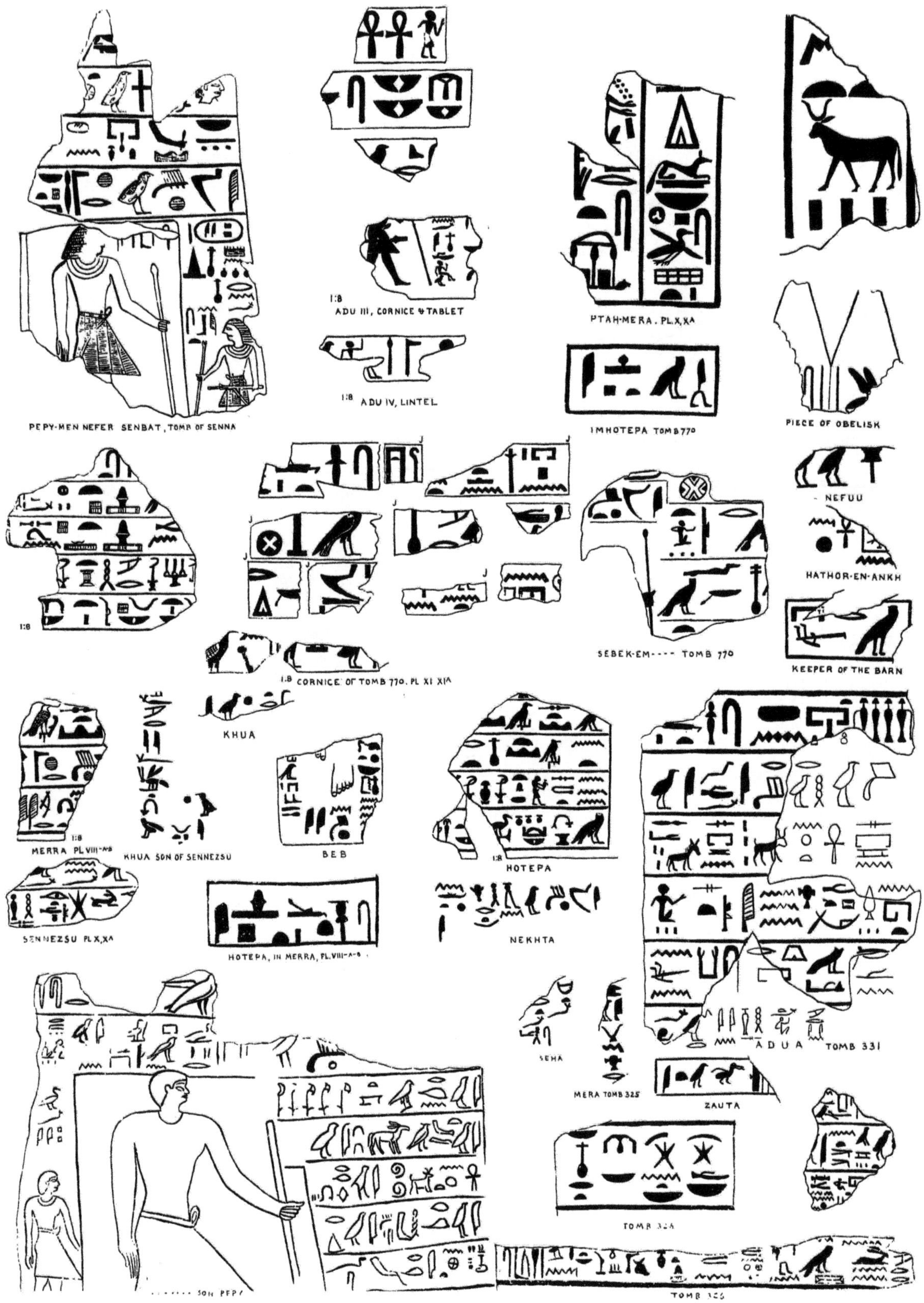
PEPY-MEN NEFER SENBAT, TOMB OF SENNA
1:8
ADU III, CORNICE & TABLET
1:8
ADU IV, LINTEL
PTAH-MERA. PL.X,XA
IMHOTEPA TOMB 770
PIECE OF OBELISK
NEFUU
HATHOR-EN-ANKH
KEEPER OF THE BARN
1:8
SEBEK-EM---- TOMB 770
1:8 CORNICE OF TOMB 770. PL XI XIA
KHUA
KHUA SON OF SENNEZSU
1:8
MERRA PL VIII-A-B
BEB
1:8
HOTEPA
SENNEZSU PL.X,XA
HOTEPA, IN MERRA, PL.VIII-A-B
NEKHTA
ADUA
TOMB 331
SEHA
MERA TOMB 325
ZAUTA
TOMB 324
.... SON PEPY
TOMB 326

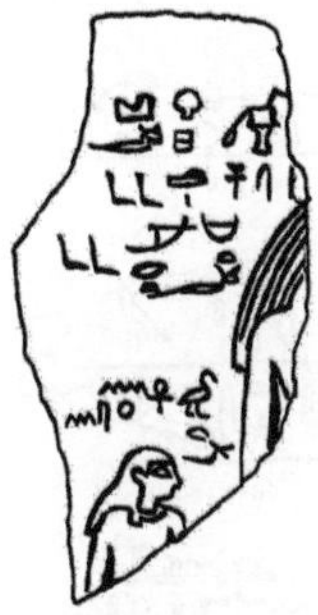

BEB & ANKHSEN TOMB 770

...ERDUTSA, BEBA-URT, & KHETPUA. TOMB 771

AZAUA SON OF BEBA γ

TOMB 336

PTAH-MERA β?

BEBA, SON BEBA

BEBA TOMB 539

MERRA B
HATHOR-HOTEP
& NEFER-MESTU

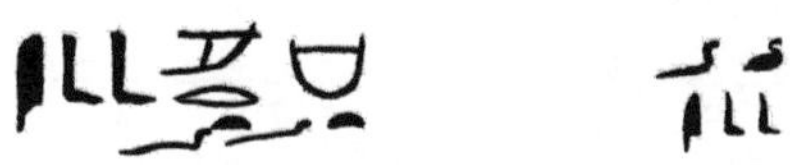

x, WIFE BEBA SON BEBA

BAU-HOTEPA, WIFE YUA SON BEBA. TOMB 323. PL. XIB

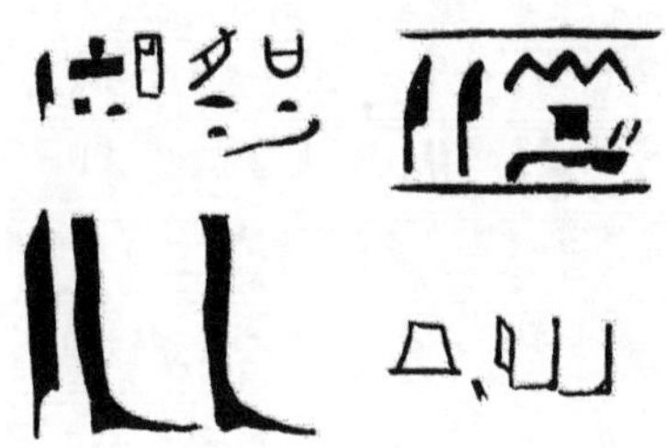

BEBA & HATHOTEP PL. XI

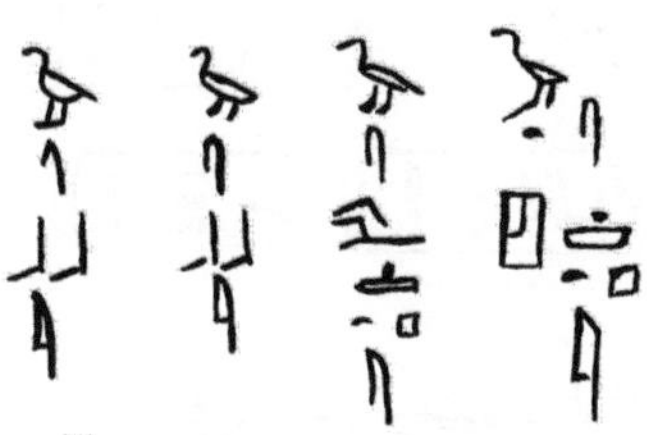

HOTEPA, SONS BEBA, BEBA, SEBEK-HOTEPA; DAU[r] HATHOR-HOTEPA TOMB 549

ANTEF & BEBA, PL. XIC

ANKHS HUA, & SERVANT RANUS

AN

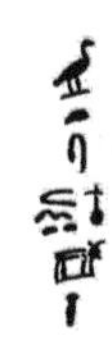

NEFER-THENT

1 : 6

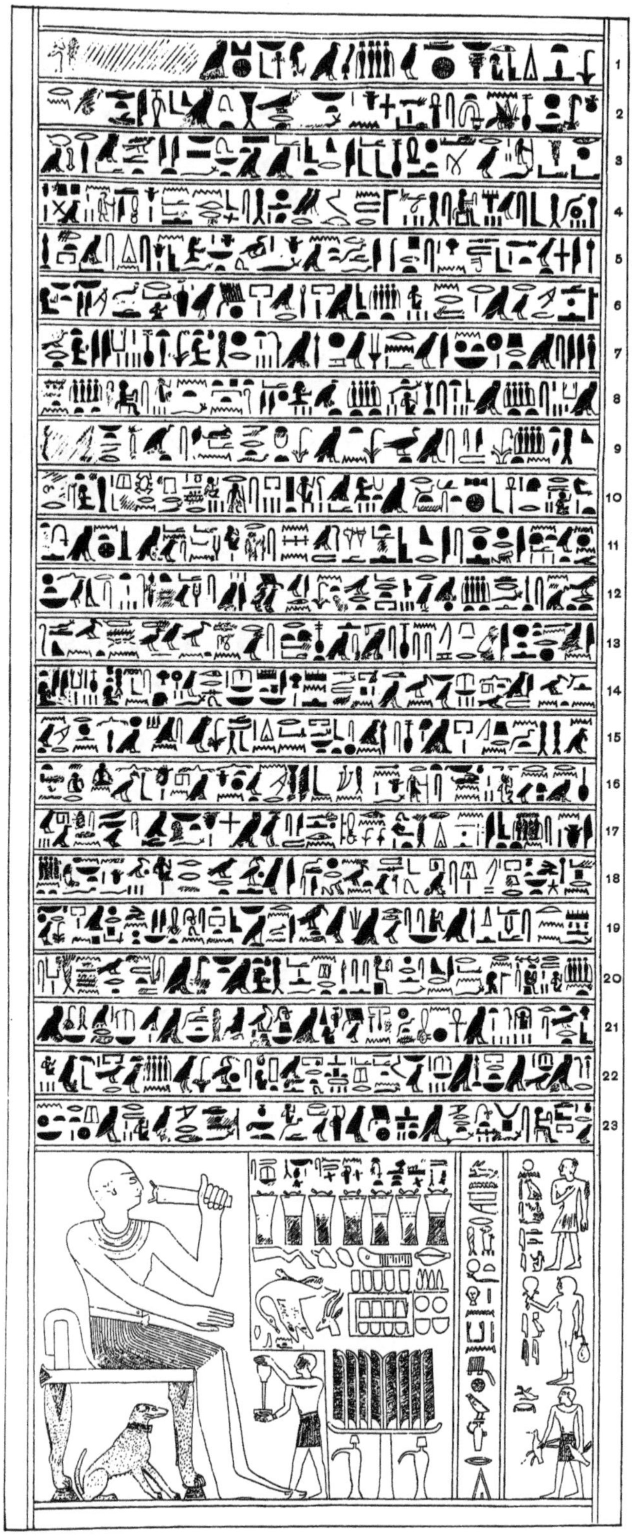
1
2
3
4
5
6
7
8
9
10
11
12
13
14
15
16
17
18
19
20
21
22
23

1 ; 5

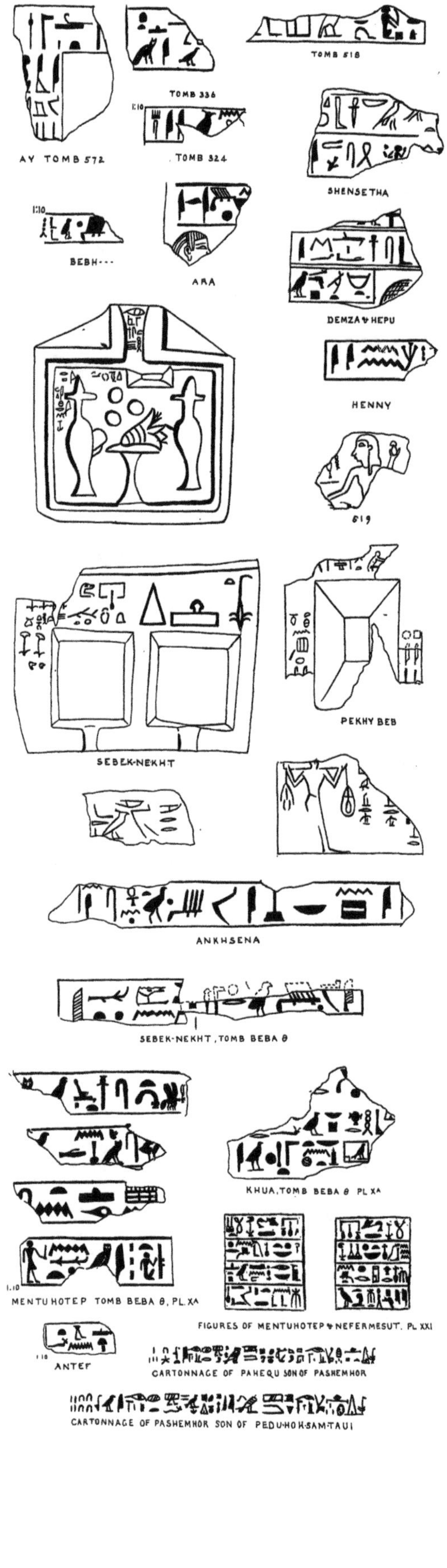
AY TOMB 572
TOMB 336
1:10
TOMB 324
TOMB 518
SHENSETHA
1:10
BEBH...
ARA
DEMZA & HEPU
HENNY
519
SEBEK-NEKHT
PEKHY BEB
ANKHSENA
SEBEK-NEKHT, TOMB BEBA θ
KHUA, TOMB BEBA θ PL. XA
1.10
MENTUHOTEP TOMB BEBA θ, PL. XA
FIGURES OF MENTUHOTEP & NEFERMESUT. PL. XXI
1.10
ANTEF
CARTONNAGE OF PAHEQU SON OF PASHEMHOR
CARTONNAGE OF PASHEMHOR SON OF PEDU-HOR-SAM-TAUI

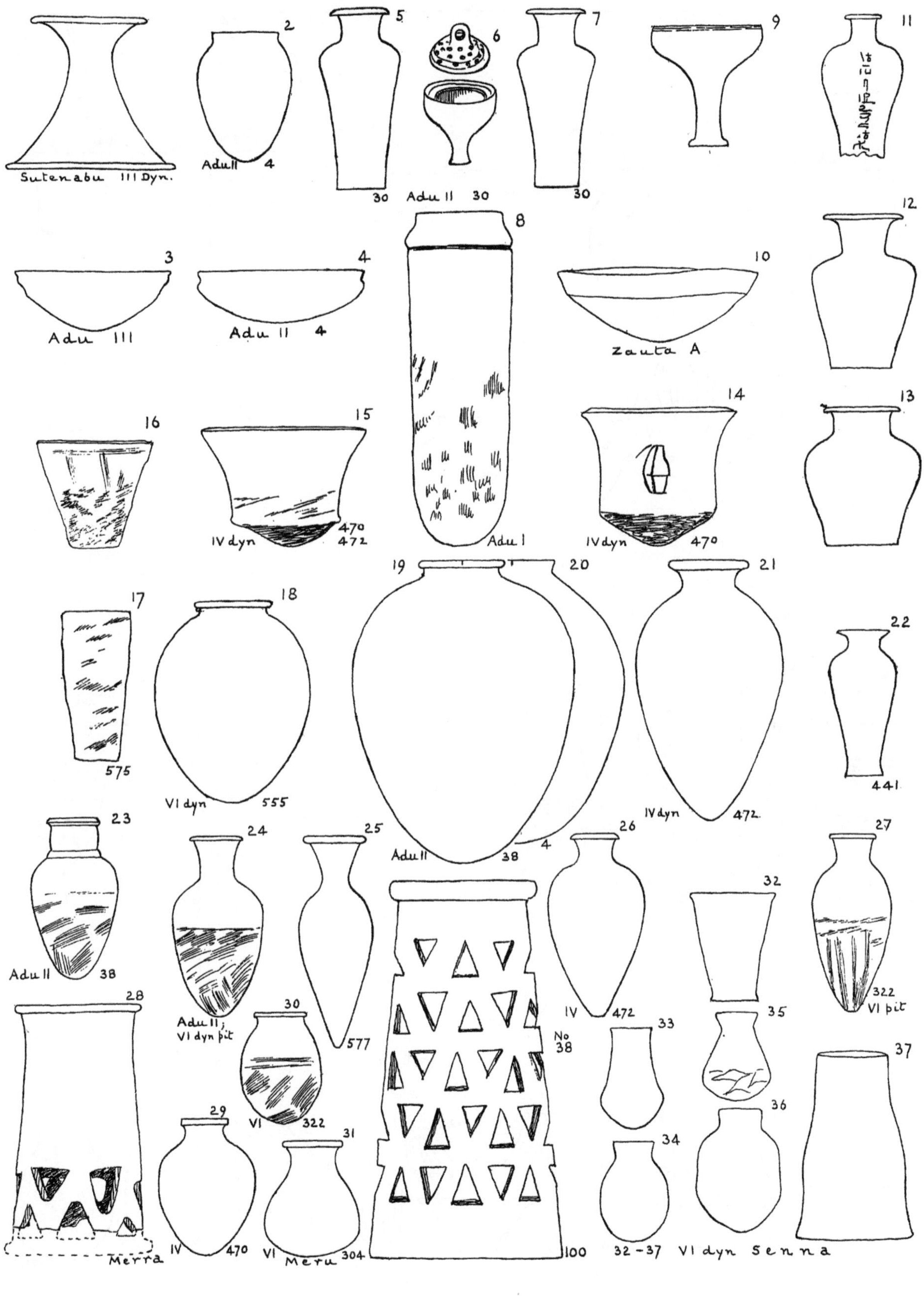
Sutenabu III Dyn.
2
Adu II 4
5
6
7
9
11
30
Adu II 30
30
8
3
Adu III
4
Adu II 4
10
Zauta A
12
16
15
IV dyn
470
472
Adu I
14
IV dyn
470
13
17
575
18
VI dyn
555
19
20
21
IV dyn
472
22
441
23
Adu II
38
24
Adu II; VI dyn pit
25
577
Adu II
38
4
26
IV
472
27
322
VI pit
32
28
Merra
30
VI
322
No 38
33
35
37
29
IV
470
31
VI
Meru
304
100
34
36
32-37 VI dyn Senna

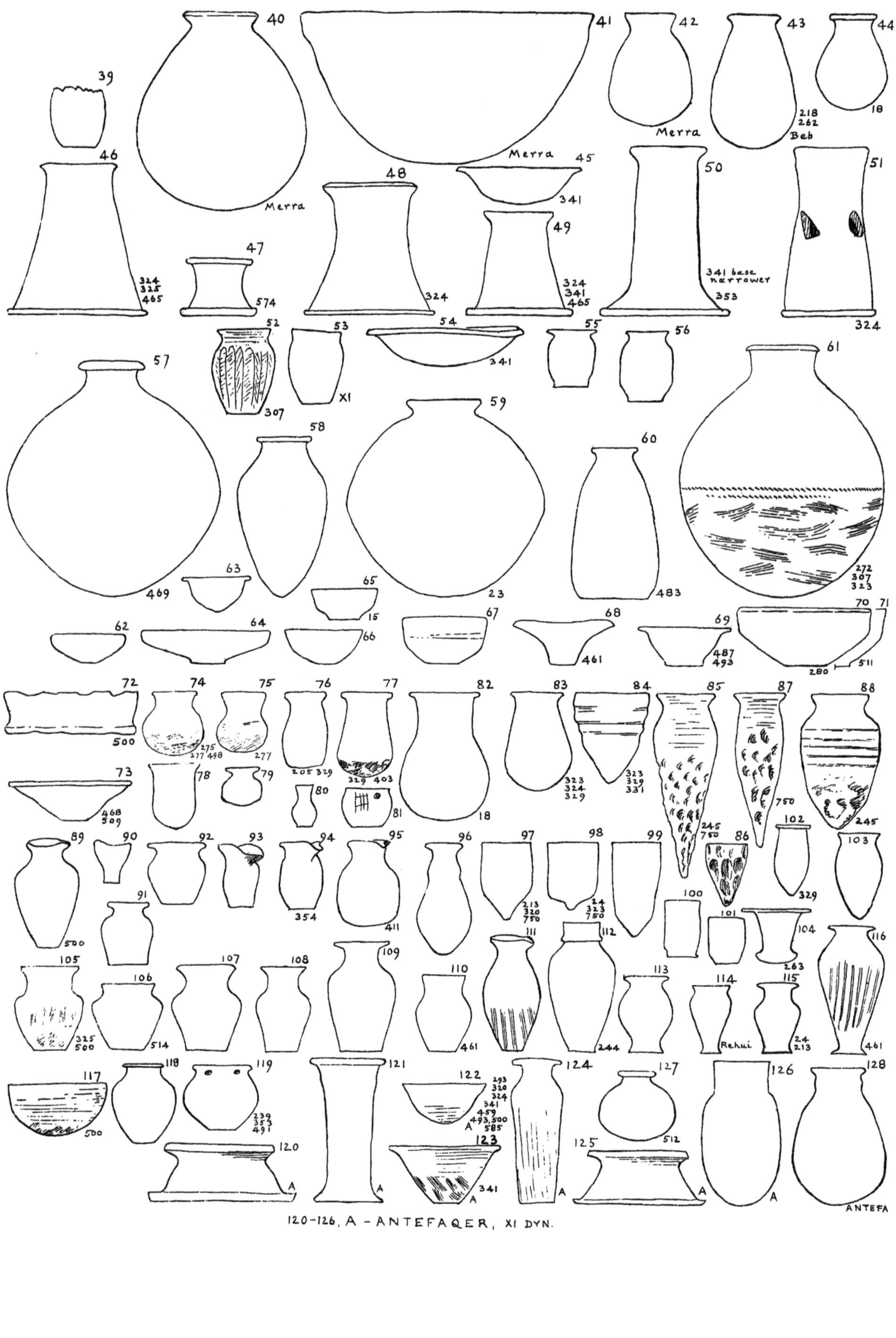

120–126, A – ANTEFAQER, XI DYN.

1:6. DENDEREH. POTTERY OF XI.–XII. DYNASTIES. XVIII.

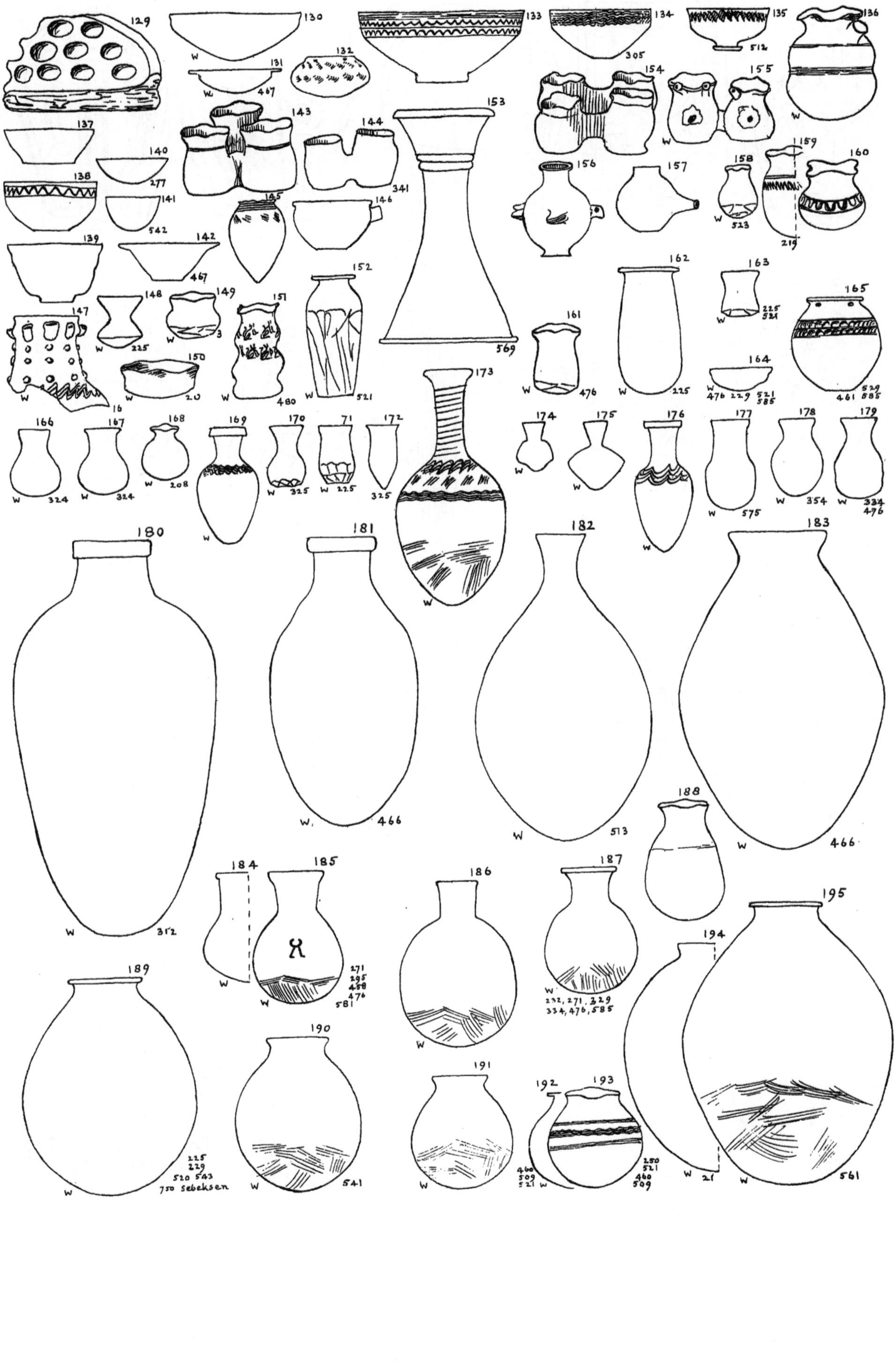

1
2
3
4
5
325
Mera
6
7
8
9
10
11
12
13
600
351
549
Hotepa and sons Pl.XIV—
14
16
15
474
17
18

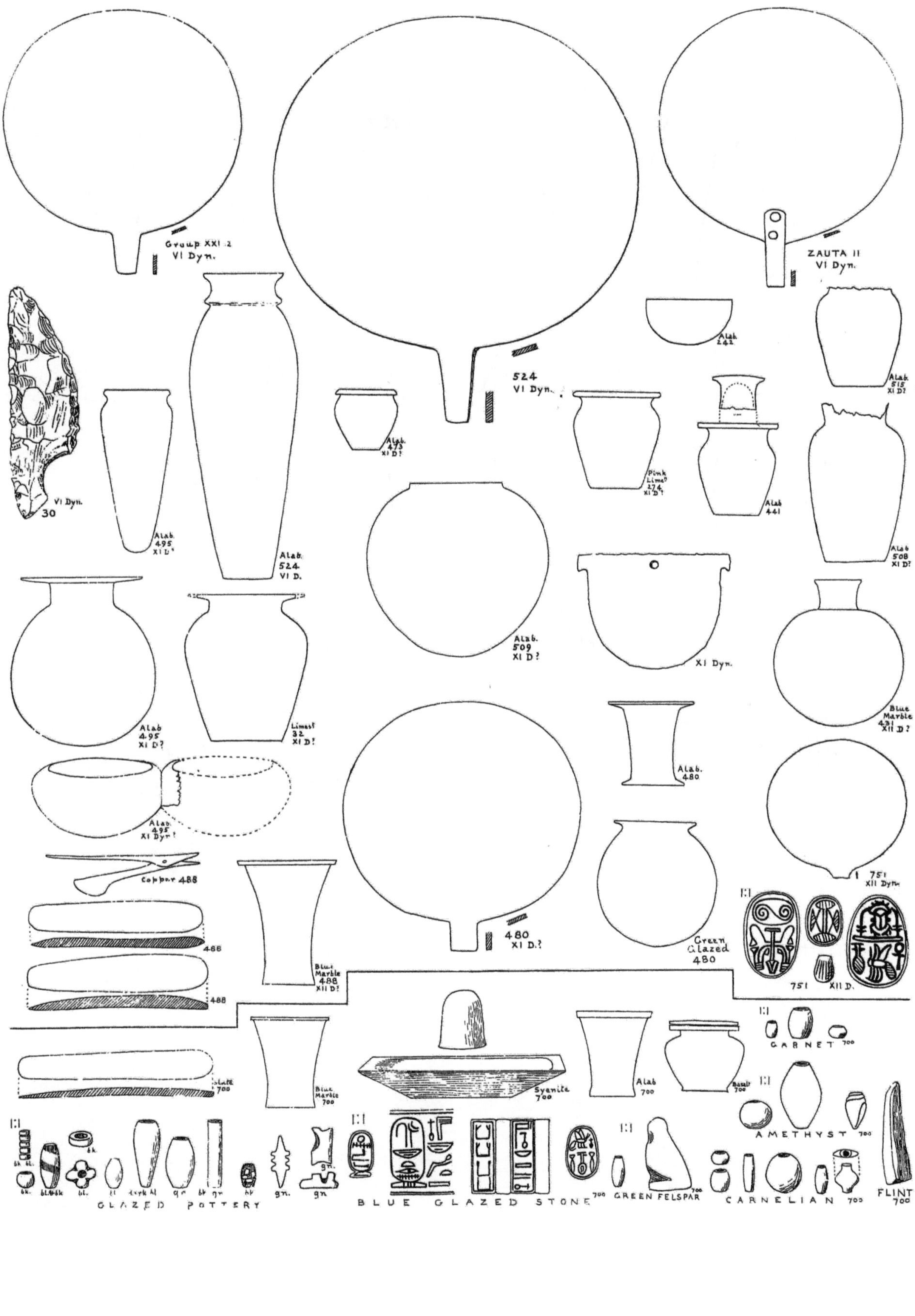
Group XXI 2
VI Dyn.
524
VI Dyn.
ZAUTA II
VI Dyn.
VI Dyn.
30
Alab.
495
XI D.?
Alab.
524
VI D.
Alab.
473
XI D?
Alab.
242
Pink Lime?
274
XI D?
Alab.
441
Alab.
515
XI D?
Alab.
508
XI D?
Alab.
509
XI D?
XI Dyn.
Alab
495
XI D?
Limest
32
XI D?
Blue Marble
431
XII D?
Alab.
480
Alab.
495
XI Dyn?
Copper 488
751
XII Dyn.
488
488
Blue Marble
488
XII D?
480
XI D.?
Green Glazed
480
751
XII D.
GARNET 700
Slate 700
Blue Marble 700
Syenite 700
Alab 700
Basalt 700
AMETHYST 700
FLINT 700
GLAZED POTTERY
BLUE GLAZED STONE 700
GREEN FELSPAR 700
CARNELIAN 700

XI dyn
in red paint
in black paint
in red paint

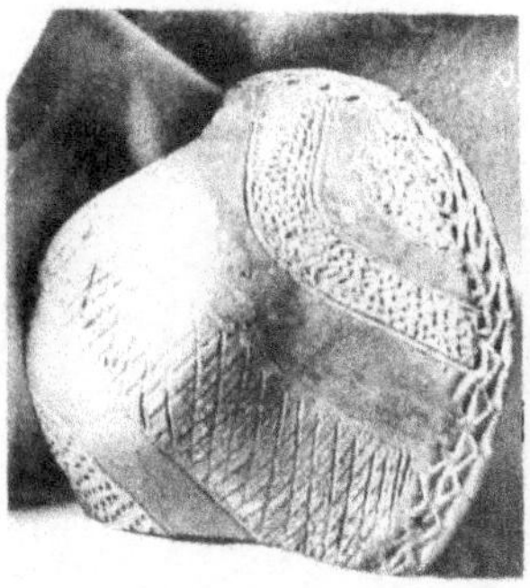

1 : 3. III. DYN.

1 : 6. VI. DYN.

3 : 10. ADU I. VI. DYN.

1 : 5

3 : 7

3 : 8

MENTU HOTEP AND MESTU. XI. DYN.

1 : 5. XI. DYN.

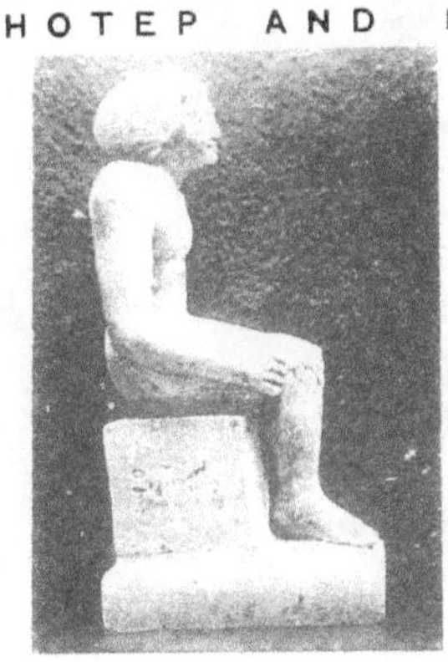

1 : 5. ATSA.
XI. DYN.

2 : 9 MOURNERS. XI. DYN.

2 : 5. VASE HEAD. XI. D.

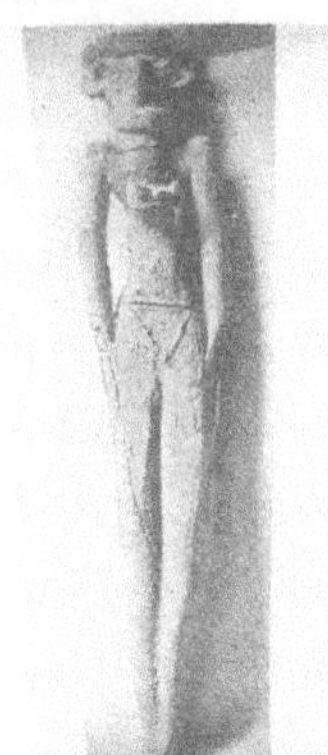

2 : 5. DOLL. XI DYN.

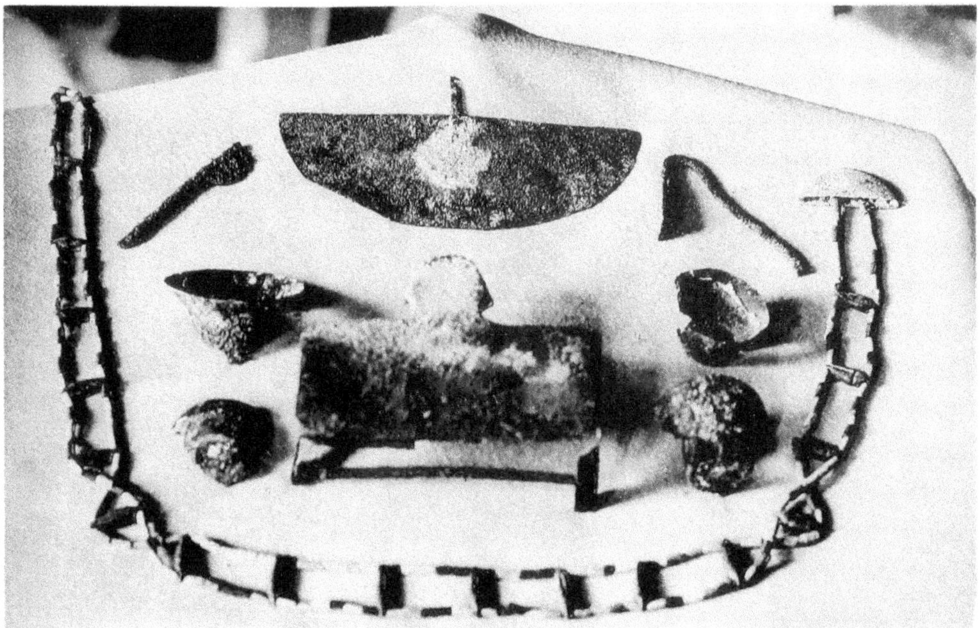

MERU. TOMB 304. VI. DYN.

GALLERY OF ANTEF AQER. XI. DYN.

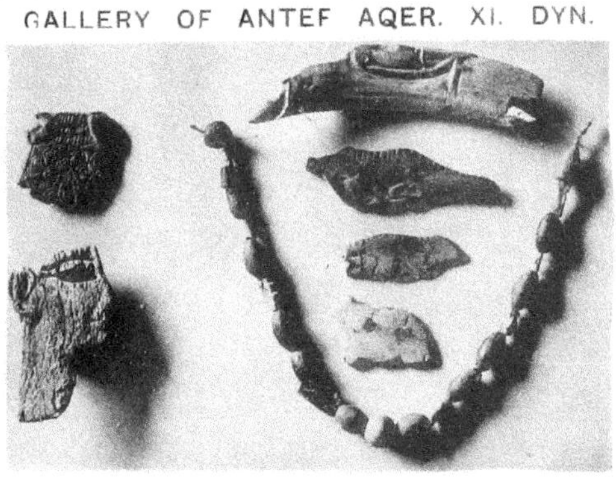

IVORY. XVIII. DYN. TOMB 309. XI. DYN.

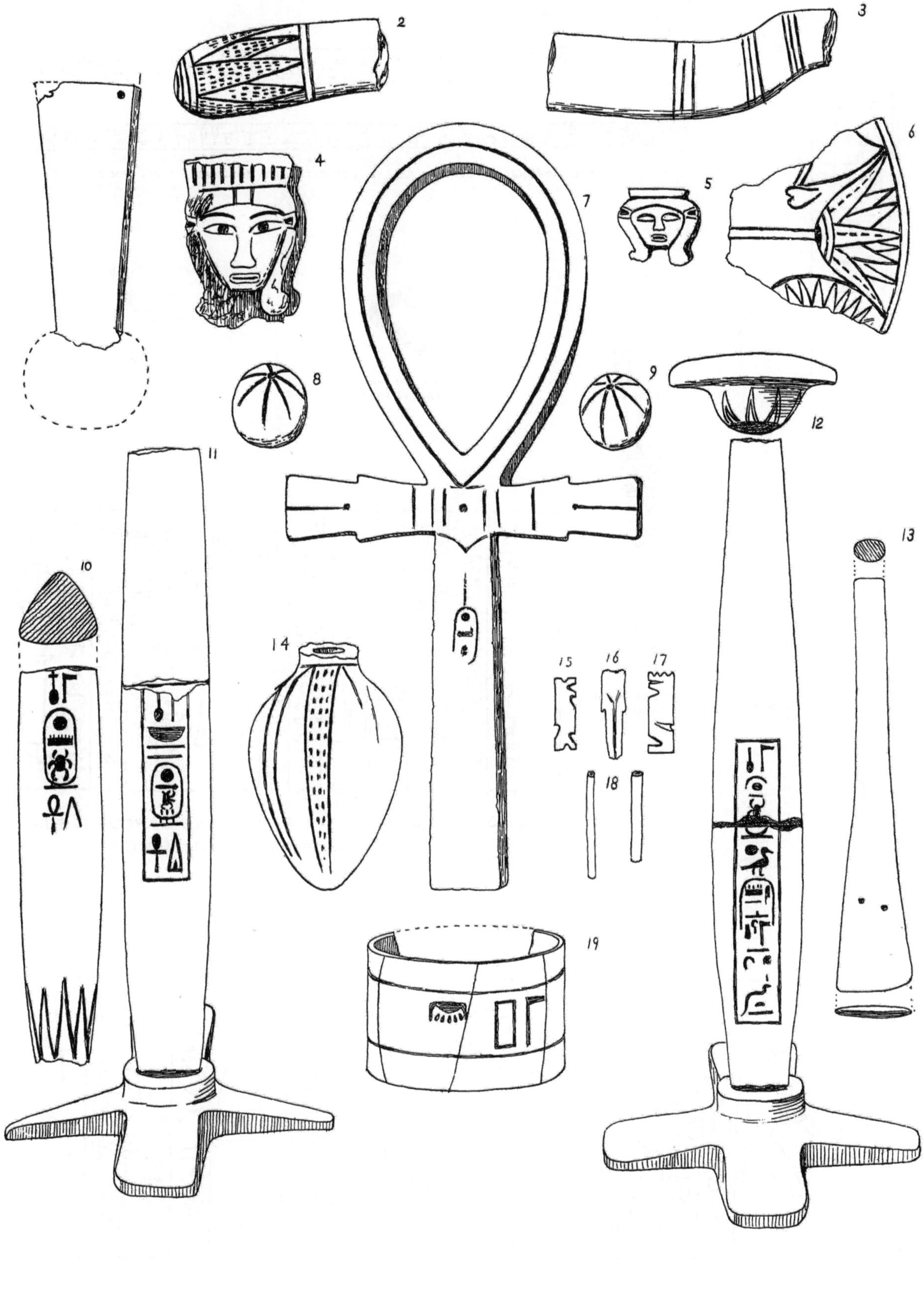
1
2
3
4
5
6
7
8
9
10
11
12
13
14
15
16
17
18
19

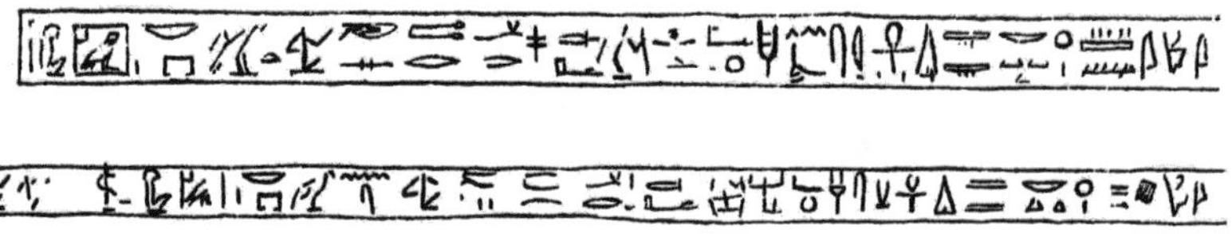

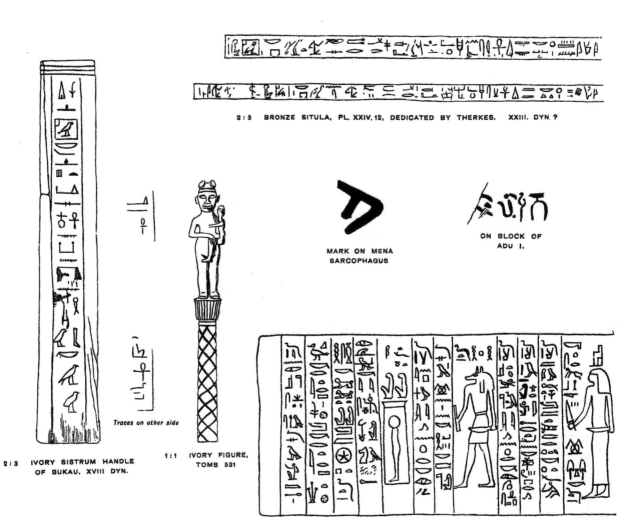

2 : 3 BRONZE SITULA, PL. XXIV. 12, DEDICATED BY THERKES. XXIII. DYN. ?

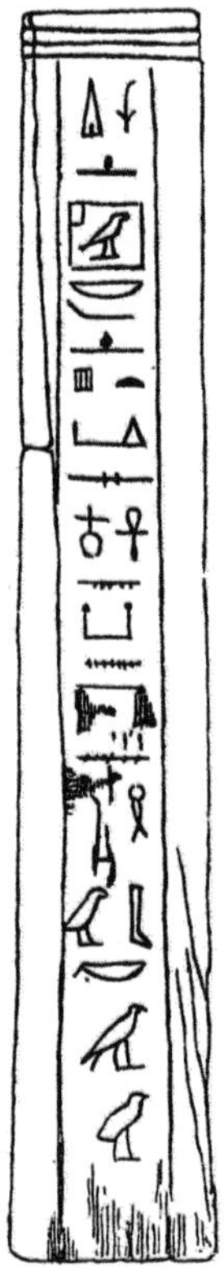

Traces on other side

2 : 3 IVORY SISTRUM HANDLE OF BUKAU. XVIII DYN.

1 : 1 IVORY FIGURE, TOMB 521

MARK ON MENA SARCOPHAGUS

ON BLOCK OF ADU I.

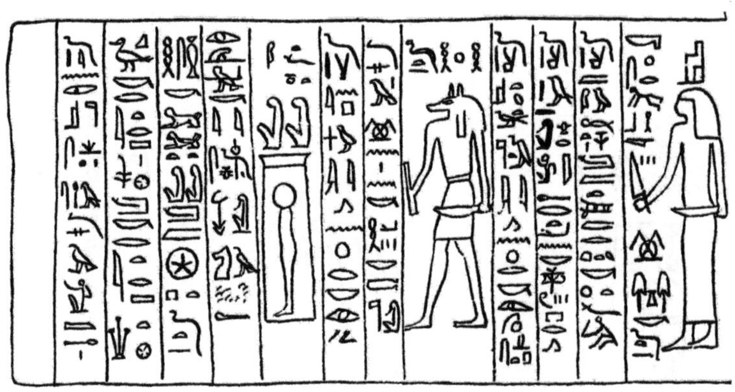

2 : 15 INSCRIPTION ON SANDSTONE SARCOPHAGUS OF NESI-HOR. PTOLEMAIC ?

continued

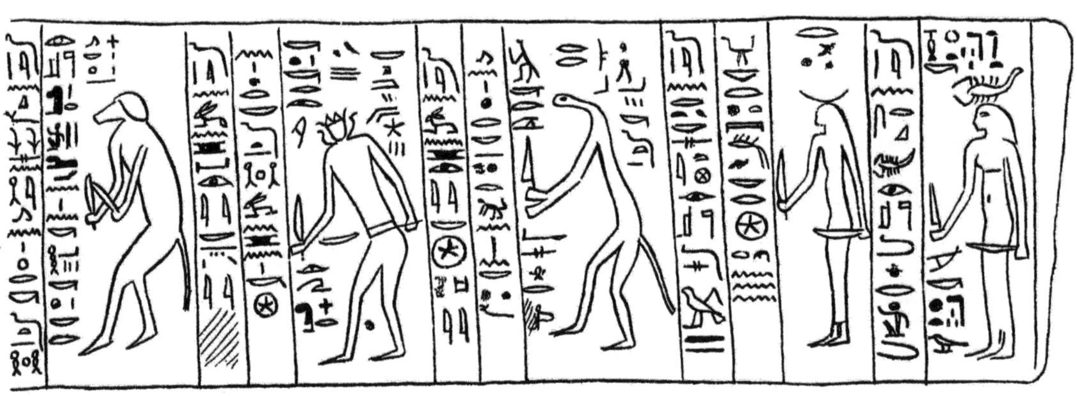

ROMAN.

POTTERY DISH, XVIII. DYN.

MUTARDUS, XXV. D.

HORSIAST, XXVI. D.

PEDU-HOR-SAM-TAUI.

DOG MUMMIES, ROMAN.

FUNEREAL TABLETS.

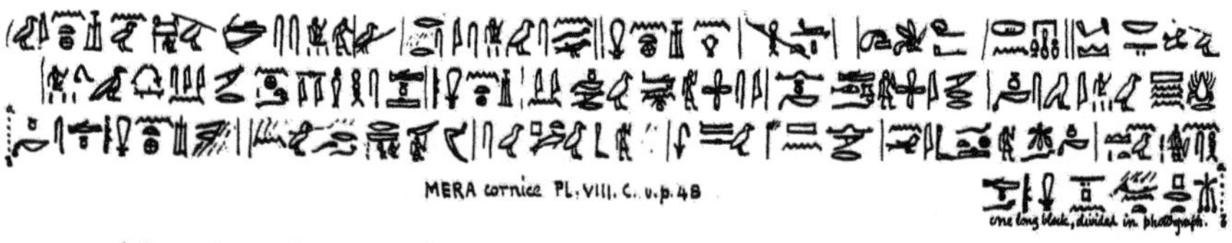

MERA cornice Pl. VIII. C. v. p. 48

one long block, divided in photograph.

Pl. XV Stela of Chnemerdu— collation by HH. Schäfer and Lange

see p. 51 and cf. Pl. XI B.

See Pl. II A and p. 44.

D

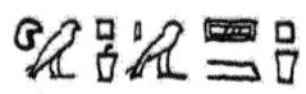

C
over figure of mummy on sandstone slab.

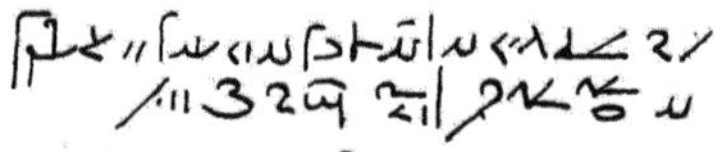

B
bier between Isis and Nephthys kneeling

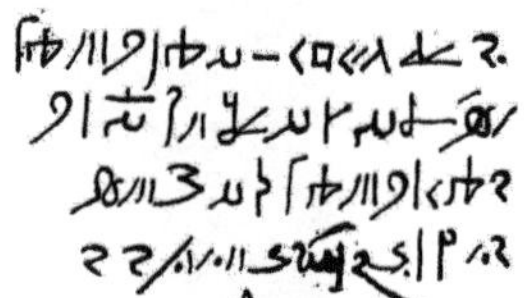

A
Anubis holding heart (?) at side of bier Isis and Nephthys kneeling. "Sons of Horus" standing behind.

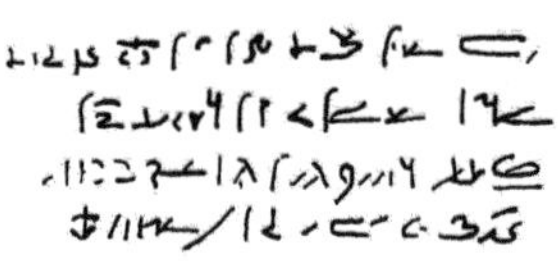

V

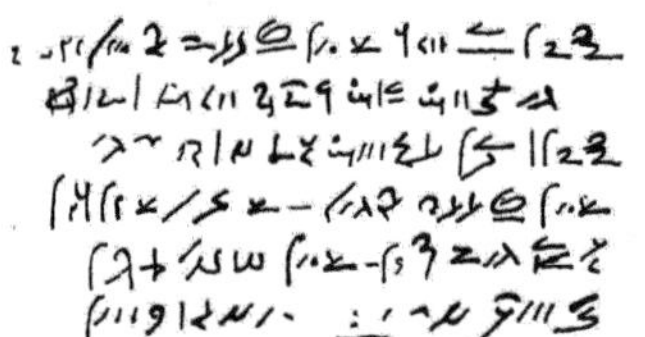

IV

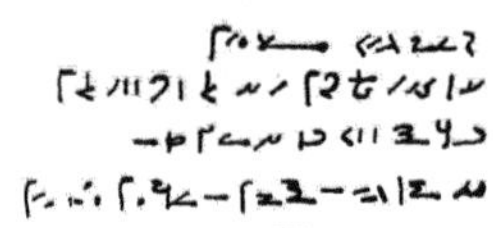

II

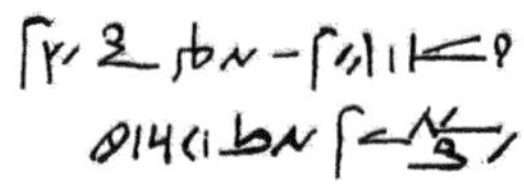

I

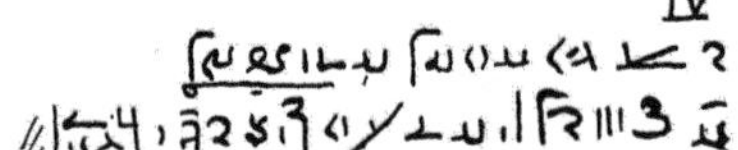

X

VIII

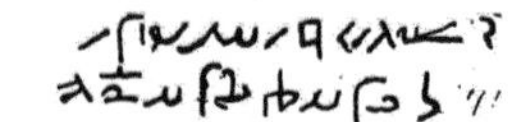

VII

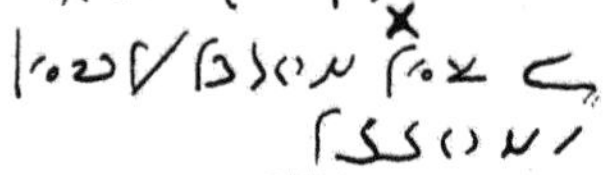

XIII

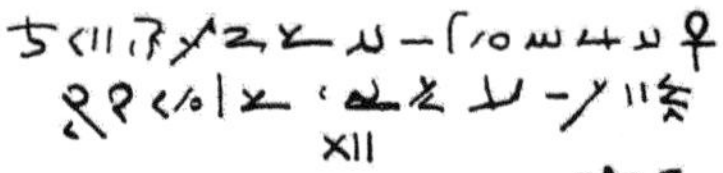

XII

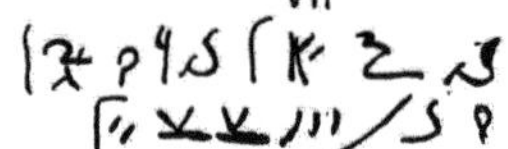

XI

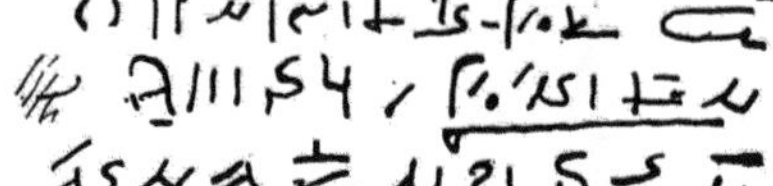

XIV

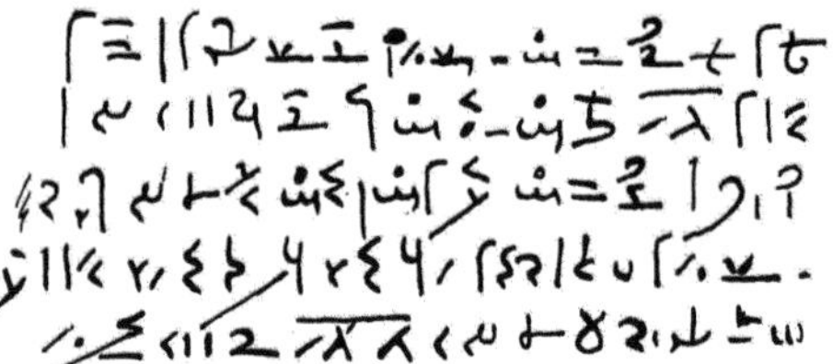

XVI.

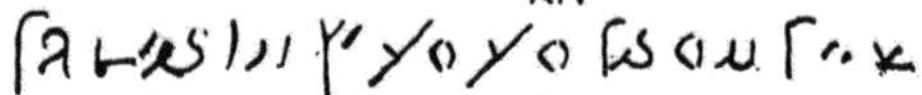

XV

Demotic inscriptions on Pl. XXV A; from squeezes

32
33
34
35
36
37
38
39
40
41
42
43
44
45
46
47
48
49
50
51
52
53
54
55
56
57
58
59

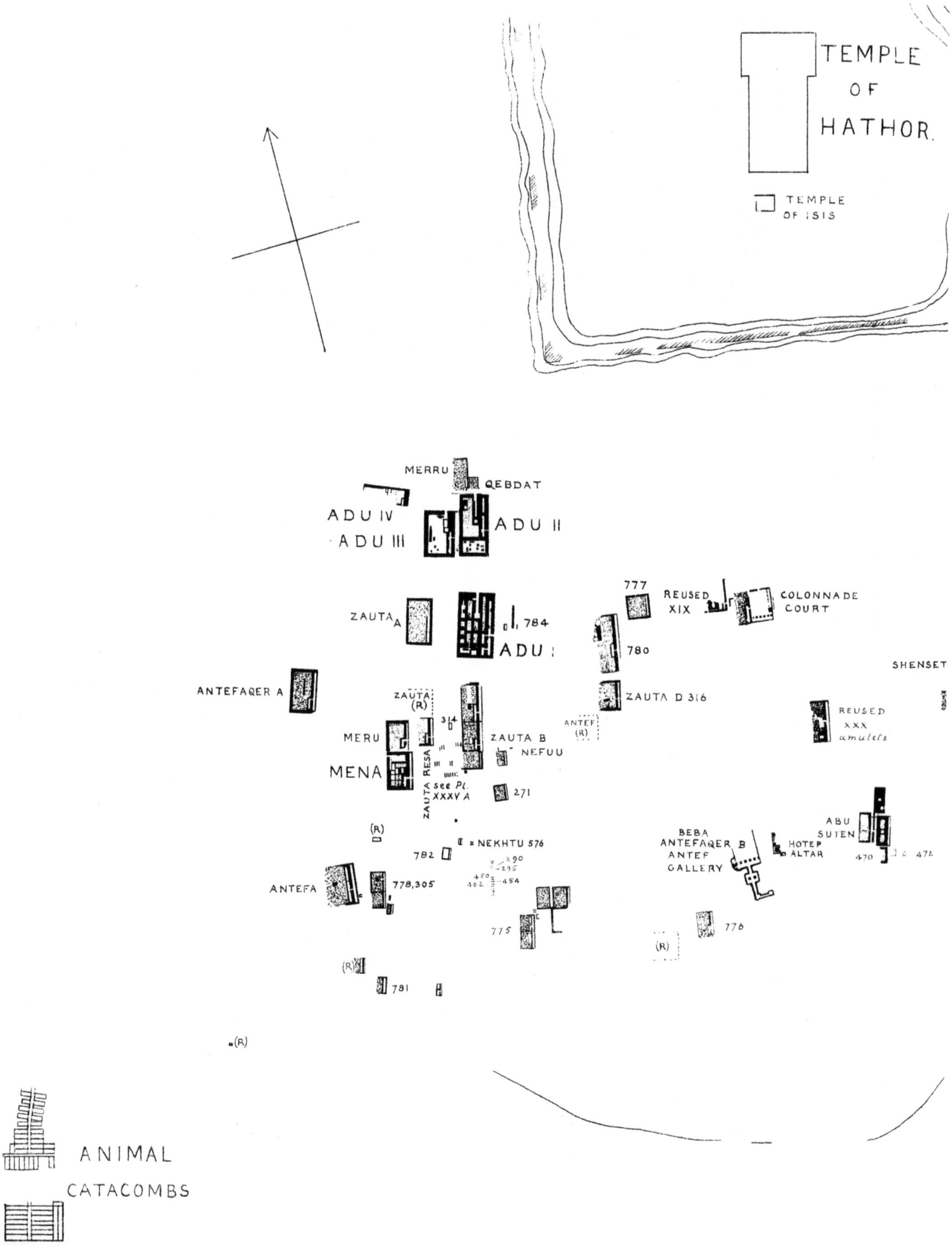

TEMPLE OF HATHOR.
TEMPLE OF ISIS
MERRU
QEBDAT
ADU IV
ADU III
ADU II
777
REUSED XIX
COLONNADE COURT
ZAUTA A
784
ADU I
780
SHENSET
ANTEFAQER A
ZAUTA (R)
ZAUTA D 316
ANTEF (R)
REUSED XXX amulets
314
MERU
ZAUTA B
NEFUU
MENA
ZAUTA RESA
see Pl. XXXV A
271
ABU SUTEN
BEBA
ANTEFAQER B
ANTEF GALLERY
HOTEP ALTAR
470
472
(R)
NEKHTU 576
782
ANTEFA
778,305
775
776
(R)
(R)
781
(R)
ANIMAL CATACOMBS

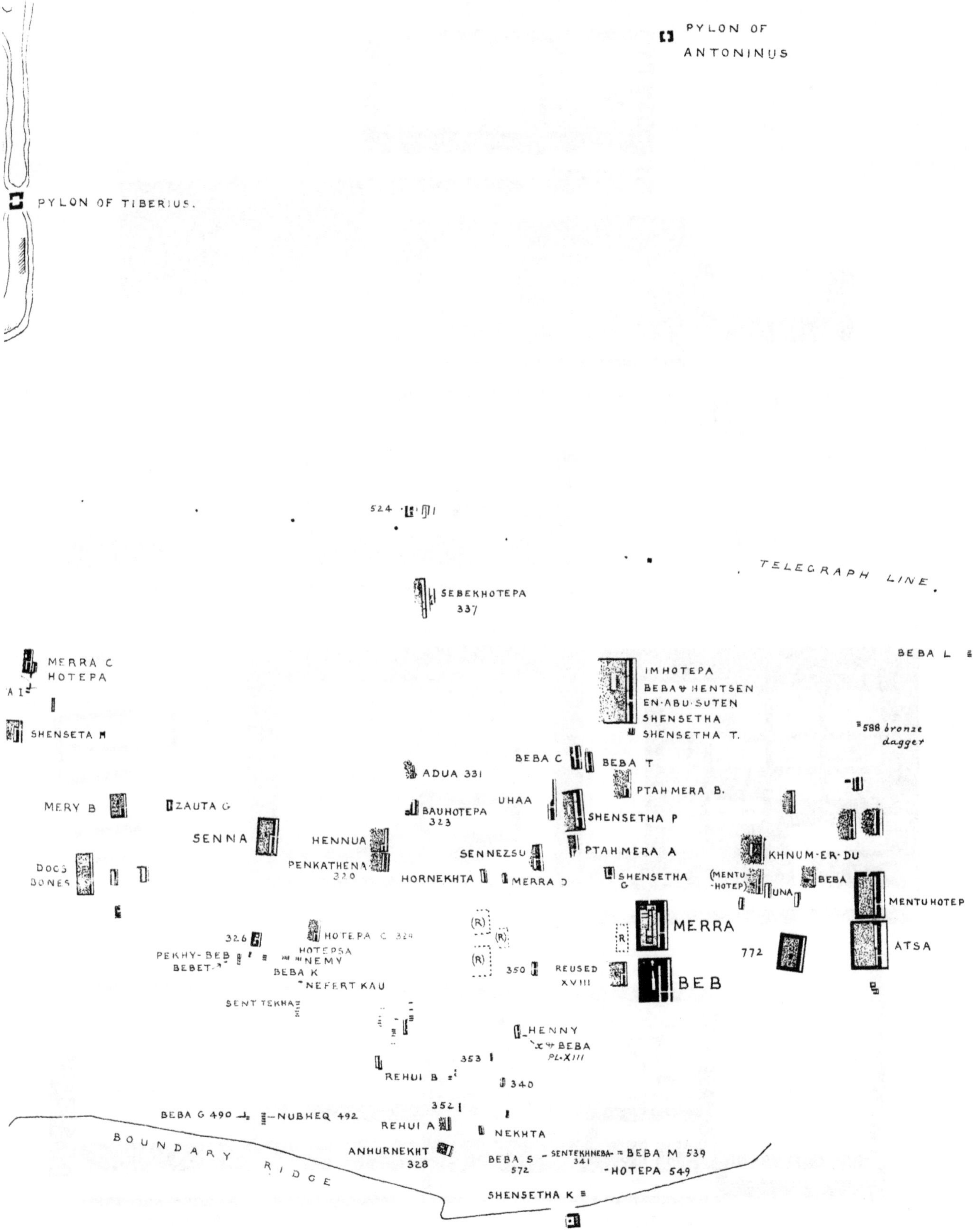
PYLON OF ANTONINUS
PYLON OF TIBERIUS.
524
TELEGRAPH LINE.
SEBEKHOTEPA 337
BEBA L
MERRA C
HOTEPA
SHENSETA H
IMHOTEPA
BEBA & HENTSEN
EN-ABU-SUTEN
SHENSETHA
SHENSETHA T.
588 bronze dagger
BEBA C
BEBA T
ADUA 331
PTAHMERA B.
MERY B
ZAUTA G
UHAA
BAUHOTEPA 323
SHENSETHA P
SENNA
HENNUA
PTAHMERA A
SENNEZSU
KHNUM-ER-DU
PENKATHENA 320
HORNEKHTA
MERRA D
SHENSETHA G
(MENTU-HOTEP)
UNA
BEBA
MENTUHOTEP
DOGS BONES
MERRA
772
ATSA
326
HOTEPA C 324
HOTEPSA
PEKHY-BEB
BEBET
NEMY
BEBA K
NEFERT KAU
350
REUSED XVIII
BEB
SENT TEKHA
HENNY
x & BEBA
PL. XIII
353
REHUI B
340
352
BEBA G 490
NUBHEQ 492
REHUI A
NEKHTA
BOUNDARY RIDGE
ANHURNEKHT 328
BEBA S 572
SENTEKHNEBA 341
BEBA M 539
HOTEPA 549
SHENSETHA K

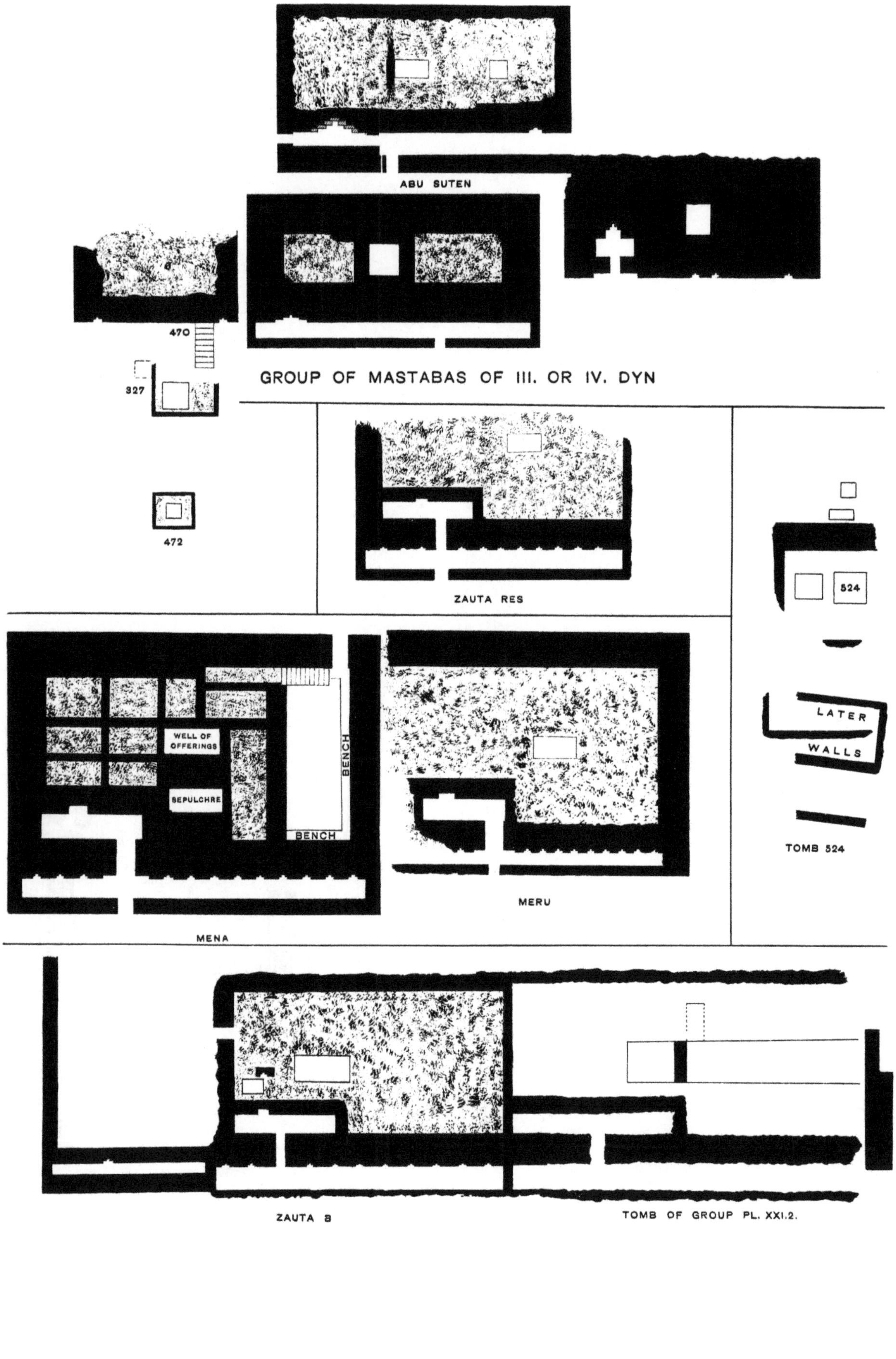
ABU SUTEN
470
327
GROUP OF MASTABAS OF III. OR IV. DYN
472
ZAUTA RES
524
TOMB 524
LATER
WALLS
WELL OF OFFERINGS
SEPULCHRE
BENCH
BENCH
MERU
MENA
ZAUTA B
TOMB OF GROUP PL. XXI.2.

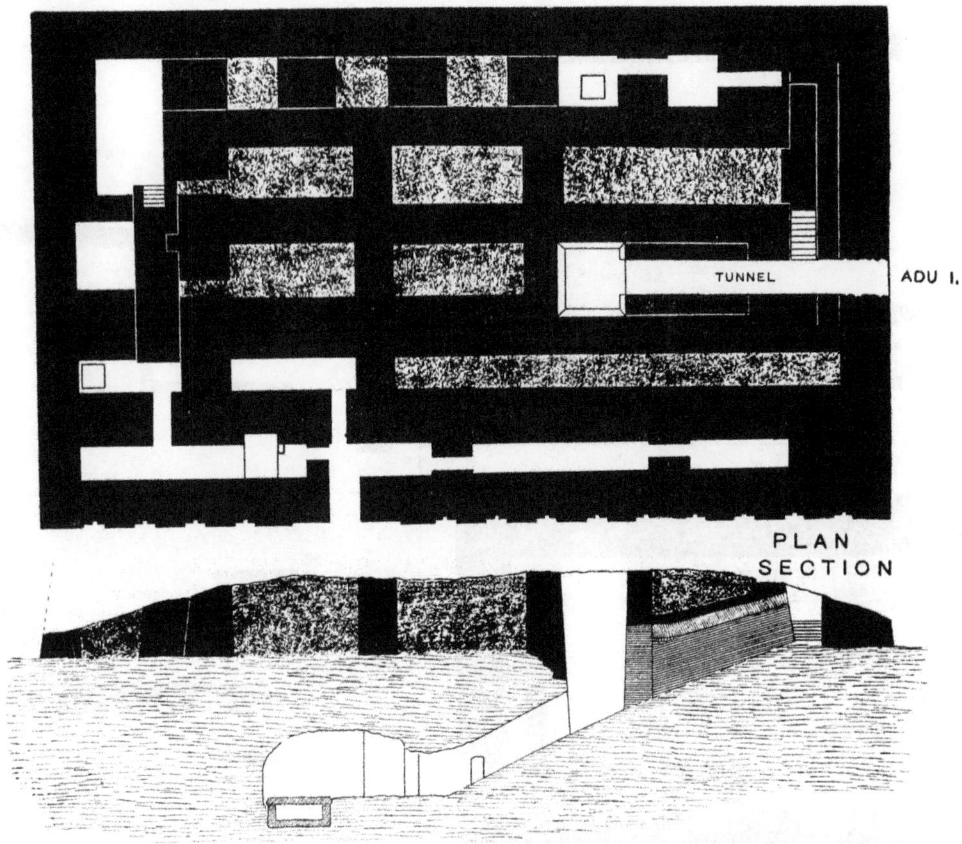
TUNNEL
ADU I.
PLAN
SECTION

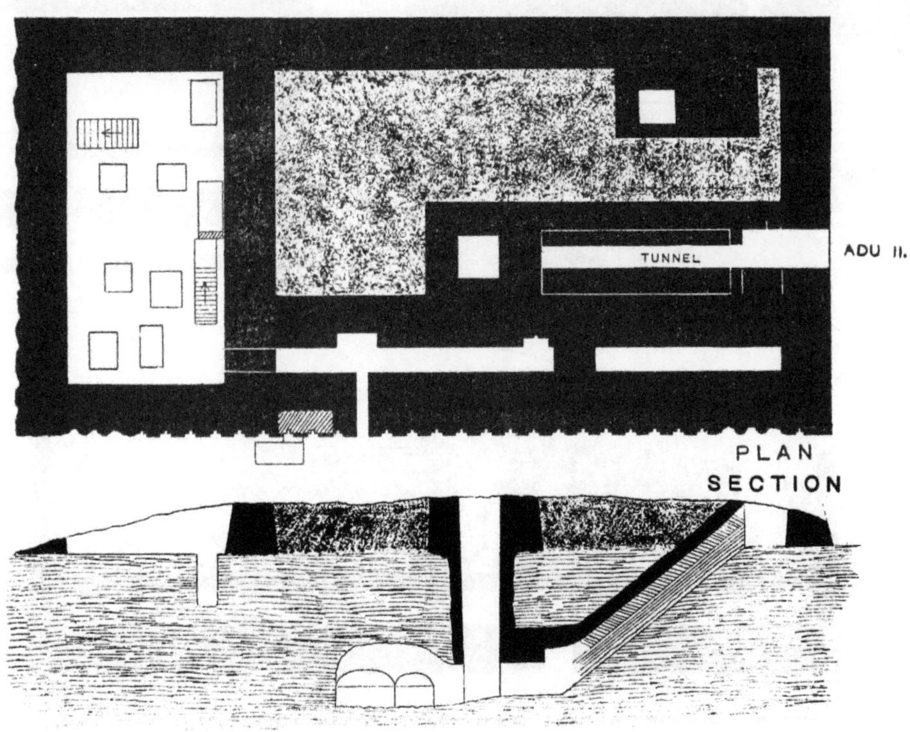
TUNNEL
ADU II.
PLAN
SECTION

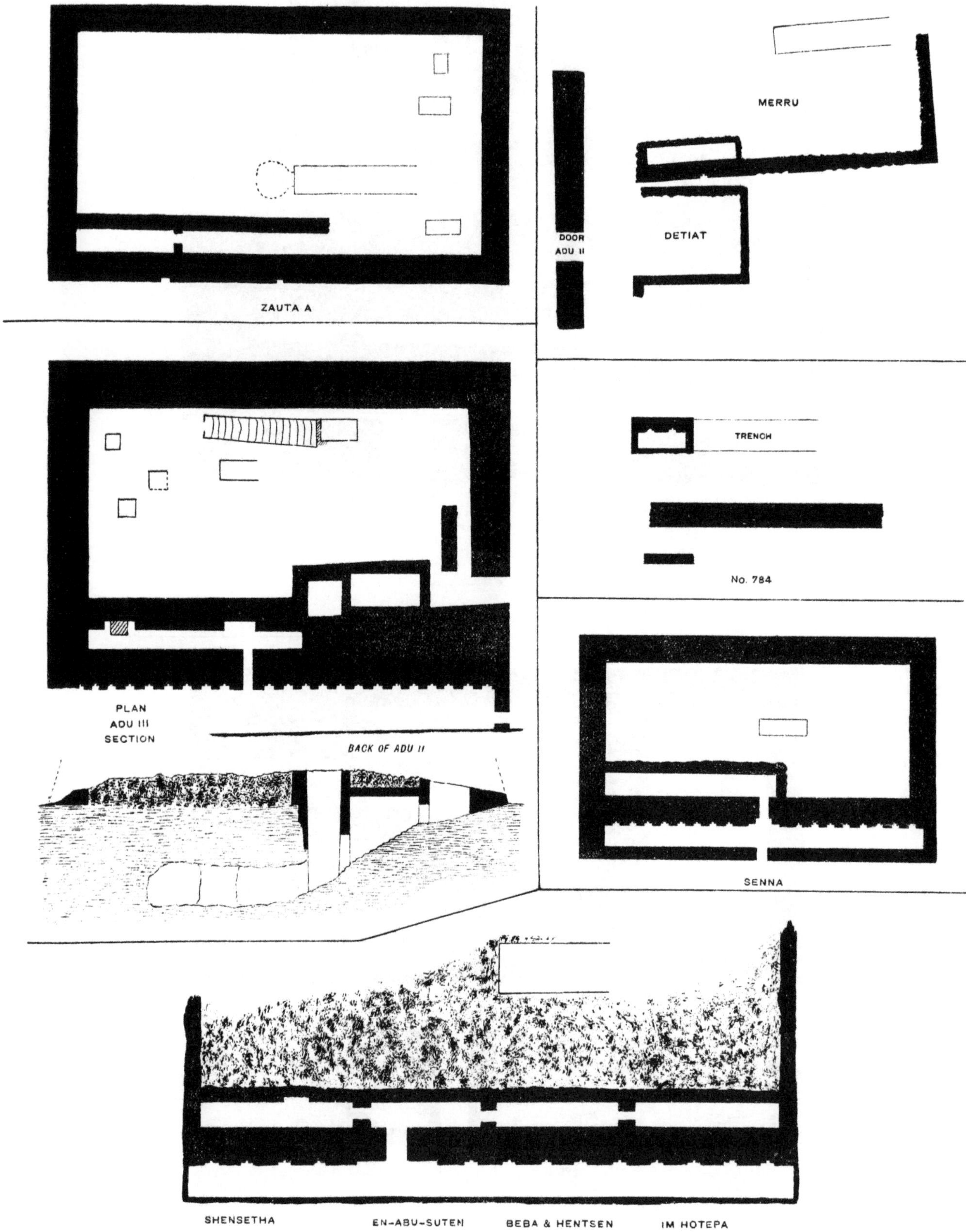
ZAUTA A
DOOR
ADU II
MERRU
DETIAT
TRENCH
No. 784
PLAN
ADU III
SECTION
BACK OF ADU II
SENNA
SHENSETHA
EN-ABU-SUTEN
BEBA & HENTSEN
IM HOTEPA

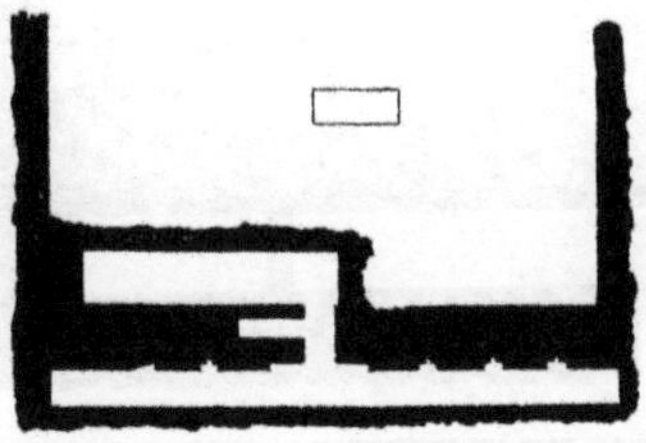

REUSED IN XVIII. DYN.

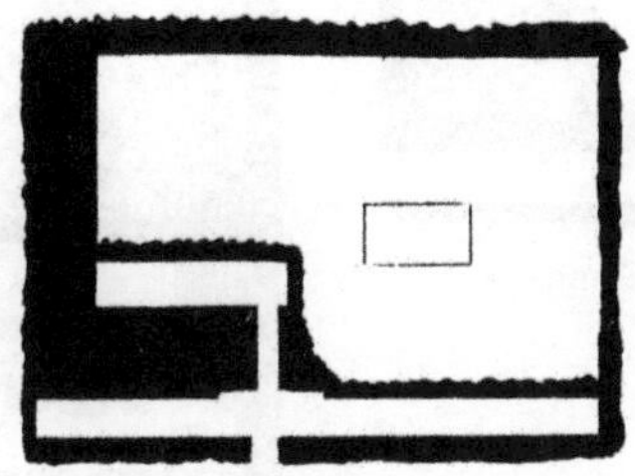

MERY B.

SEN-NEZ-SU

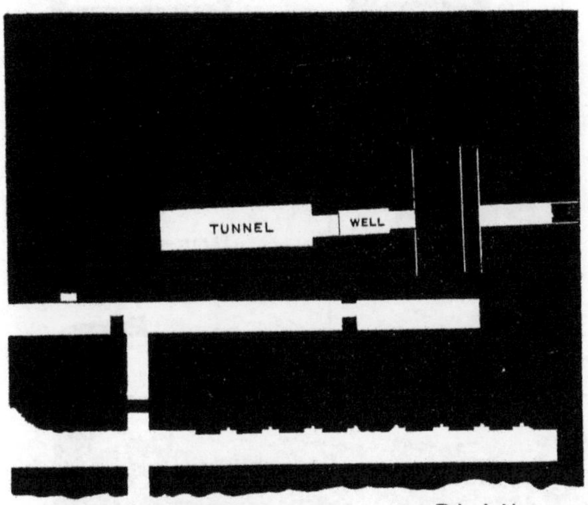

PLAN
BEB
SECTION

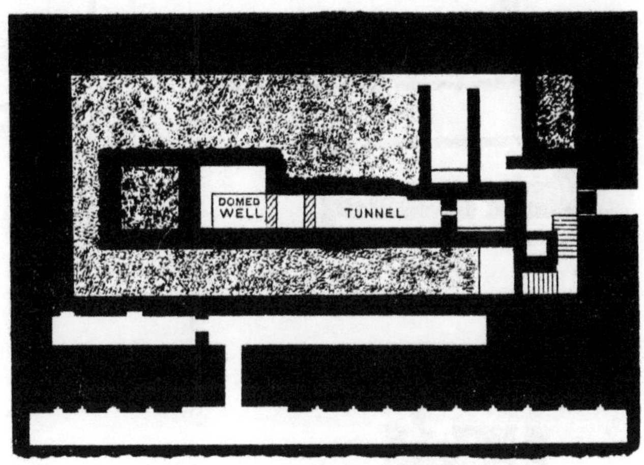

PLAN
MERRA
SECTION

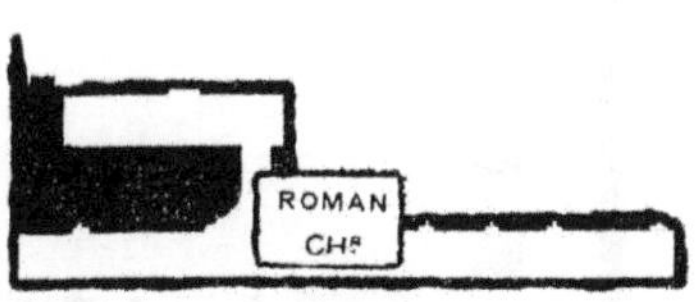

PTAH-MERA B.

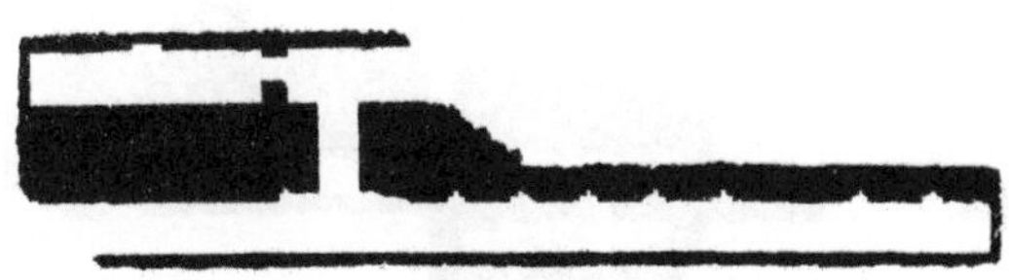

UHAA

PTAHMERA A

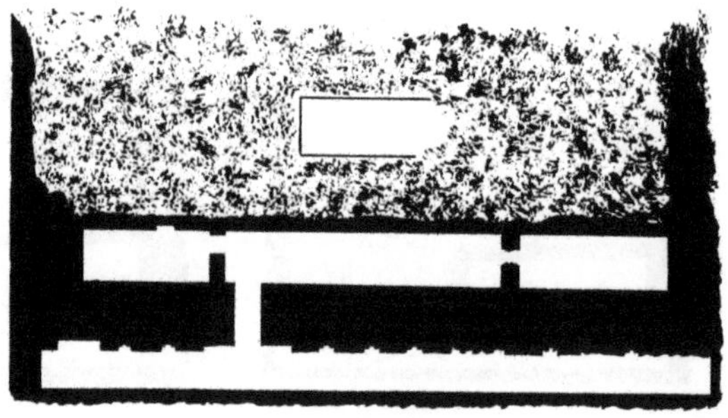

SHENSETHA P

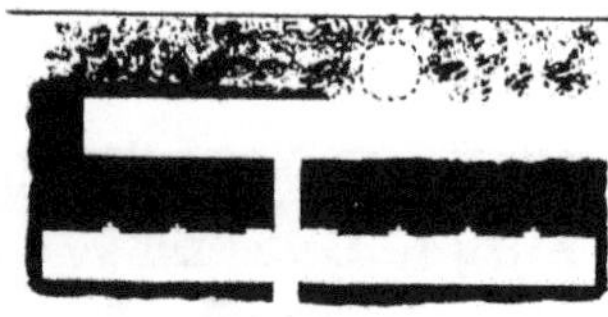

BEBA C

SHENSETHA G

MERRA D

HORNEKHTA

BEBA T

NEKHTA

ZAUTA E

PEKHY-BEB

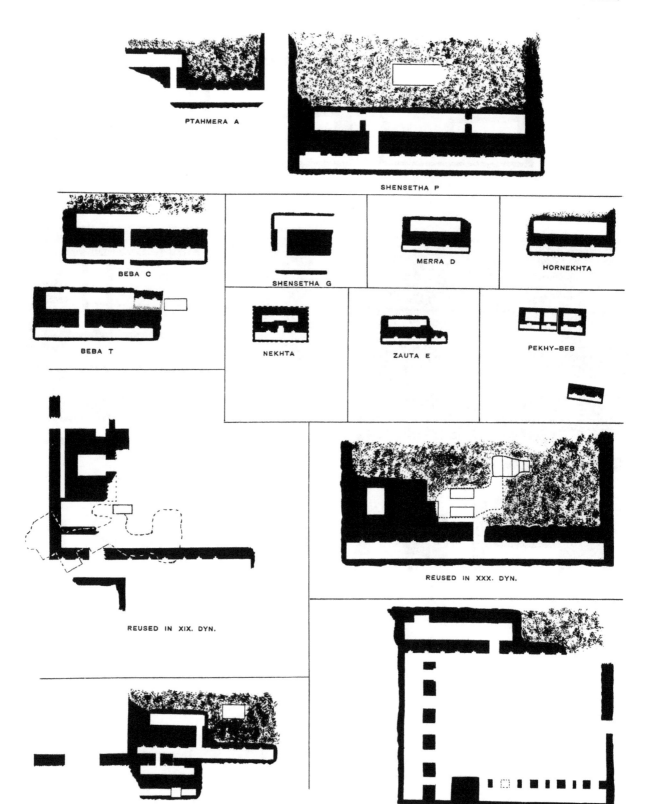

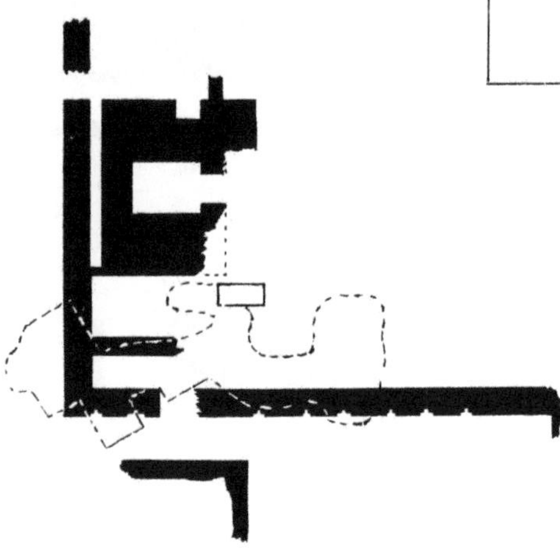

REUSED IN XIX. DYN.

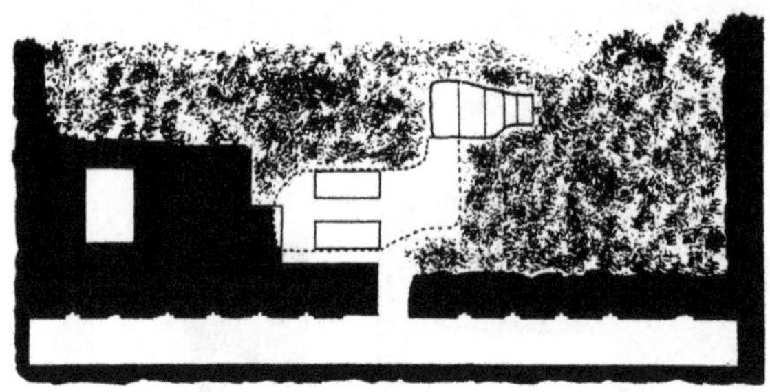

REUSED IN XXX. DYN.

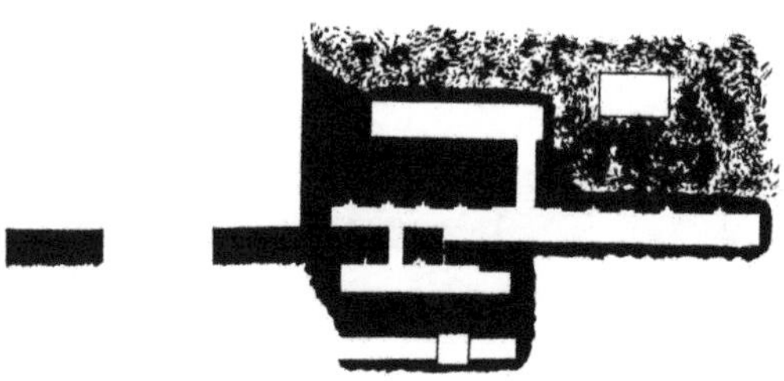

MERRA C HOTEPA

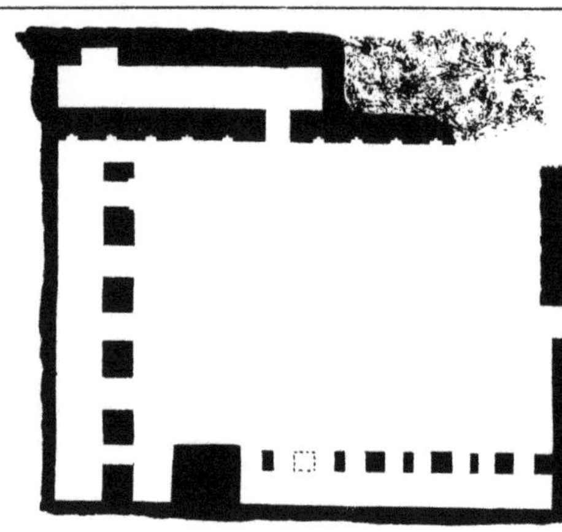

COLONNADE COURT

DENDEREH. MASTABAS OF XI. DYNASTY.

772. E. OF BEB

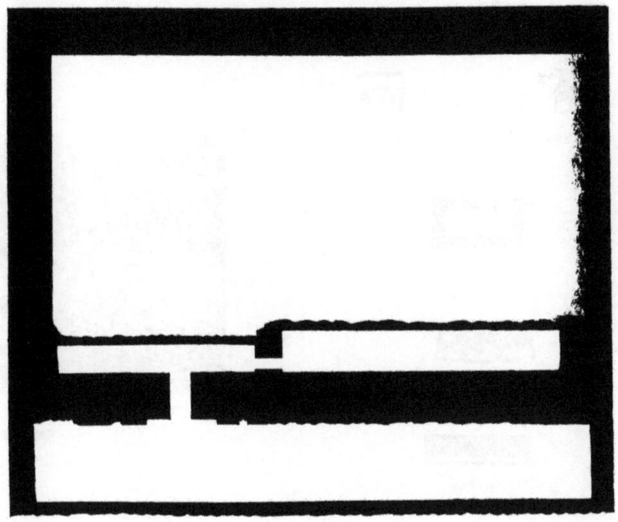

773. S. OF MENTUHOTEP

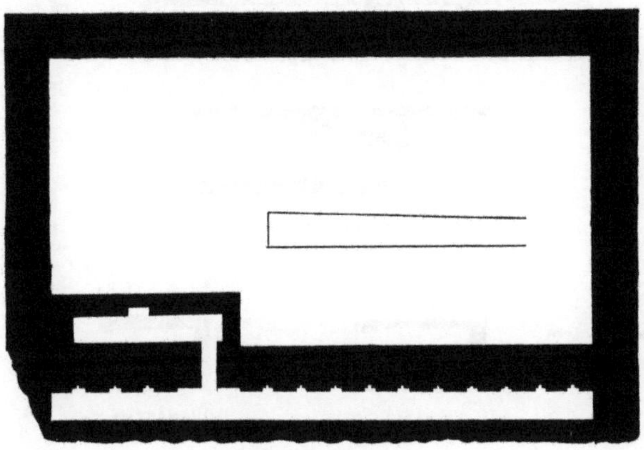

ANTEFAQER A

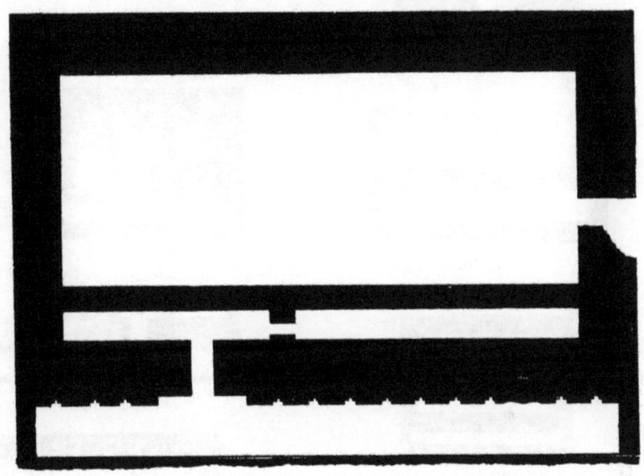

774 MENTUHOTEP

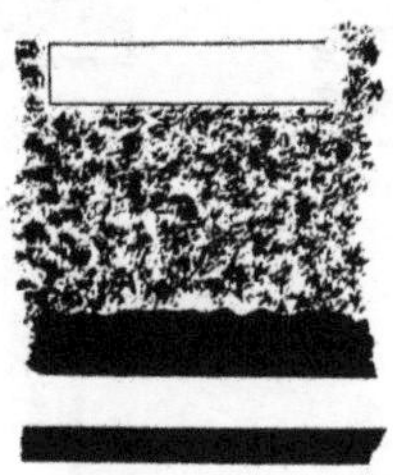

KHNUM-ER-DU

HOTEP ALTAR

E. OF XI. DYN. GALLERY

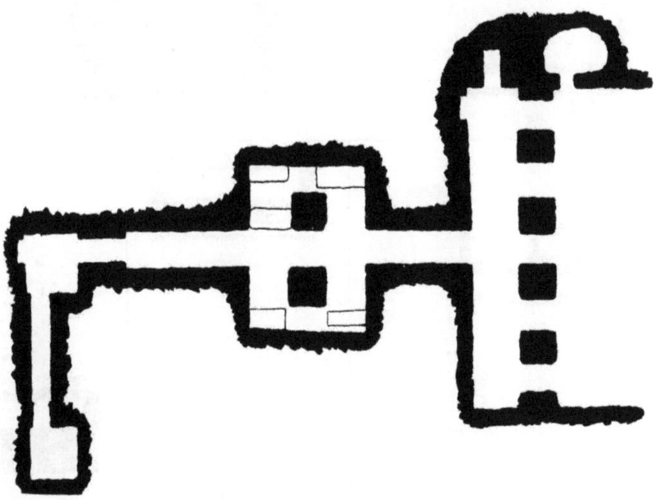

750 GALLERY TOMB OF BEBA, ANTEFAQER AND ANTEF

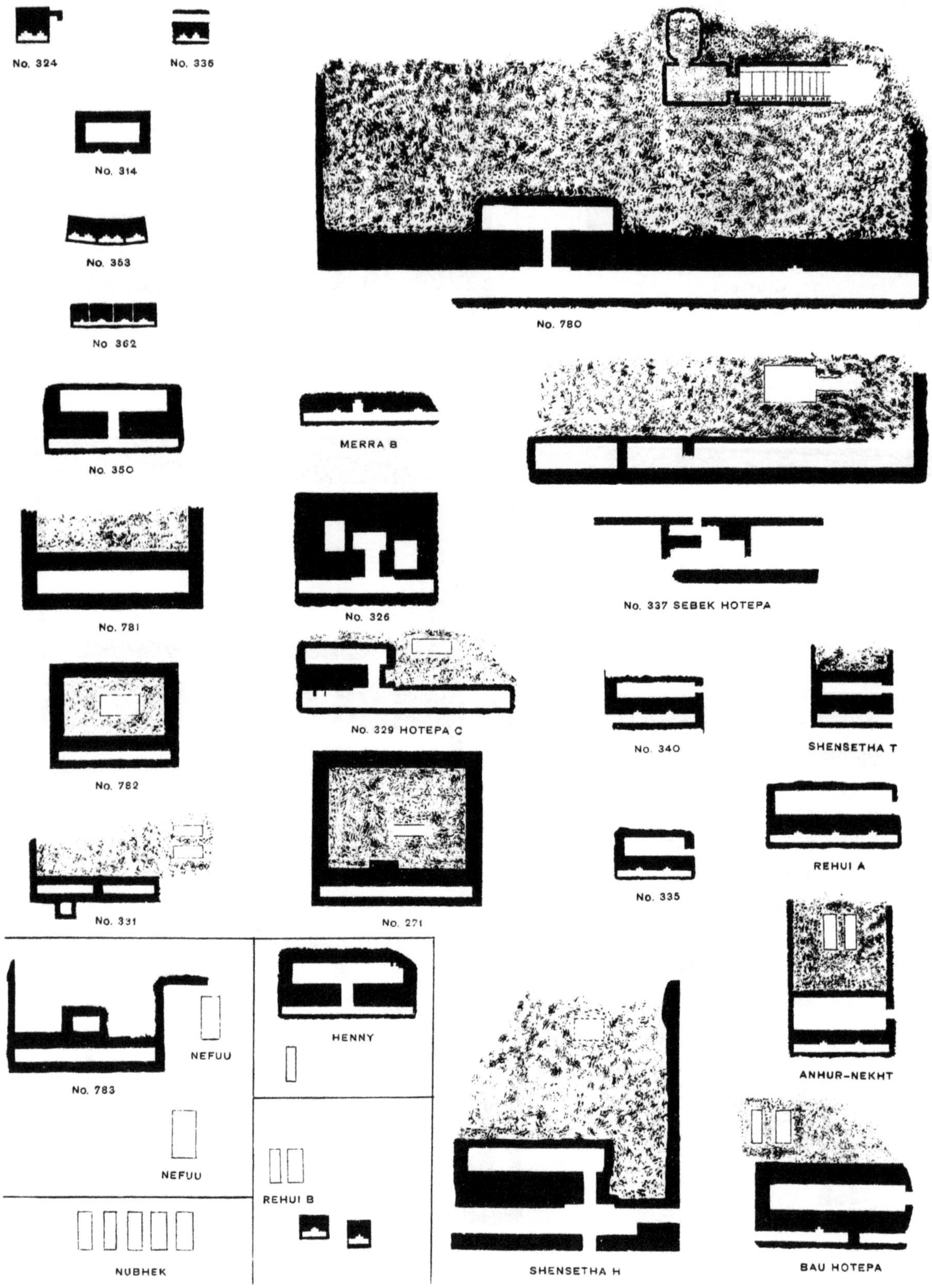
No. 324
No. 336
No. 314
No. 353
No. 362
No. 780
No. 350
MERRA B
No. 781
No. 326
No. 337 SEBEK HOTEPA
No. 782
No. 329 HOTEPA C
No. 340
SHENSETHA T
REHUI A
No. 335
No. 331
No. 271
HENNY
No. 783
NEFUU
NEFUU
ANHUR-NEKHT
REHUI B
NUBHEK
SHENSETHA H
BAU HOTEPA

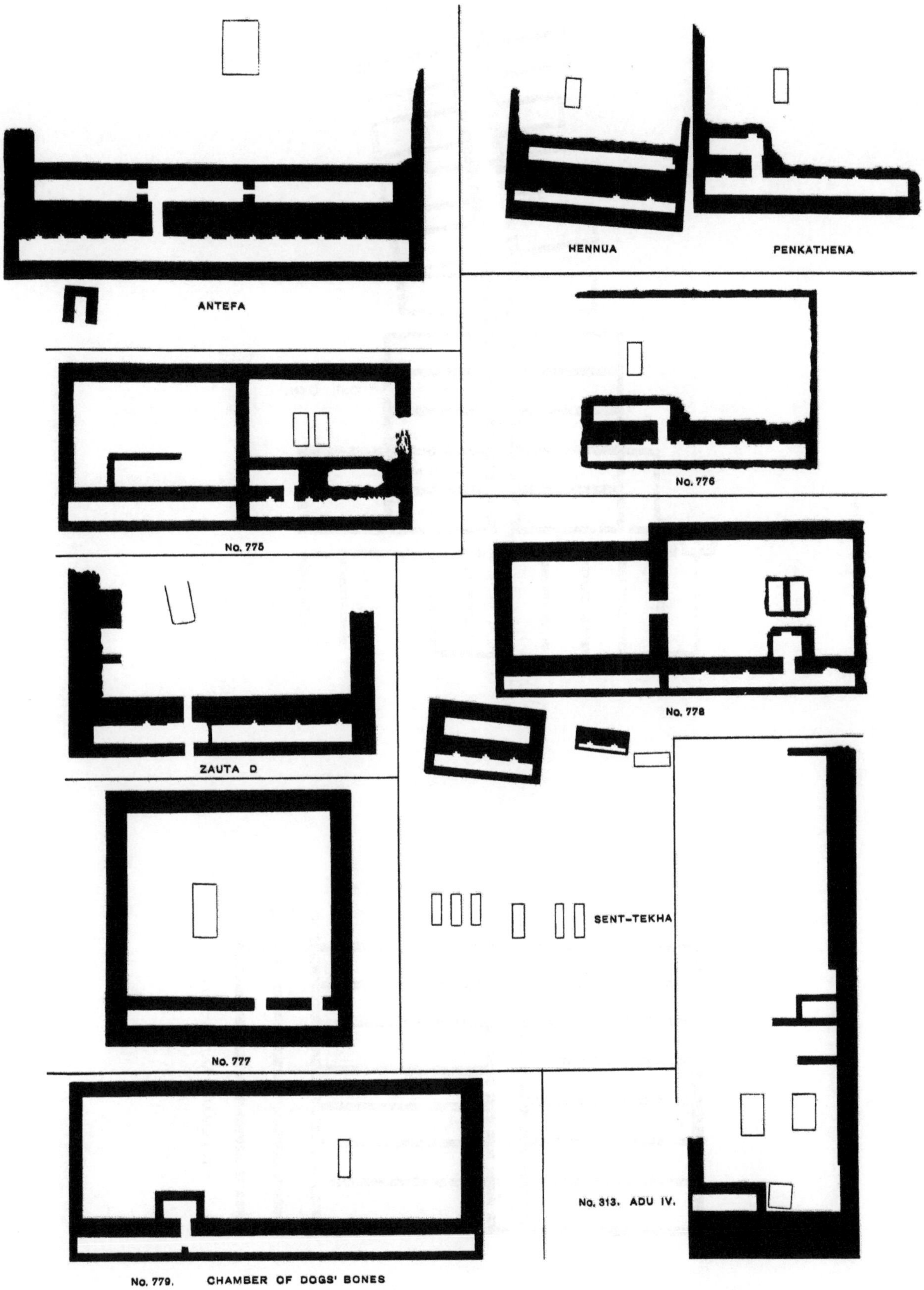
HENNUA
PENKATHENA
ANTEFA
No. 776
No. 775
No. 778
ZAUTA D
SENT–TEKHA
No. 777
No. 313. ADU IV.
No. 779. CHAMBER OF DOGS' BONES

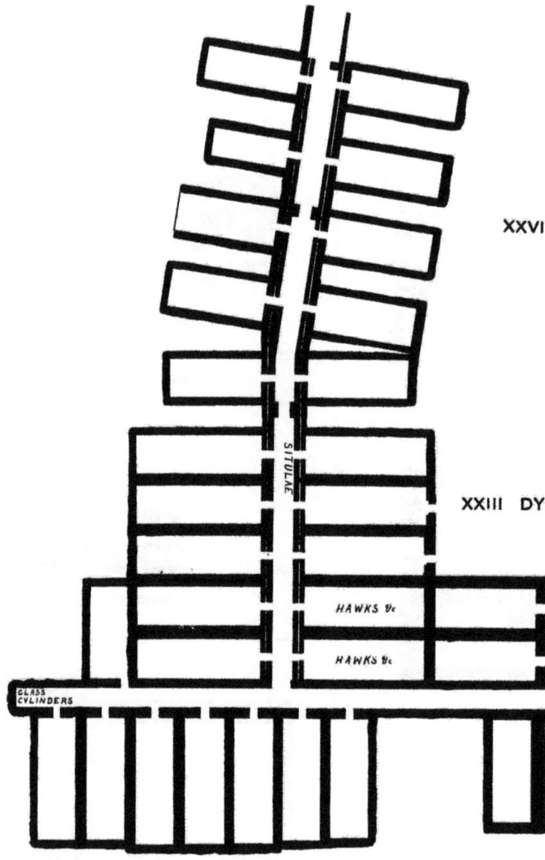
XXVI ? DYN.
SITULAE
XXIII DYN.
HAWKS &c
HAWKS &c
GLASS CYLINDERS
XVIII DYN.

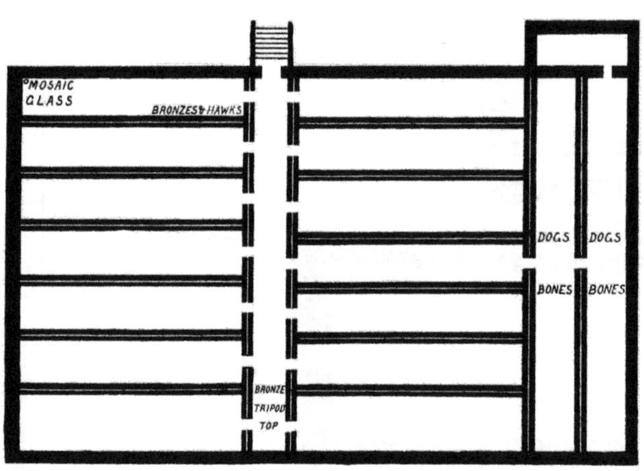
MOSAIC GLASS
BRONZES & HAWKS
DOGS
DOGS
BONES
BONES
BRONZE TRIPOD TOP
PTOLEMAIC AND ROMAN

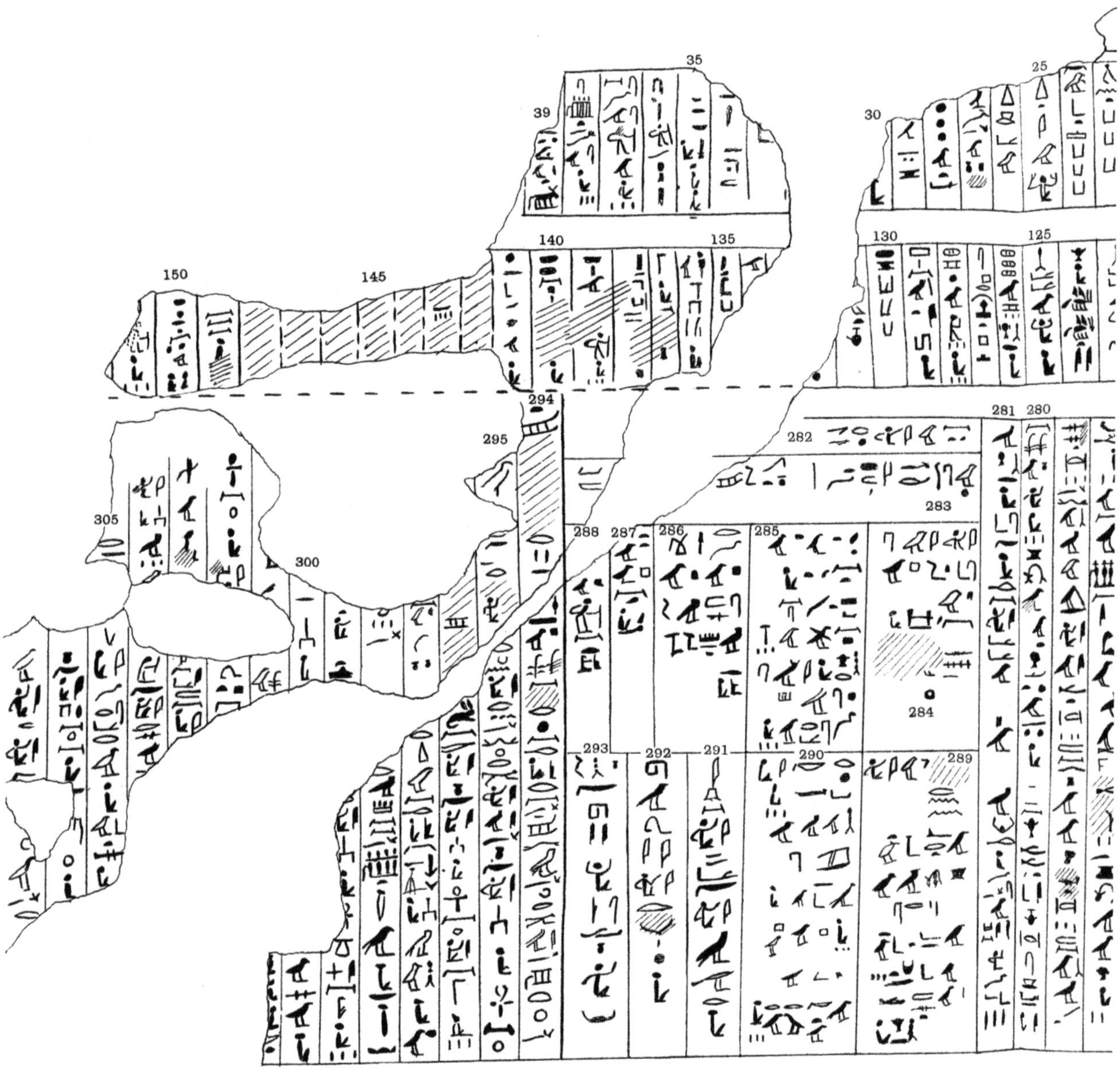

KEY PLAN OF SARCOPHAGUS OF BEB, WITH NUMBER

S. END	W. SIDE		
PL.XXXVII K	PL.XXXVII J	PL.XXXVII H	PL.XXXVII G
828-851	722-744	699-721	671-698
852-873	803-827	779-802	745-778

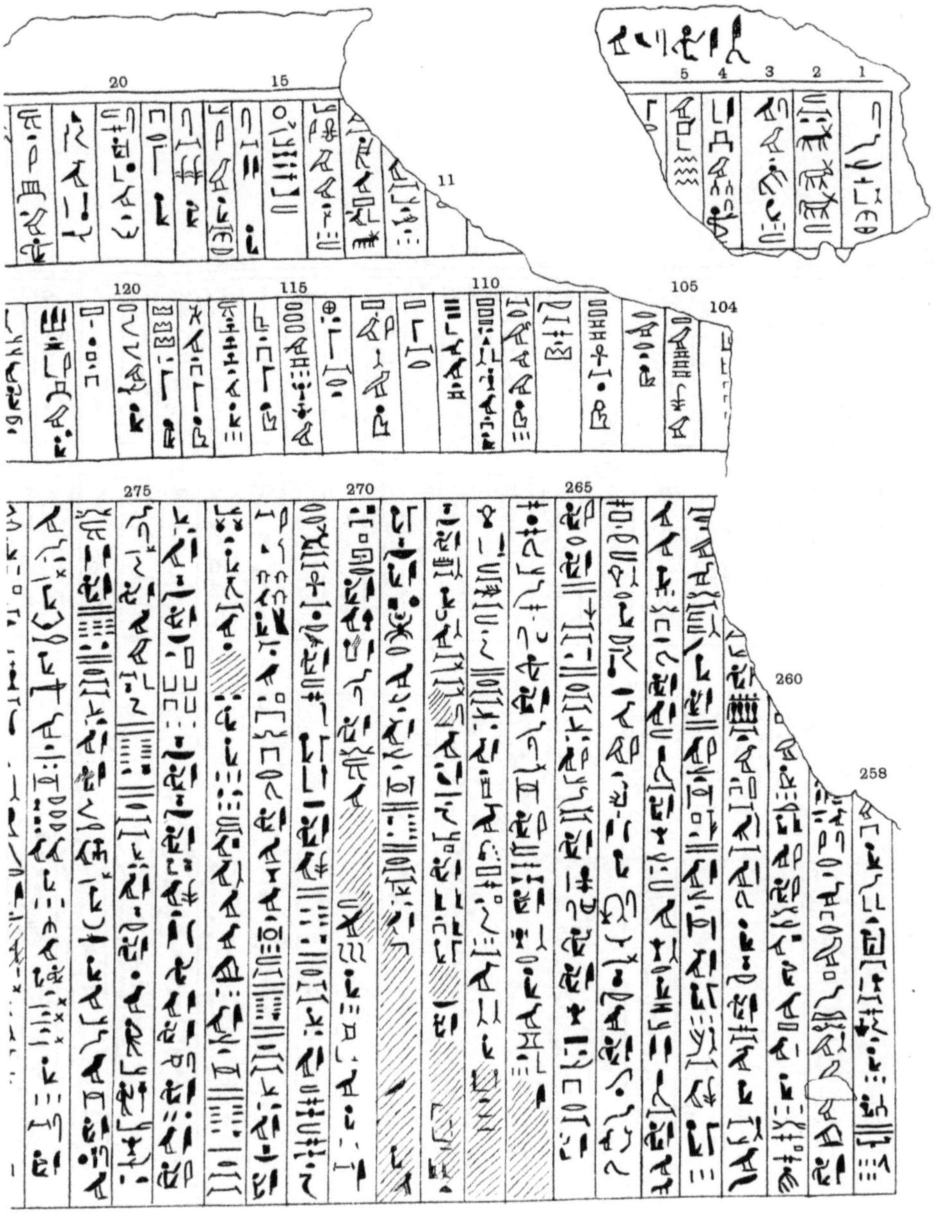

ING OF PLATES AND COLUMNS.

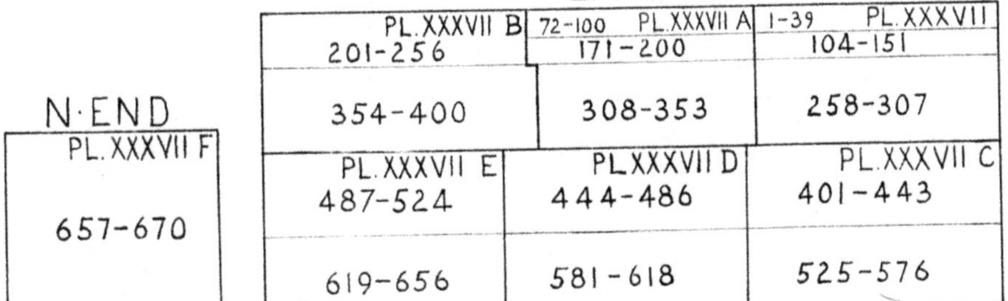

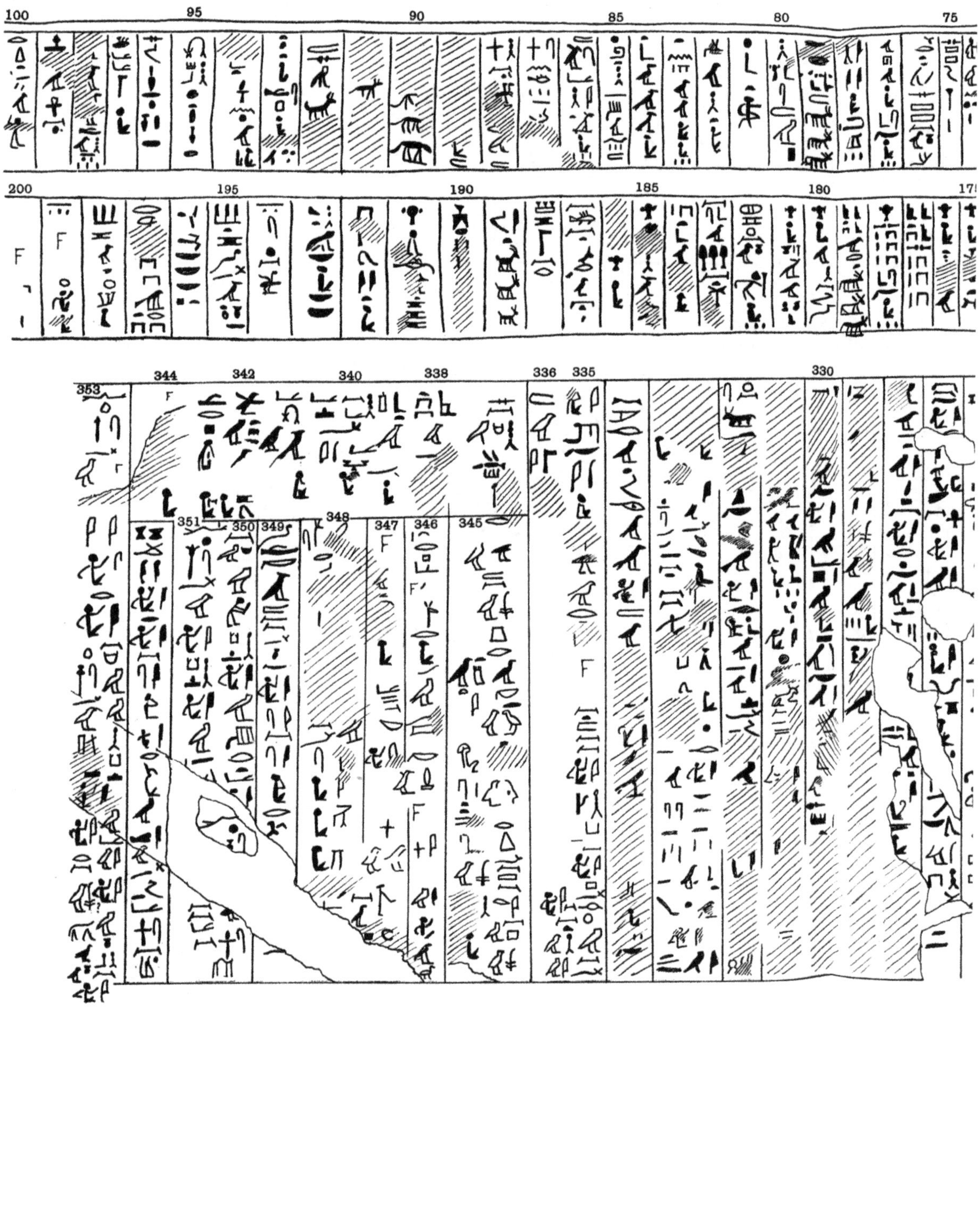
100 95 90 85 80 75
200 195 190 185 180 175
353 344 342 340 338 336 335 330
351 350 349 348 347 346 345

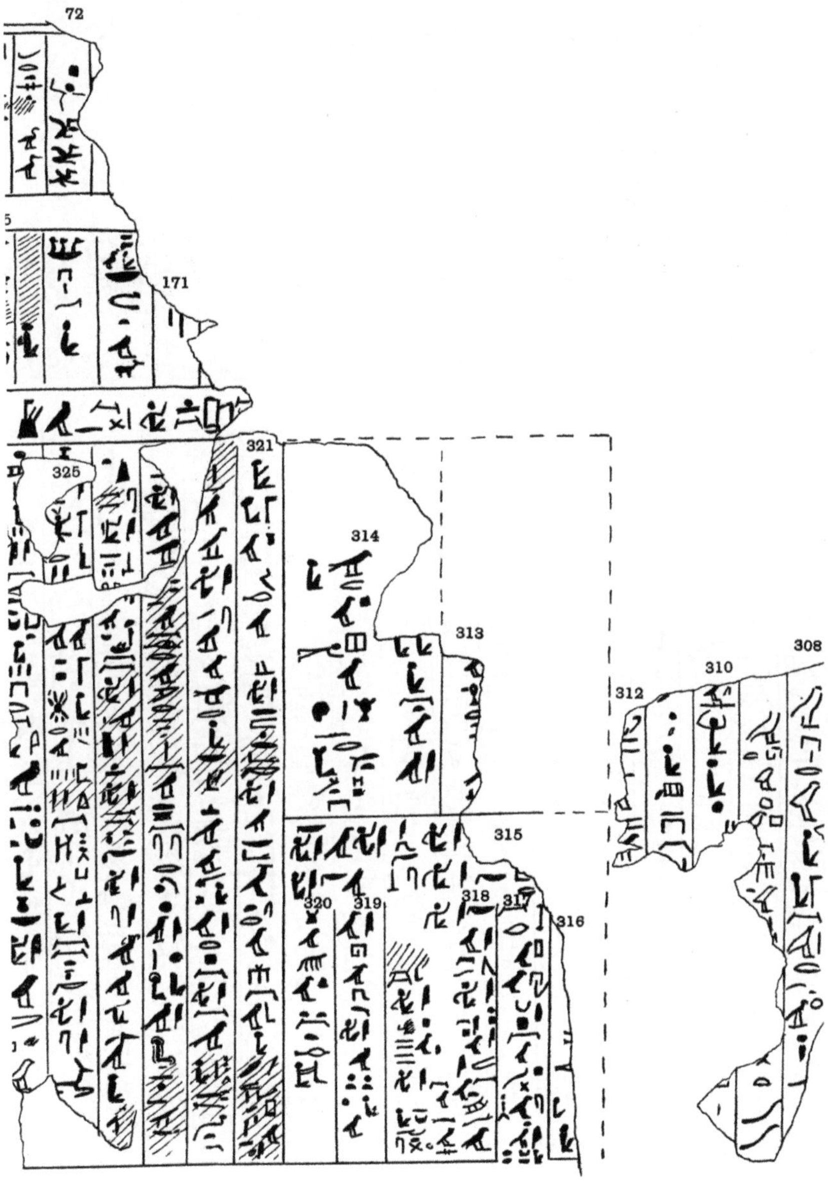
72
171
321
325
314
313
310
308
312
315
320
319
318
317
316

250
245
240
235
230
256
255
FLINT
400
395
390
385
380
BLANK

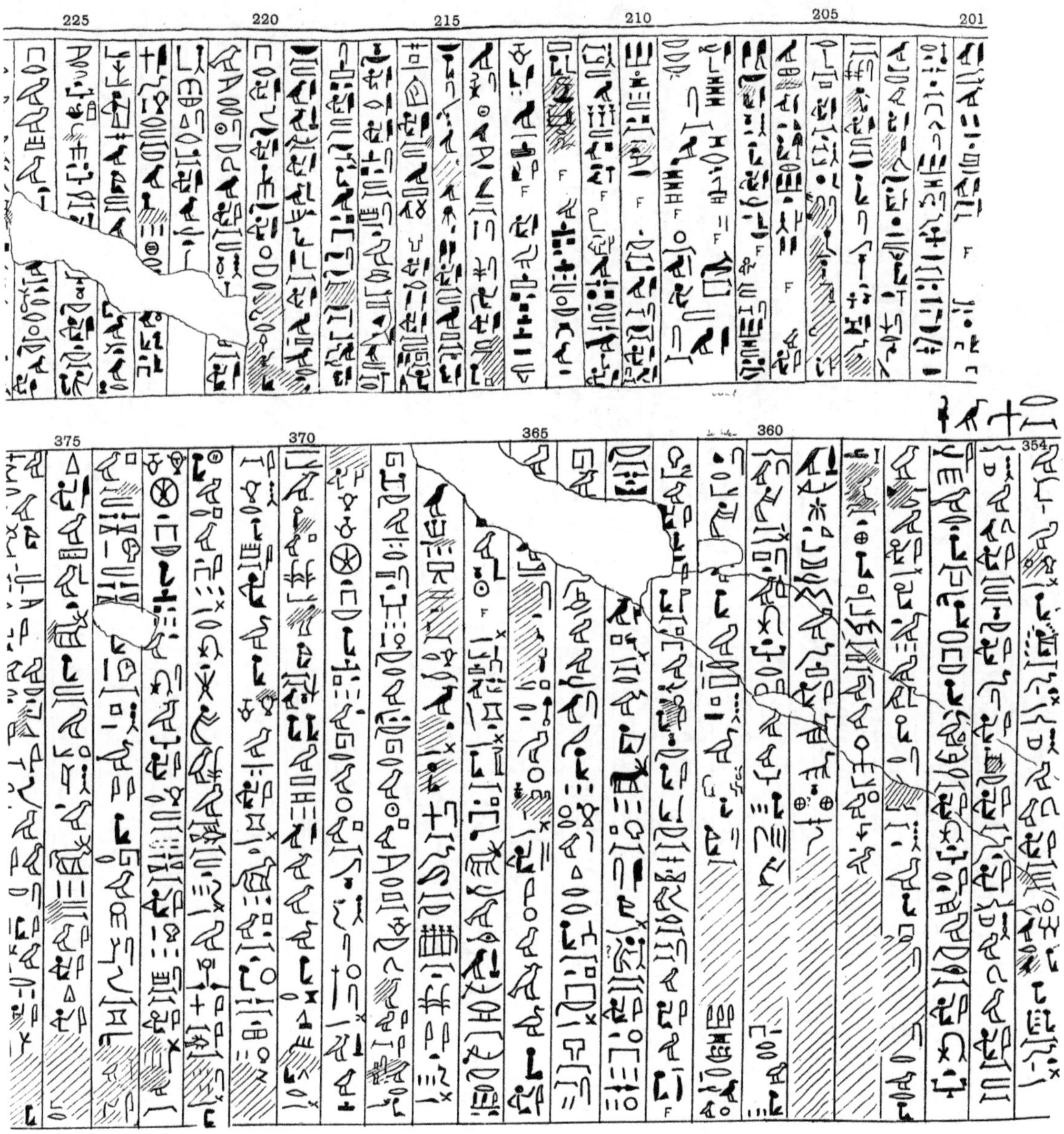
225
220
215
210
205
201
375
370
365
360
354

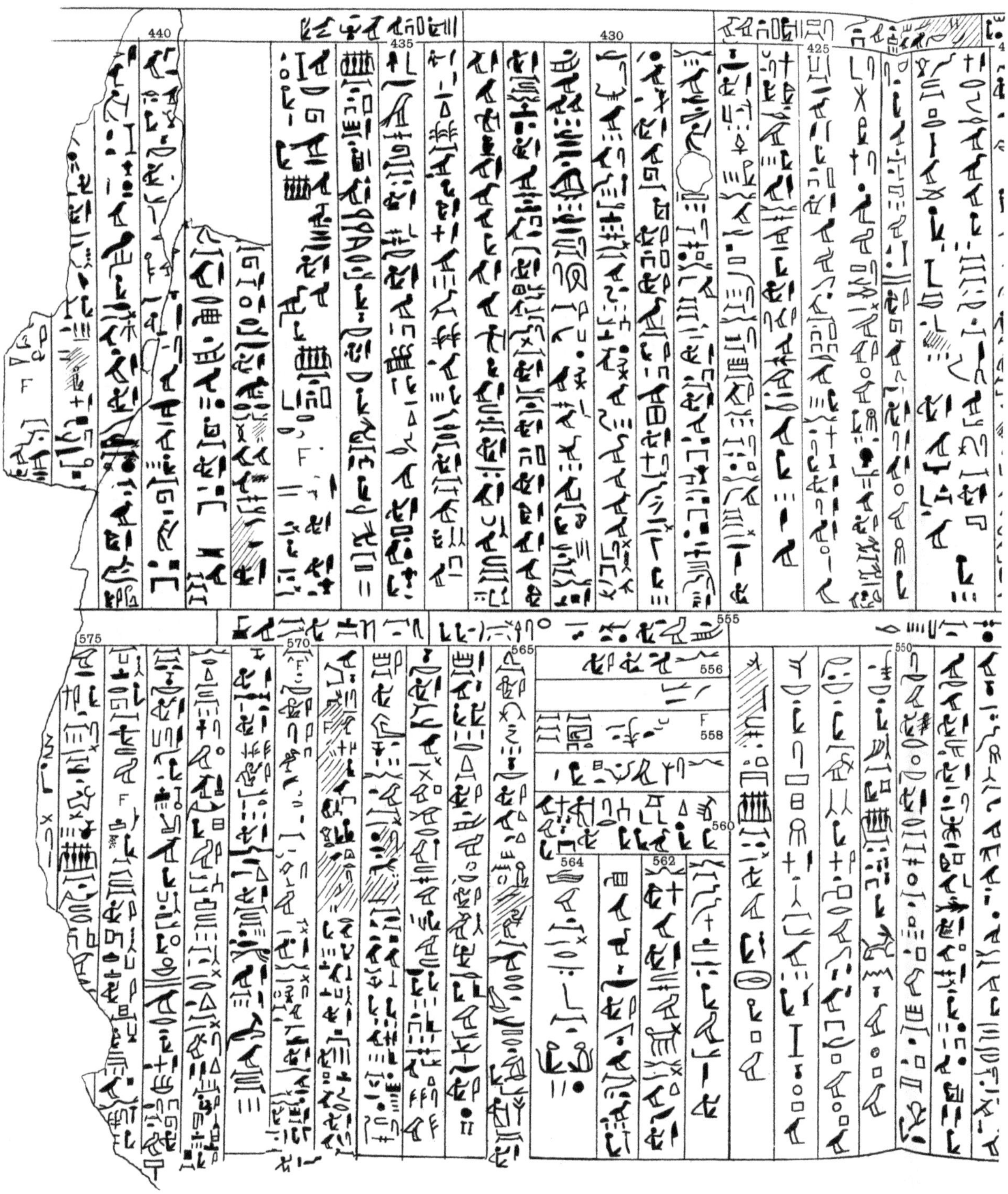
440
435
430
425
575
570
565
555
556
558
560
564
562
550

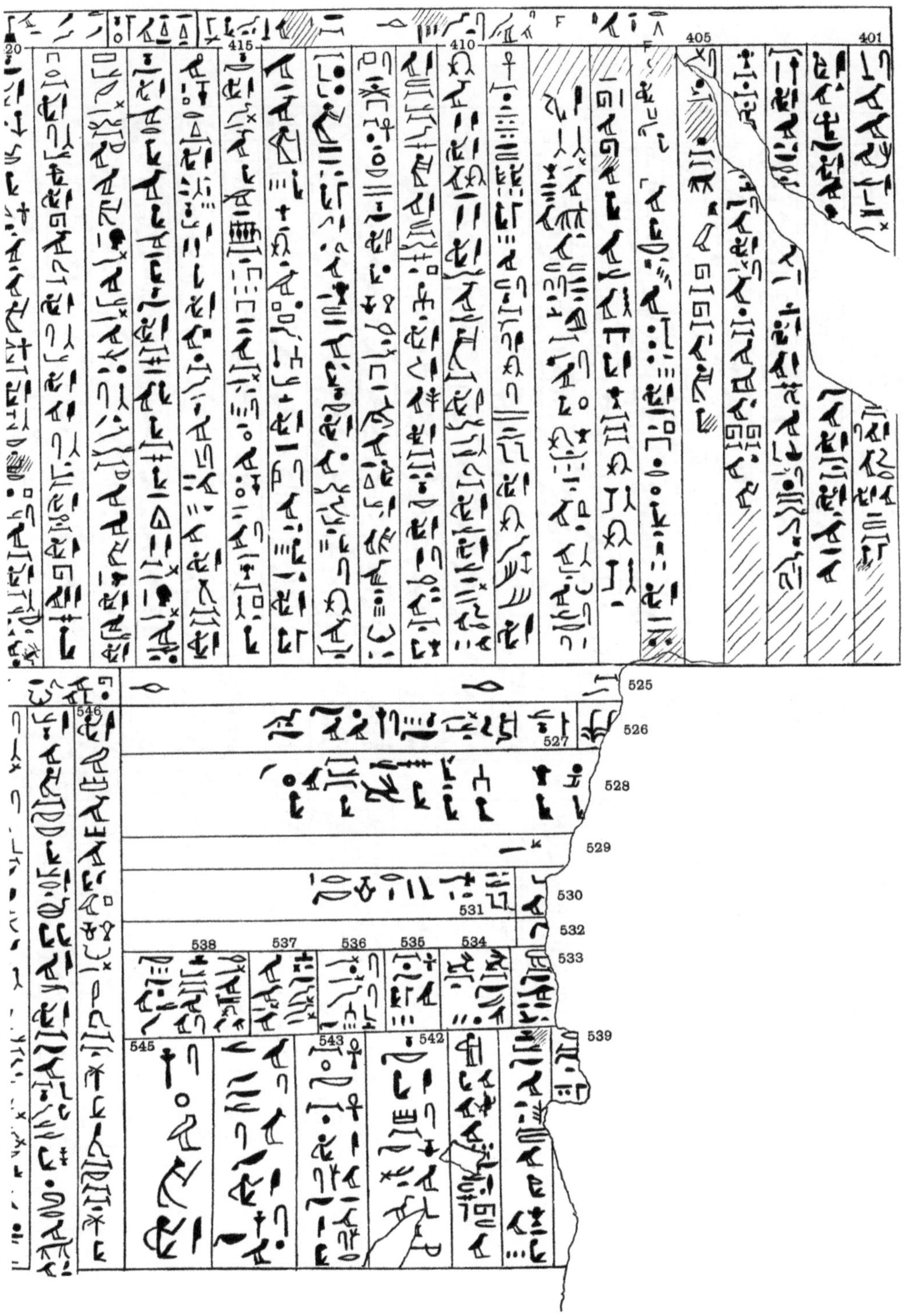
420
415
410
405
401
525
526
527
528
529
530
531
532
533
534
535
536
537
538
539
542
543
545
546

485
480
475
470
465
610
605
615
600
599
594
595
598
592

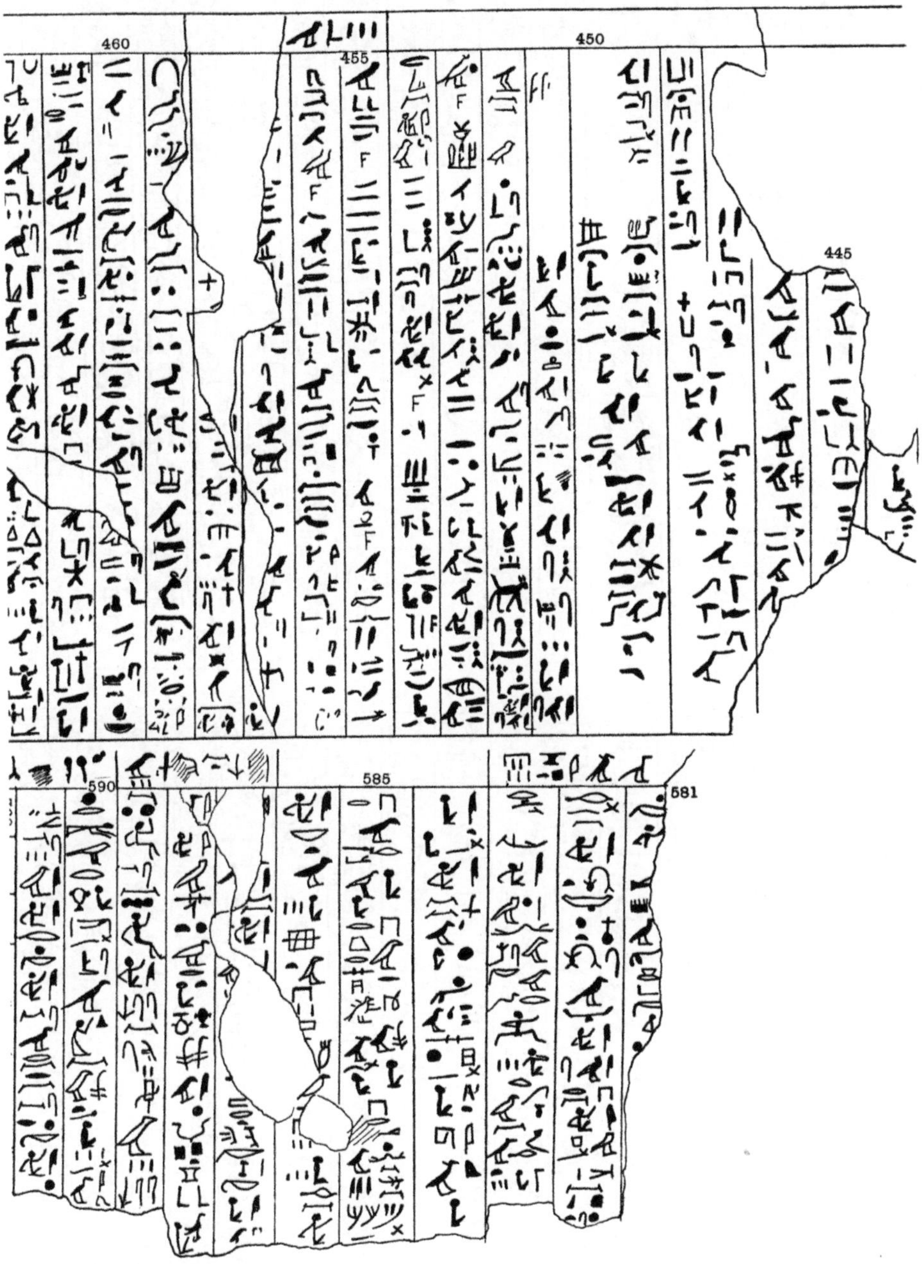
460
455
450
445
590
585
581

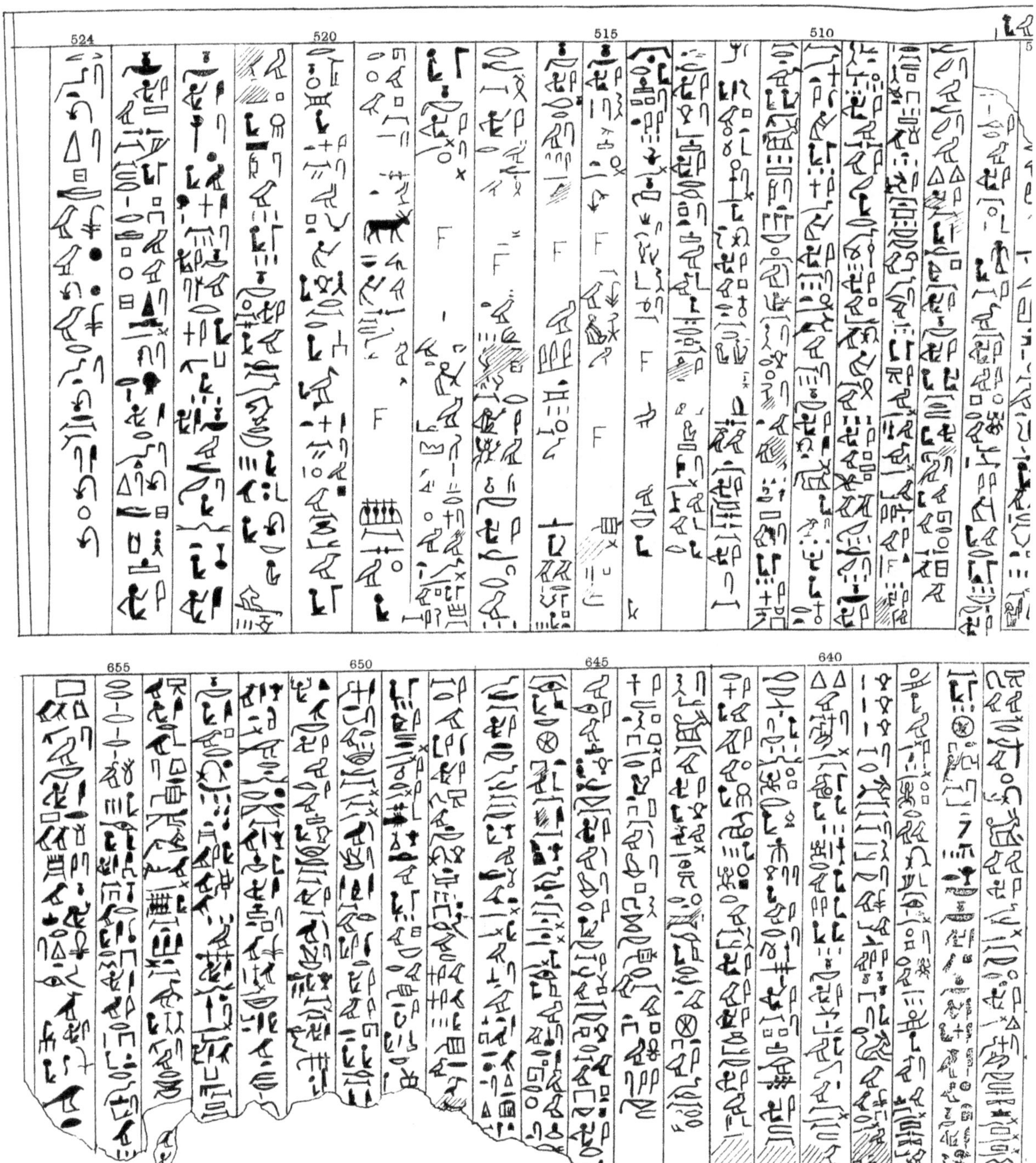

524
520
515
510
655
650
645
640

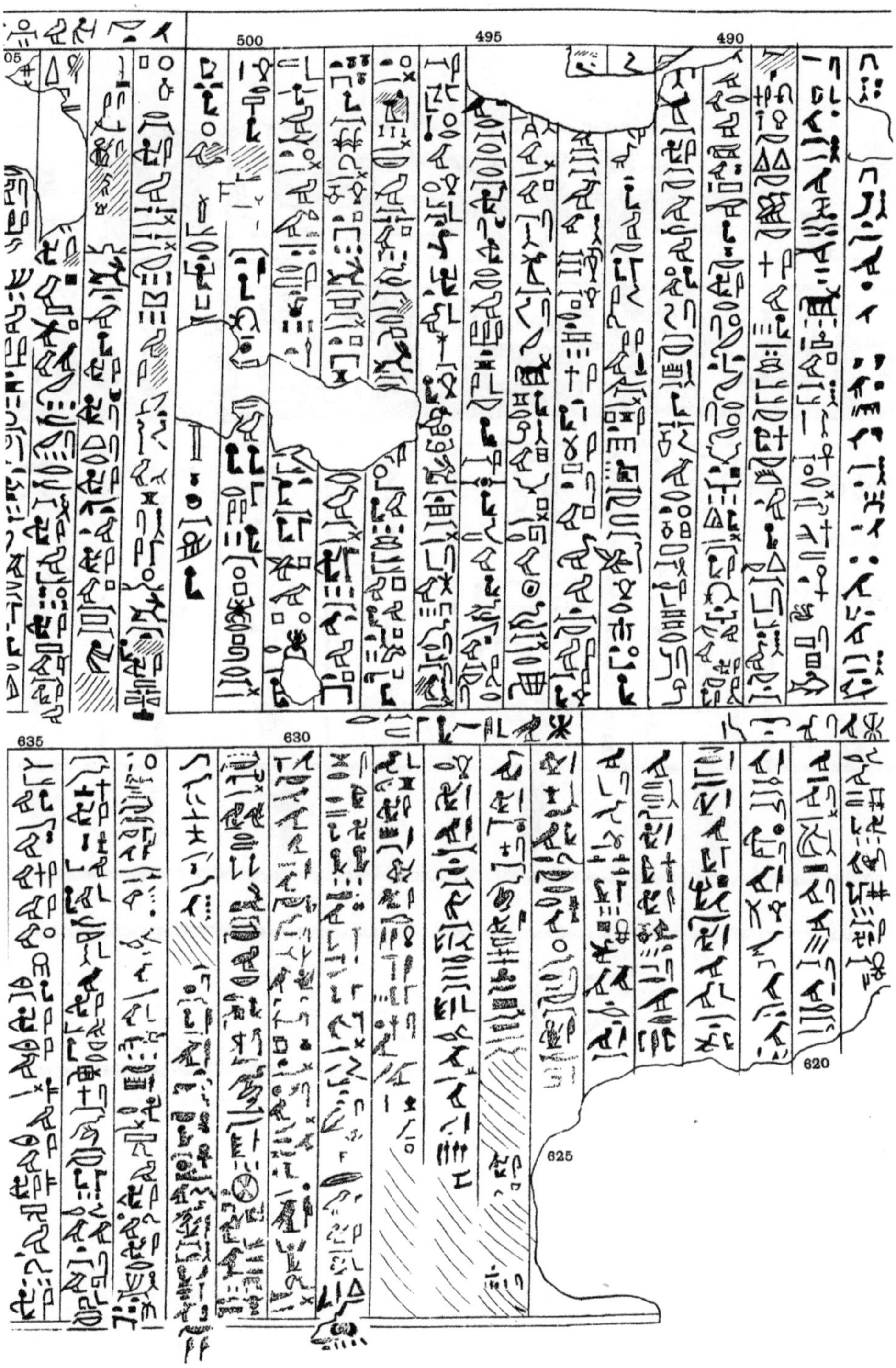
500
495
490
635
630
625
620

1 : 2

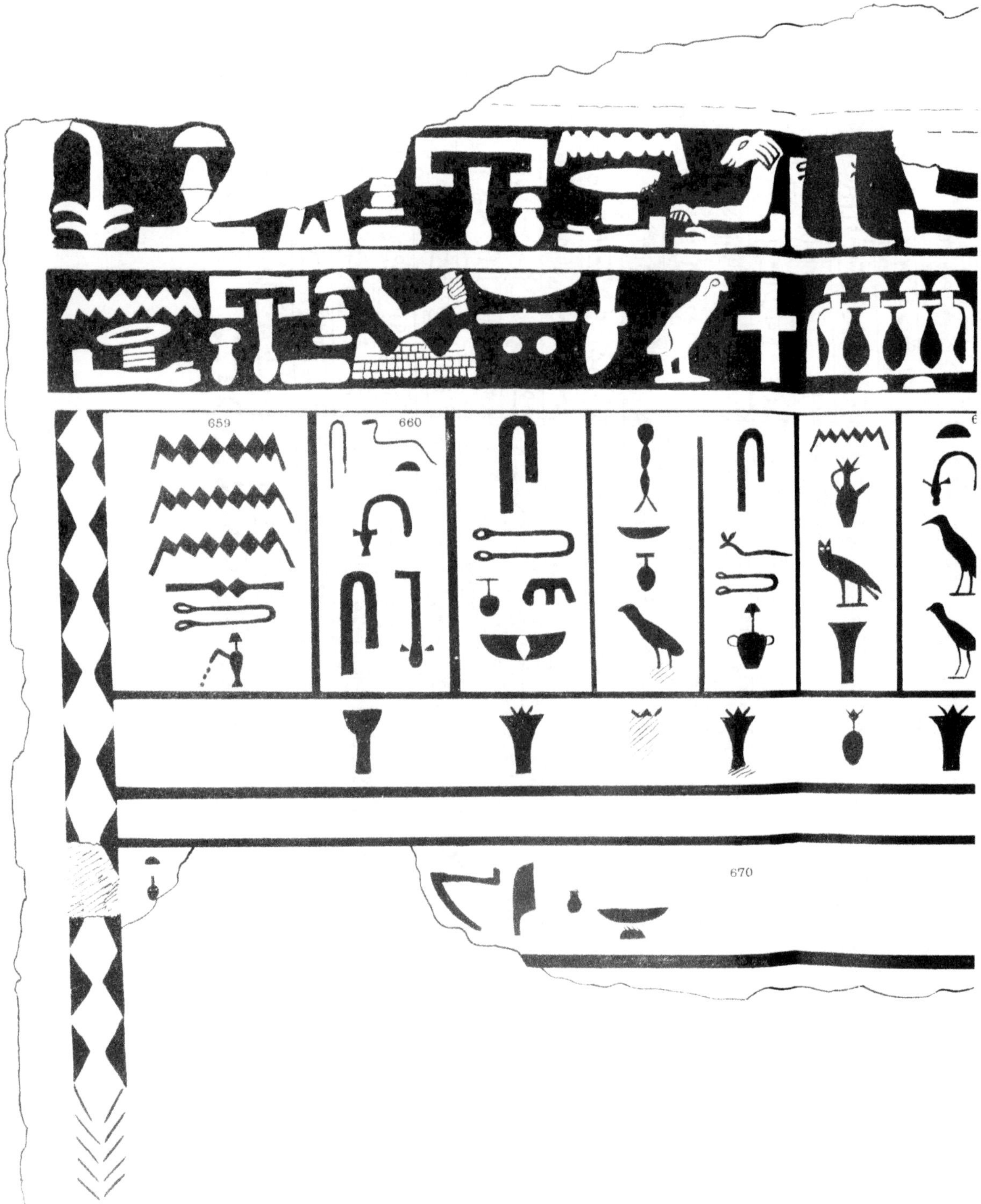

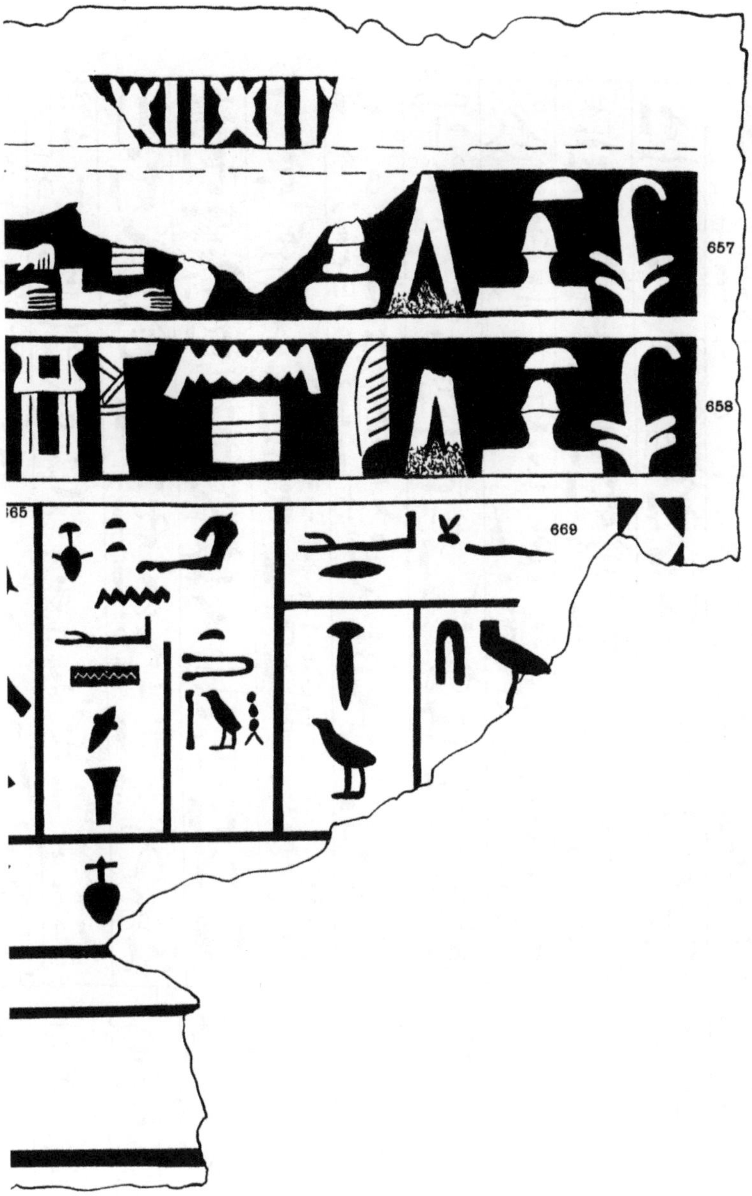
657
658
665
669

695
690
685
775
770
765

675
680
671
755
750
745

1:2

705
700
779
785
780

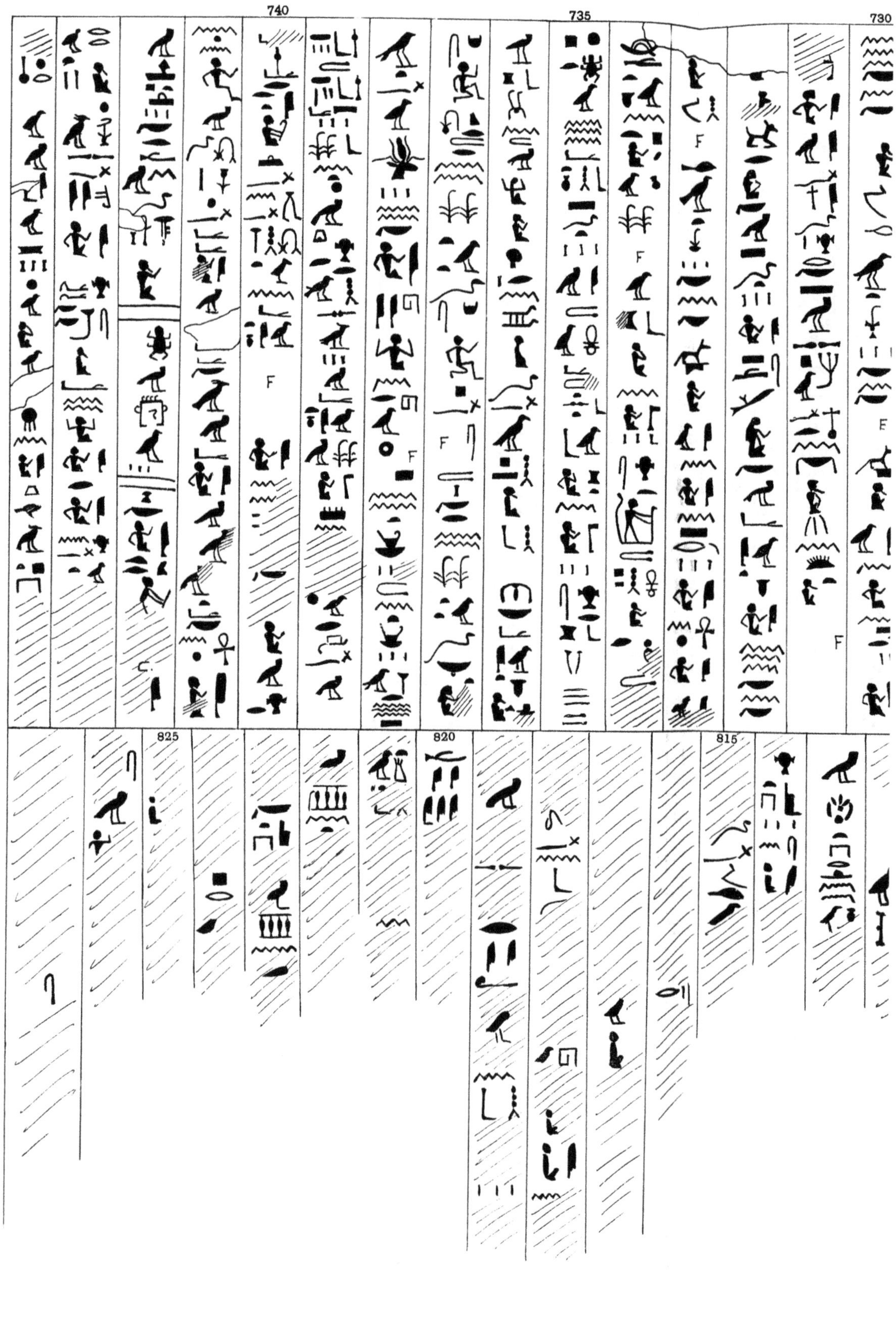
740
735
730
825
820
815

725
810
805
F
F
F
F

1:2

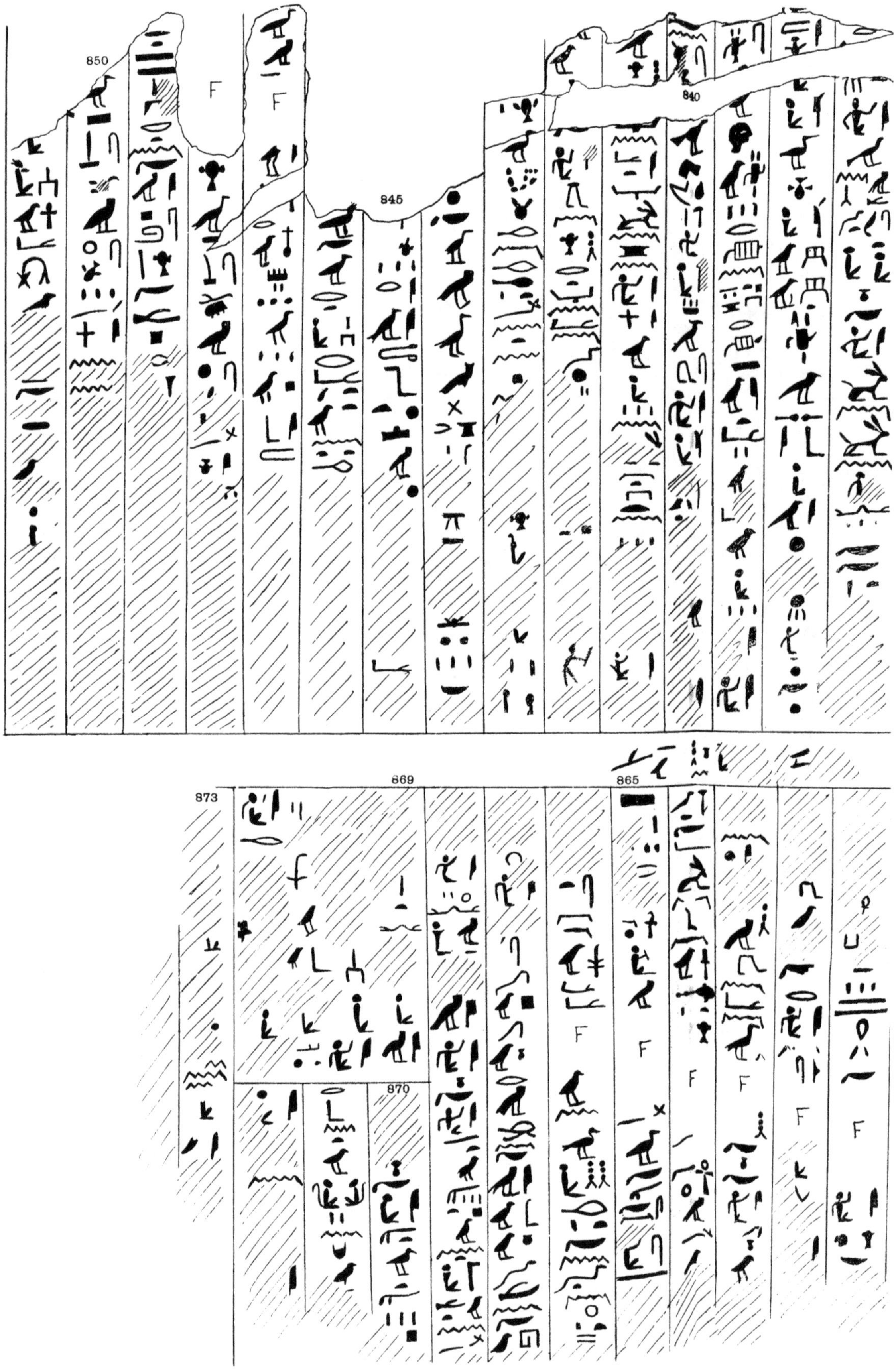

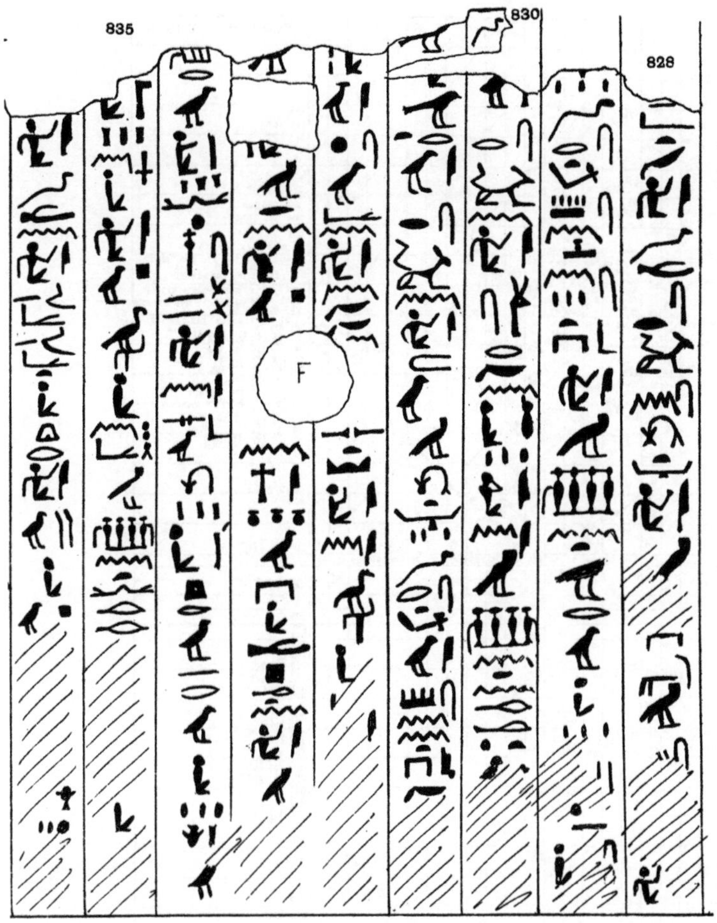
835
830
828
F

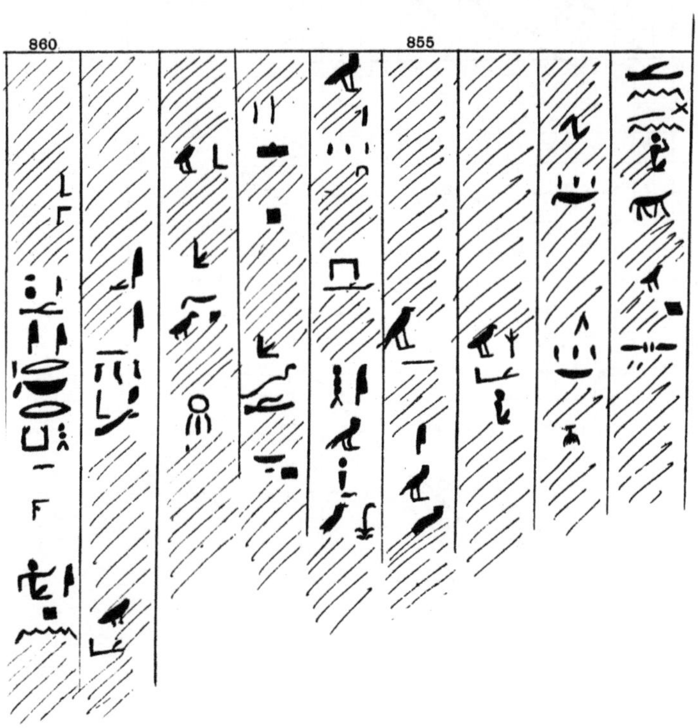
860
855
F

DENDEREH. MAXIMUM LENGTH, BREADTH AND INDEX, MALE SKULLS. PL. A.

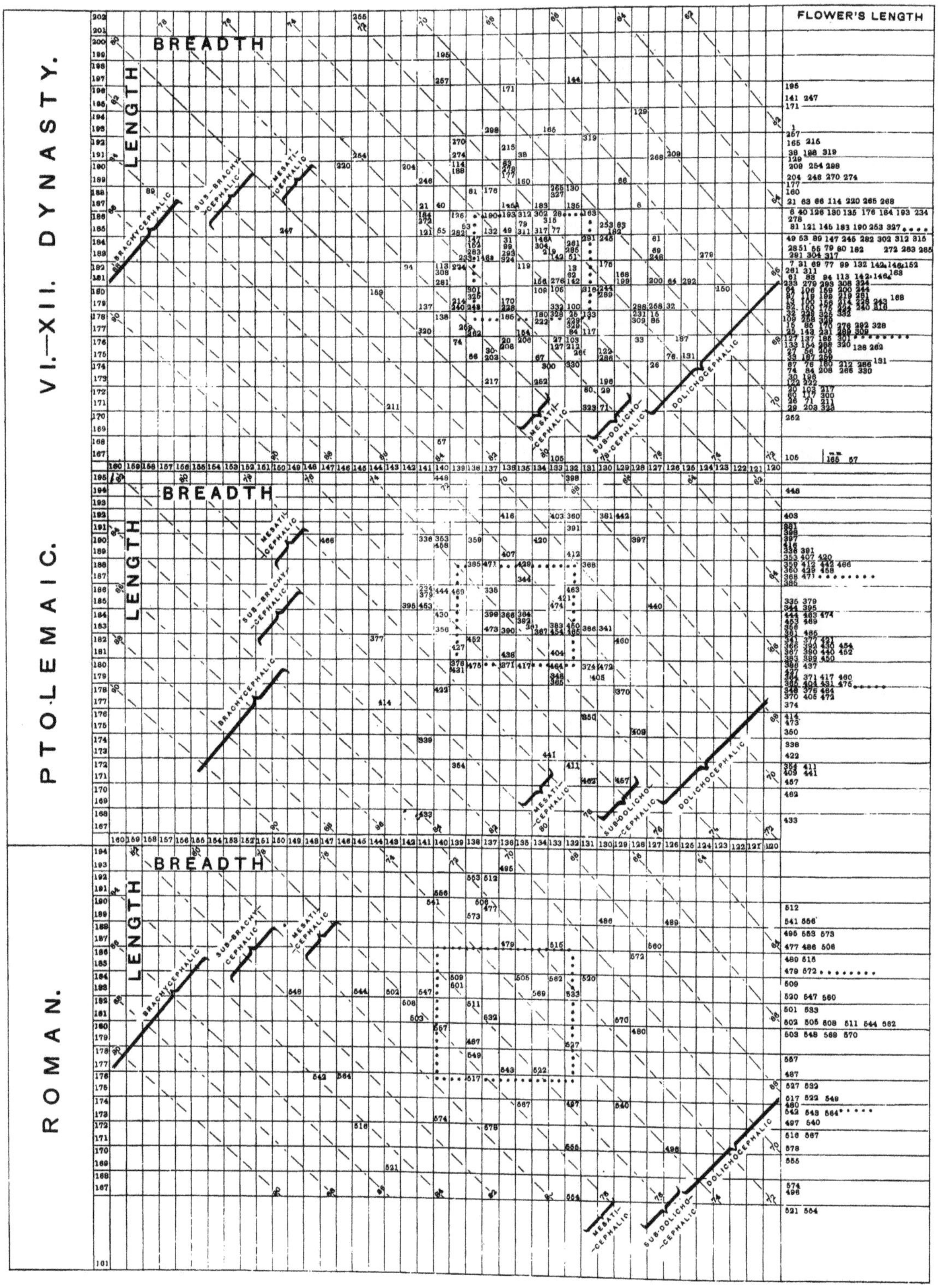

DENDEREH. MAXIMUM LENGTH, BREADTH AND INDEX, FEMALE SKULLS. PL. B.

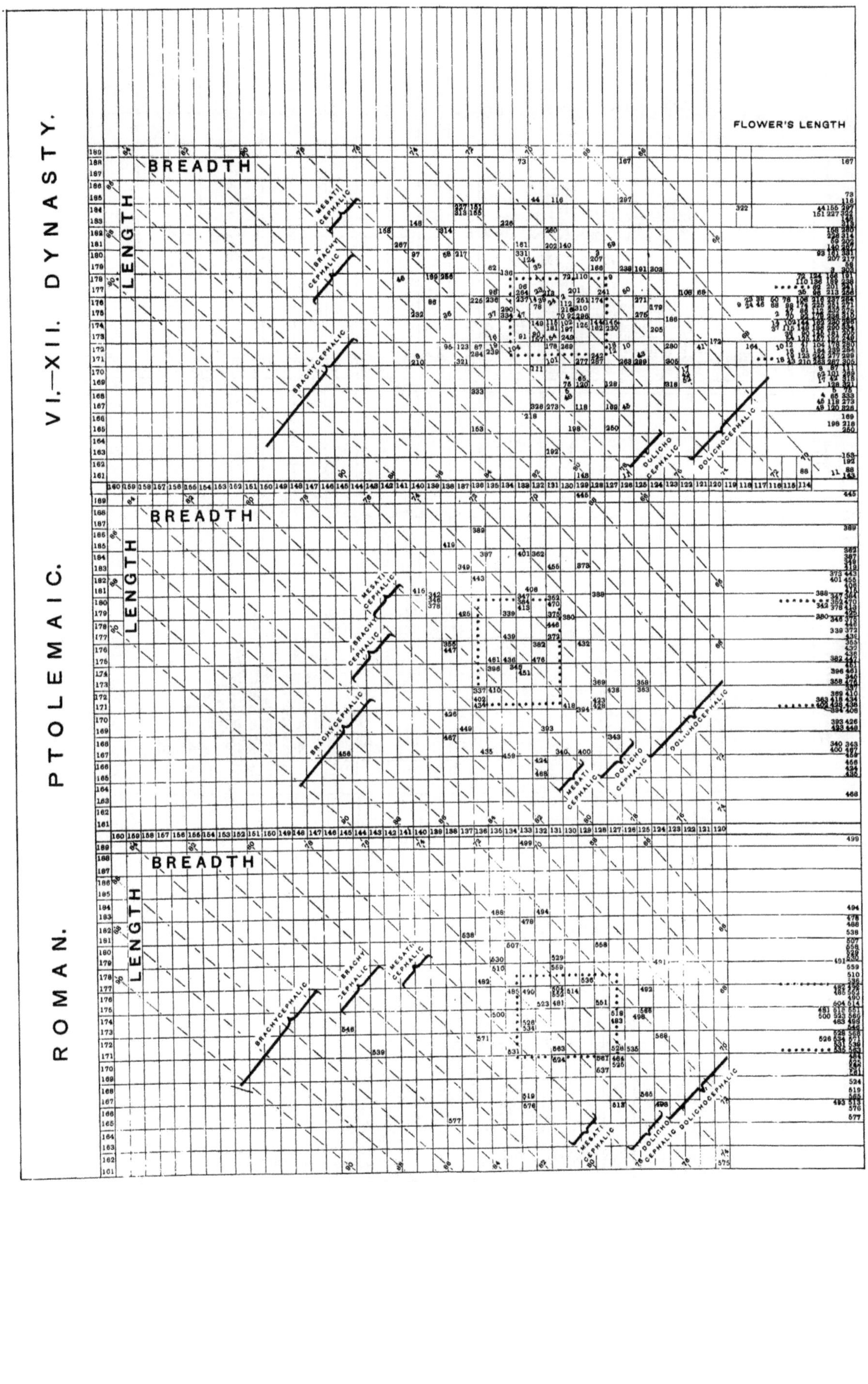

DENDEREH. BREADTHS OF SKULLS, MALE. PL. C.

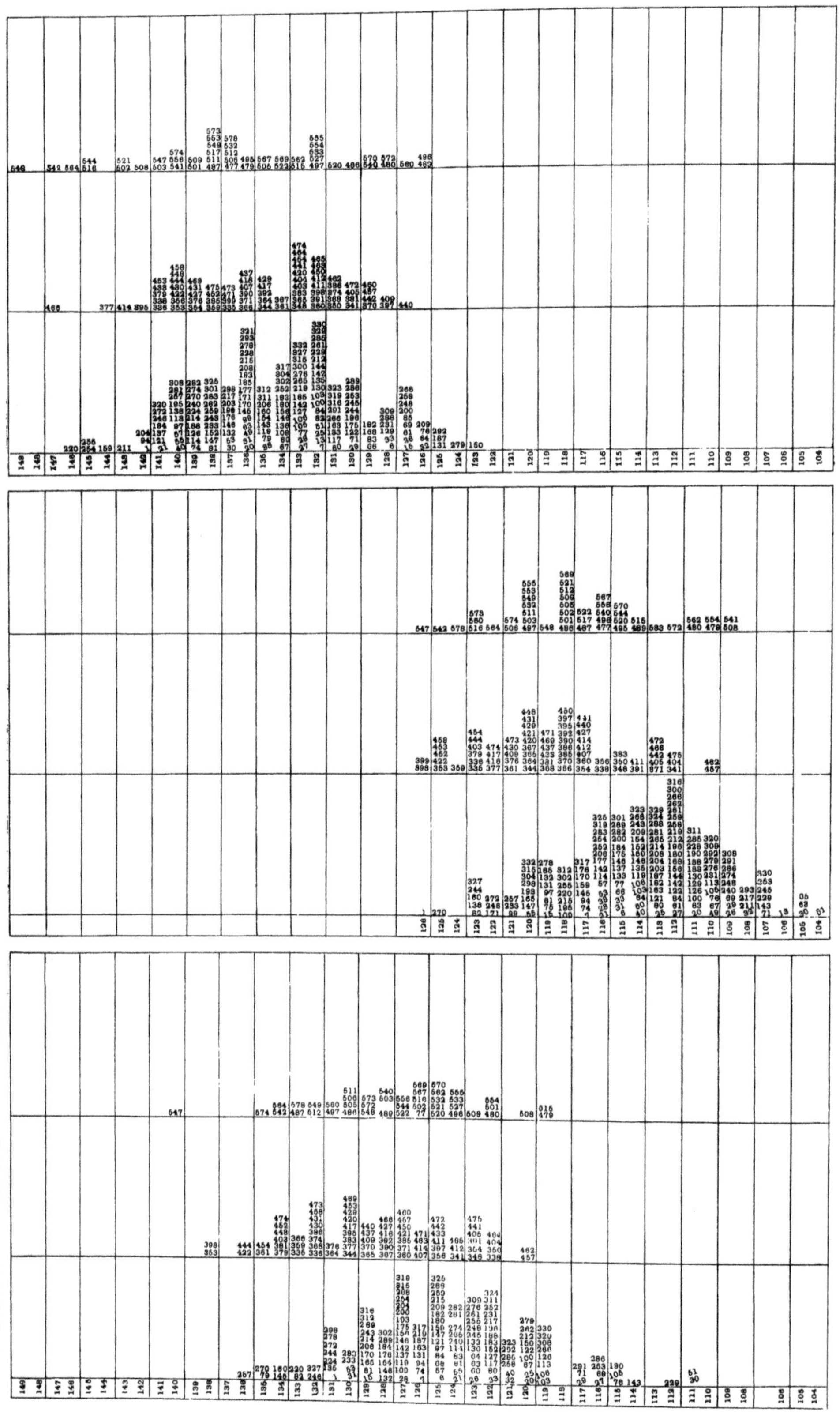

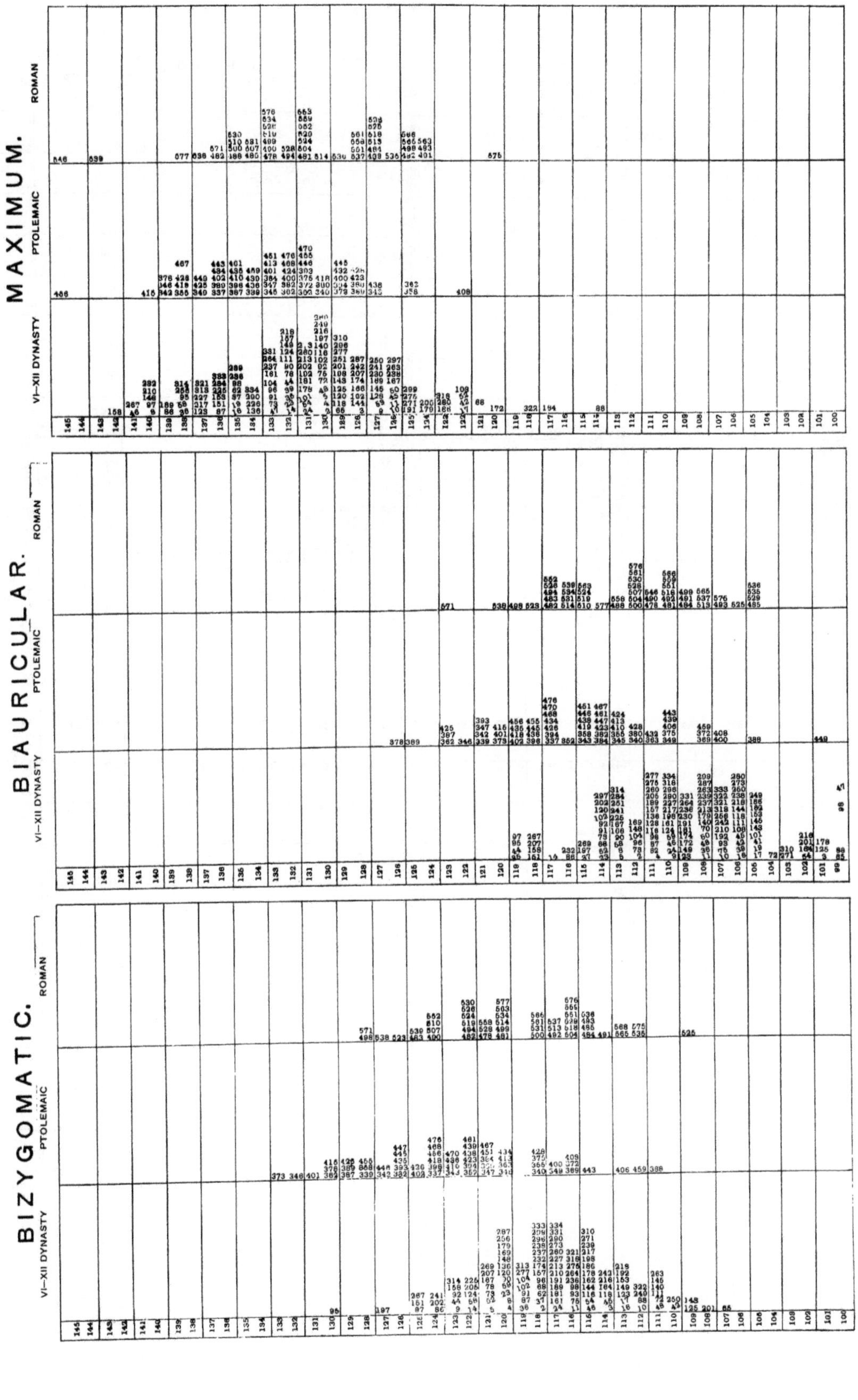
MAXIMUM.
ROMAN
PTOLEMAIC
VI–XII DYNASTY
BIAURICULAR.
ROMAN
PTOLEMAIC
VI–XII DYNASTY
BIZYGOMATIC.
ROMAN
PTOLEMAIC
VI–XII DYNASTY

	MALE			FEMALE		
	VI–XII DYNASTY	PTOLEMAIC	ROMAN	VI–XII DYNASTY	PTOLEMAIC	ROMAN
834						
836				172		
838						
840						
842						
844						
846					445	
848						563
850						
852						
854				198		
856					382	
858						
860						
862						
864		403				
866	316		480 572			
868						
870		353				
872	320					
874				167	428	
876				9	413	
878						
880						
882					362	
884	278					
886	329	360	487	73		537
888				237		
890			540			
892	82				378	
894				120 44		492
896	57 171 229	377 386	505 512	125	389	
898			486	318		
900		368?		86 207	358	
902	265	367 448		41	388	
904				218		
906	195	412	532			504 518
908		361	555	98	461	523 524
910	122 246 330					
912		407 465	506 560		346 373 426	482
914	220 288 27 255 268		489	116 321		
916		391 437 464 374 383	542 547			
918	89·206·272 13	350 452	522	23 12	363 387 393 339	546
920		427 430 458				
922	64 74 154 332 28 276	422	570 574 553	111		491
924	40 7 163	379 442 473		35		
926	160 252	371		322 191	468	481 507
928		356	515·517·567	118	419 406·425	535 526
930	253·132·150 215 188	433 370 421	578		434 435 446	
932	180 291 292 254 53 262	381 398 366		296		
934	204 257				400	577 538
936	31 165 319	338		162 227 287 3 24 95 181	423	493 510
938	33·212·279 109	441 475	495 501	2·251	372·424·439	530
940		376 405		202 92 205	349 375 436 345	490
942	66 142 177 199 274 311 129 38 243 81 325	454	508	166	449	
944	55	348				
946				87 192 236 18 37 201 213 230 232 242 256 10 17 46 169 197	467	539 500
948	49 228 258 71 137·240 248 281	354 417	533 516	102 140 145·151·241–297 179 299	415 394	
950	138	420·440	502 509 554		380 470 443	
952	117 79 156 214 183 244 270	429 390	497			
954		469				
956	286			42 48 96 143 250 93 97 263	402 455 410	568 488
958	97 145 196 261 300 323 67 185	409	564 521	52 178	476	514 551
960	69 80 142∧231 285 302 308 309 312 324 83	416 344	479	124 158 267	447	528
962	114 222 327 235	359 404				
964			477	174		
966	219 100			11		534
968	266 60	365 431	569	269 72-226-273	396 418	484 525
970	26 29 113·317	364	520			558 536
972	103 146-175 182 184 283 200 298	411				
974						
976	135					494
978	25			115 8-68-101-110-123-260-271	337·347·384·408	552
980	20 30 133 152 293 315 301	395 414 471 463	527 543 496	59 290		478
982	1 32 247	335	541	284 149 186		
984				238 153		498 576
986						
988	217		549			
990	6 105 127 168 170 176 193 203 209 282	392 397	511 544 556 562 573	75 136 148 225 65 90-264-280	340·451 401	519
992						
994						
996	121			275 313		
998						561 575
1000	126 143 159	444 462 472 474	557	43 45 47 54'58 78 104 144 249 314 333 334	342	485 513
2						
4						
6	190			310	438	499
8						
1010	84 94 187 224 147	399	503	164 189 239 277	352 456 459	529 559
12						566
14						
16						
18						
1020	15 77·130	466 457		217		
22	51			36 88 157 91		
24						
26						
28				216	343	
1030	131 259					
32		460		62 5		
34		385		161		
36						
38	304					
1040	21					
42		450		108 4		571
44						
46						
48	119					
1050						483
52					432	
54						
56						
58						
1060						
62				16		
64						
66	245					
68						
1070						
72						
74						
76						
78						
1080						
82						
84						
86						
88						
1090						
92						
94						
96						
98						
1100						
102	61					

Index	MALE VI–XII DYNASTY	MALE PTOLEMAIC	MALE ROMAN	FEMALE VI–XII DYNASTY	FEMALE PTOLEMAIC	FEMALE ROMAN
556–568	7			12		
570–578				321 18		563
580–588	185 15			24		
590–598	171 82			3 172 210?		526
600–608						
610–618	109 126 67	474	512	275	338 446 432	537
620–628	282 206		480 541	227 78 42		491 523 529
630–638	55 255 262 160	412 360	564 487 553	164 17 125 207 218	339 470 443 349	513 535
640–648	74 327 270 292 329 83 154 220	473 348 368	520 517	41 166 88 318 167 144 9	394	
650–658	21 246 69 311 182 187 316 274 122 247 265	483 370 390	572 515	124 153 314 73 102 116	388 373 418 461	525 528 485 559
660–668	66 129 28 105 117 145 184 175 180 133 288 315	453 359 361? 433? 354 465	479 560 480 547	8 16 37 260 136 296 178 52 93 191 217	382 434 447 337 406 402	478 488 538 494 576 534 483 492
670–678	13 176 33 131 212 31 81 121 203	430 403 416 379 391	509 544 557 578	59 14 43 140 35 143 192 236 284	362 415 424 439 401 384 407	499 518 565 493 552
680–688	258 156 135 285 289 293 324 40 142A 257 152 248	442 392 471	570 543	98 242 120 179 273 92 145 205 101 4 251 44 334 158 181 115 162	372 393 459	539
690–698	60 281 147 64 312 183 199 168 233 1 150 32 163-177	448 383 336 437 397 356	496 555 505 574	198 235 2 72 267 68 263 239 23 104 46 65 111 197	425 435 380 455 476	581 576 536 568
700–708	130 193 254 319 6 113 127 138 27 283 159 298 304 219 26 231 309 317 119 200	366-422 381 429 450 335 371 374 414 367-420	497 477 502 506 542	161 237 47 98 96 174 45 86 108 110 151	428 467 426 436 340 346	481 566
710–718	80 165 261 308 51-53 146A 224 240 320 29 20 300 170 332 132 268 272	462 398 440 364 405 338	516 508 562	186 58 287 299 241 256 11 90 149 169 75	423 438 387 389 413 419 363	577 558 482 498 514
720–728	188 253 266 244 278 143 325 61 291 215	344-452 395 404 457	503 511 522 527	264 226 322 48 157 54 262 271 333 297 87	378 343 445 449 400 410	524 504 484 490
730–738	142-323 222 245 276 30 137 228 190 196 89 195	377 441 460 350 431 444	486	216 225 148 230 238 290 310 91 277 36 189	352 375 451	510
740–748	84 259 204 286 301 330 94	399 365		202 5 123	342 456 468	571 551
750–758	302 49 57	353 458	554 573 501	97 313 232 280	345 347	
760–768	229 114 217 79	376 464 417	532	249		507
770–778	209 77	411 475 427	540 569 549	269	396	519
780–788		454	495	10		500
790–798	25 100	381				
800–808	243		556			
810–818	146	466	567			
820–828						
830–838	103	469				
840–848		472	548			546
850–858						
860–870			521			

Index	MALE: VI–XII Dynasty	MALE: Ptolemaic	MALE: Roman	FEMALE: VI–XII Dynasty	FEMALE: Ptolemaic	FEMALE: Roman
362–368				143		
370–378						
380–388						
390–398	81				389	
400–408	89		567 521		400	492
410–418	146B 274				345	482 510
420–428	13 142 A 288	475 353 457		9 48		
430–438	252 122 77 31	390 398	557 540	87 230 35	456	500 568
440–448	40 1	367 391 464 422	515 569 495	24 10	362 424 451 428	561
450–458	129 79 166 243 332 163 133 288	444 404 420	502 543 506 532 572 · · · ·	181 4 251		538 483
460–468	132 246 255 61 268 130 278 293	397 427 361 466 344 383 471 · · · · · ·	508 501 505	23 153 148 95 210	346 387 445 378 476	363 468 488 507 · · · · · 551
470–478	265 325 20 97 259 262 195 209 53 114	356 336 360 433 437 405 421 371 354 374	570	238 241 250 145 205 151 232 97 218 104 277 101 125 197 201	340 419 · · · · 447 349 425	575 518
480–488	102 105 100 · · · · · · · 38 184 233 245 317 26 117 136 188 200 316 320 323 261 180	385 442 359 365 448 338	480 489 560 578	166 12 17 18 · · · · · · · 11 45 58 62 111 322	375 396 352 388 467	490 524
490–498	51 76 137 330 146A 219 276 281 217 119 55 113 170 176 193 229 266	370 429 463 465 368 376 381 386 453 458 469 473 · · ·	544 555 522 548 574 · · 400	68 86 120 162 217 271 321 46 116 157 225 263 269	435 380 373	577 484
500–509	57 152 175 183 206 244 272 177 196 291 · · · · · · · · 214 302	341 403 412 430 377 409 417 472 395	477 486 512 547 556	73 118 213 227 264 334 169 198 297 161	384 402 436 · · · · · ·	514 535 546 571
510–518	29 64 80 159 190 228 231 240 283 285 301 27 60 67 71 187 212 204 30 84 319	399 · · · · · · 379	503 573 527 · · 516 · · ·	90 140 149 102 202 296 · · · 16 47 65 164 216 172 123 44	347 413 439 406 393	504 528 · · · · 493 523
520–528	32 33 312 85 131 156 142B 298 7 199 215 247 327	460 350 440 452		108 310 52 37 235 267 237 93 144 72	438 337 434 443 449	491 537
530–538	6 25 168 203 258 308 · · · · · · 143 254 127 182 224	392 411 364 335 431	511 479 496 487 509	36 98 158 174 314 5 59 290 333 54	426 432 339	498 519 566 576
540–548	82 185 315 150 160 248 253 292 21 15 126 304	348 462 414	541 562 517	236 192 289 2 · · · · · · 299	423 372 · · · · · ·	563 499 513 534 · · · · · 552
550–558	289 69 83 105 270 279 28	454 407	542	226 75 96 124 242 256 91 284 318 275	382 459 415 342 401	529 536 494 481
560–568	121 154 300	474		239 178 189 191 167 249	446 358 394 461 410	565 539 559
570–578	135 282 109	441 450	564	186		
580–588	171 311	366		14 110	343	525 558
590–598			553			526
600–608	257 329			3 8 207 41 43		
610–618	324	416		179 42	408 418 470	
620–628						
630–638				260 78 287 88 273		
640–648	220					
650–658	147					485
660–668						
670–678						
680–688						
690–698	m.m. 830 74		m.m. 864 520			

Index	MALE VI–XII DYNASTY	MALE PTOLEMAIC	MALE ROMAN	FEMALE VI–XII DYNASTY	FEMALE PTOLEMAIC	FEMALE ROMAN
700–708	21 851mm 278; 82; 185					
710–718						
720–728		371				
730–738						
740–748	175; 67 220	440		43		
750–758	31 154; 203; 26 133 293 312	364	512 574; 564	48		
760–768		430; 397	487	47–88		
770–778	40; 29 30; 171 159	407	560	62	407	
780–788	13 55 69 311 315; 176; 219	367 386 450; 392	543; 515	12 24 54	358 461	493 482; 523
790–798	142A 60 114 160 270; 57 89	370; 366	547	8 35 36 42 189	432; 373	
800–808	180 33 109 254 272; 141 27 81 122 204		562	78; 104 45 90	446 468; 363 394 476	536
810–818	330; 196 49 66 83 152 298	452; 341 437 454 463; 472		267 136; 299; 334; 17 210	413; 459	552
820–828	32 147 215 247; 168 325 38 135 182 259 324; 285	354 . . . . .; 335; 368 421	479	3 116 216; 92 115 207 239; 23 225	447	478 483 518 561; 538
830–838	80 132 156 165 195 217; 224 268 279 281 286 309; 15 119 288; 262	412 469 374; 404 409 444; 344 361 474	477 511 542 572 . . . . . .; 557	. . . . . .; 18 87 153 205 271; 237 41 58 124	401; 400 443 445	498; 559
840–848	304; 252 308; 184 231; 7 84 127 137 300	353 359 462; 414 420; 466	489; 570; 541 554 555	95; 93 201 162 167; 75 123 178	423 375 387	. . . . .
850–858	85 245; 61 71 74 77 145A 170 193 258; 20 94 138	360 395 411 . . . 431; 399 433 458 460	501 553; 516 569; 544	191 9 140 144 148 161 226; 73 108 164 275; 44 149 198	346 406 428; 415 425	491 558 526; 539
860–868	53 327 183; 121; 25 257 323	379; 381; 398 441	567 573 . . . .; 486 556 540	46; 232 37 227 . . . . . .; 91 110 321	470; 380 426; 384	566; 535 568 481
870–878	6 163; 233 200 289; 79 126 229 291	448; 350 383 416; 336 365 390 442	480; 502; 548	166 2 11 172 277; 59 86 96 264; 158 256	488 . . . . 352 388 449 467; 439 451	484 490 510 537 . . . . . .; 494 534
880–888	131 244 246 274 282 283; 209 222; 146A	403 422; 376; 348		314; 174	337; 424	528; 500
890–898	113; 103 187 198 261; 278 1 76; 106 143 243 248 292 301 317	338 356 405	496; 497	318; 72 213; 5 14 65; 179 273	419; 362	525; 499 529 565; 504 576
900–908	117 206 212 240 320; 214 253 329	385; 471	503 527 578	181 68 101 151; 157 197 284 . . . .; 287; 192	372 378 395 436 455; 456	575 . . . . .; 546; 571; 524
910–918	142B; 26			260; 145B 143B; 263	343; 339 393	507
920–928	51 266 316; 105; 146B 199 302; 130 332	465; 391; 427	508; 509; 533	16 202; 52 241 250 251 296 333; 102 230; 98 186 242 269; 169	340 438; 435; 402; 418	485
930–938		453	505; 549 532	297; 111	345	551 519
940–948	100 190; 64	417	517	118 125; 290 97	349 389	513; 514 563; 577
950–958	265 319	457 377	506 522	120 238	347; 382	
960–968						492
970–978	255	464 429	521 520	4 10; 322; 235 310	410; 342	
980–988			495			
990–1000	150	475		218 249		

ULNA AXIAL

mm	MALE VI–XII DYNASTY	MALE PTOL	MALE RO	FEMALE VI–XII DYNASTY	FEMALE PTOLEM	FEMALE RO
202						
204						
206						
208						
210						
212						
214						
216				110		
218				213		
220						
222				198		
224				249		
226				153 213		
228					455	
230				263 333	467	499
232				120 201 305 68 194 242	361	488 481
234				96 205 239 260 .... 88 218 236 331	461	
236		338		72 111 277 173 275 321		
238				299 90	451	
240				178 264 322 202 284 287		
242	87 194			125 167 ..... 322 ..	340 339 459 349 451	484
244	135 159 312	350		179 91	342	
246		474		123 158 197 118 186 210	468	493
248	133 185			221 232 250 297 314 318		
250	211 329 127 247 276			78 181 155 .... 82 120	347 346 456	
252	84 144A 283 328 278			313		
254	217 281 142 195			148 241 256 223 83	476	
256	124 274 330 298			124		
258	177 219 131 200 286	452		296		
260	170 183 214 320	250 464 472 ..				
262	139 281 257 285 209 175 309	336 465 466		194		
264	113 132 134 142 171 187 152 291 308 327 ...	453		334		
266	165 229 326 145	335 475 ..				
268	83					478
270	204 292 74 126 163 196 324	469 457 344		73		
272	298	348				
274	130 80 279 300	 471				
276	129 168 206 301 119 121 189 222 243 ..					
278	203 265 316 317 319 117 302			151		
280	182 311	460				
282	146B	454 462				
284	77 251 307					
286	114 245 288	458	495	273		
288	89 332 85 186 99					
290						
292						
294	248		489			
296		473				
298						
300						
302						
304						
306	122					
308						
310	233					
312						
314						
316						

RADIUS MAXIMUM

mm	MALE VI–XII DYNASTY	MALE PTOL	MALE RO	FEMALE VI–XII DYNASTY	FEMALE PTOL	FEMALE ROMAN
194						
196						
198						
200						
202						
204				153 213		
206				249 144 198 280		
208				213 333		
210						
212				68 86		
214			496	201	351	492 499
216				82 128 331 277	455	
218				72 90 205 263 86 111 128 .... 96 242		
220				88 92 143 260 303	345 461 467	481 488
222				218 299 96 153 322		
224		338		181 202 264 173 78 149 321	451	
226	184			90 125 238 239 .. 210 322		
228				202 284	459 342 349	
230	185 211			290 314 98 318 115 136 167	451 339 340	
232	87 159	474 350		123 157 186 191 179	347 488	
234	278 194 135 144A 283			165 197 118 216 232 158 250 313	346	
236	312 69 328			120 120 221 256 124		
238	142			297 305 325	456	493
240	61 247 217			148 310 223		483
242	84 180 281 127 177	450		241 267		
244	131 141 257 274 .. 292	472 452				
246	83 219 238 82 113 200 308 326	... 466		194 164		
248	152 175 231 320 109 134 166 309			334		
250	199 294 327 74 122 139 187 ..	465 464 475		214 73	476	485
252	285 132 133	335 469				
254	171 208 220 315 126 145A 240 261 317	453		166		
256	204 324 86					478
258	129 319 160 196 286	344	497	97		
260	130 163 168 206 298 301	348				
262	77 300 302 80 243 279	471 .. 454				
264	203 222 117 146A 209 289	460 457		151		
266	311 215 265					
268	83 307					
270	114 195 188 245					498
272	332	458	495	273		
274	89	462 473				
276			486			
278						
280						
282	248 99					
284						
286	306					

HUMERUS MAXIMUM

mm	MALE VI–XII DYNASTY	MALE PTOLEM	MALE RO	FEMALE VI–XII DYNASTY	FEMALE PTOLEM	FEMALE RO
262						
264				153 110 249 275		
266				153		
268						
270				125 70		
272						
274				280 115 213 207 229		
276				128 236 111 333 198	340	
278						
280	184		498	68 263 96 213 218 242		499
282				126 297 143 237 .... 72 79 28 181	345 347	
284				86 305 321		492
286				149 140 232 174	455	484 488
288				88 322		
290	329 283	338		138 169 260 86 96 197 273 284 313 318	347	481
292	159 278 293			92	468	
294	94 135 183 83 185			98 167 192 194 210 225 .... 178 264 322	342 451 451	
296		474		108 118 173 174 201 202 155 297 123 318	339 ...	
298	87			90 277 90 269 303	459	..
300	131 231 257 312	350	487	179 284	470 349	
302	180 211			191 256 ...... 299 81 93 95B 148 186 202 241	339 346 467 461	485
304	144A 309			120		
306	109 186 231 257 323 199 215		477	205 325 97		
308	69 276 133 171					
310	66 113 247 301 ...... 81 122 142 217 240 304 308 328	450		238 298 120 260 267		493 490
312	212 262					
314	145 240 261 286 296 219 285 294	336 464		221 223 296 216 271 334	476	
316	64 67 117 132 138 147 168 170 187 160 300 319	463		73 158		
318	152 330 292 317				456	
320	84 139 200 281 326 127 163 222			214		
322	164 177 285 279	453 472 452 454 475 460 463 ..		314		
324	80 129 220 243 315 126 175 176 204					478
326	289 85 134 188 195 228					494
328	234					
330	311 316 82 274	471 465 466				
332	198 254 77					
334	130 146B 209 298					
336	114 119 266 268					
338	244 288 63 182 261	344				
340	332 203 270	348 469	489			
342		 492				
344	307	344	495			
346	245					
348	206 272	458 335	497			
350	79					
352	248					
354			486			
356		457				
358						
360	99					
362	306	462				
364		473				
366						
368						
370	233					

ULNA MAXIMUM

mm	Male VI–XII Dynasty	Male Ptol	Male Ro	Female VI–XII Dynasty	Female Ptol	Female Roman
202						
204						
206						
208						
210						
212						
214						
216						
218						
220				110		
222				153		
224				213		
226				198		
228				249		
230				153 207 213		
232				86		
234				62 263	456	499
236				333 96 125 68	467 361	481 488
238				70 277 218 305 331 ••••		
240		338		72 96 102 201 260 174 205 242	461 ••••	
242				49 235 239 321 90 299	451	
244				173		
246	184			125 178 323 202 275 ••••••	459	
248	87			135 264 167 322 78 264	340 349 •••	484
250	135 329	350			339 451	
252	312 159			91 158 314 318 123 210 284	342 468	
254	69 185			118 179 250 188		
256	144A 281 137 247			120 197 221 •••• 92 232 297	346 456	
258				93 155 313		493
260	94 276 278 330 150 283			111 148 256 241		
262	274			124 296	476	
264	219					
266	82 122 131 177 286 320 •••••• 131 200 231 257	452 472 460 465 ••		213		
268	109 133 285 309	336 466				
270	84 139 152 134 142A 183 195 231 308	464		194 334		
272	165 171 175 83 113 132 187 240 326	453				
274	220 74 337 145A 189	475 •••		73		478
276	204	459 335				
278	79 85 324 126 198	348 457 344				
280	298	••••				
282	279 300 80 243 301 119 129 289	471		151		
284	121 160 203 206 265 316 130 168 302					
286	117 222 317 311					
288		454 460				
290	83 77 182	462				
292	146B					
294	114 245 251 99 288 307 89	468	495	273		
296						
298	188					
300						
302	248		486			
304		473				
306						
308						
310						
312						
314						
316						

223

RADIUS AXIAL

mm	Male VI–XII Dynasty	Male Ptolem	Male Ro	Female VI–XII Dynasty	Female Ptol	Female Ro
194				153		
196				144 249 280		
198				198 213 236 333		
200						
202			496	207 88 86 126		492
204				201		499
206				128 277 331 92 242	351 465	488
208				62 86 90 95 148 173 205 218 263 303		481
210				72 111 260	345 461 467 •••	
212	184	336		88 96 181 299 321 149 202 239 264 322 174	451	
214				76 125 90		
216	185 87			167 173 238 202 210 212 314 322 ••••••	459 461	
218	159 135	350		96 294 290 318 155	349 ••• 342 339 340 408	493
220	92 76	474		191		
222	144A 283 312			116 156 179 197 236 120 120 167 218 232 305 ••• 115 136 250 313 124	347 346	
224	69 142B			297		
226	61 247 84 211 177 180 257 328			221 326 207 310	456	483
228	281 274	472		123 148 166 228 267		
230	127 141 219 231 292 306 •••• 131 142A 144	452 450 ••••		194 241		
232	83 176 200 294 231 326	465				
234	82 109 134 309 122 165 187 320	464		164		
236	74 113 139 152 199 285 •••• 133 327	453		73 214 334	476	
238	132 220 240 261 171	336 475 ••• 469				485 478
240	145A 315 317 324 126 319					
242	286	344		166		
244	85 117 130 160 204 298 129 163 168 300	348 466		97		
246	198	471 454 ••••	497			
248	206 222 279 203			151		
250	77 80 243 307 316 •• 146A 209 289 291 302	460				
252	301 311 63 146B	457				
254	265 166 195					
256	114 251B 245		495	273		
258	332 89	462				498
260		458 473				
262	215		466			
264						
266						
268	99 248					
270						
272						
274	306					
276						
278						
280						
282						
284						
286						

HUMERUS OBLIQUE

mm	Male VI–XII Dynasty	Male Ptol	Male Ro	Female VI–XII Dynasty	Female Ptol	Female Roman
262				110 153		
264				249 275		
266				153		
268						
270				125 189 70 207 280		
272				213 229		
274				115 263		
276			496	199 111 126	340	
278	184			143 181 333 88 96 242 219		499 492
280				86 126 213 237 257 ••••••	345 347	
282				72 79 128 305	456	
284				313 321 140 149	347	488 ••• 484
286				232 322	•••	
288	278 293 329	338		88 92 197 86 273 319		
290	183 169 283 186			90 136 169 173 192 194 202 284 118 178 260 322	468 342 457 451 459	491
292			487	98 167 108 201 210 225 297	339 349	
294	83 94 136 174	474		120 155 174 318	348	
296	131 257 312	350		277 90 123 299 269 284	467 470 •• 339	
298	87 144A 231			120 186 202 256 303 ••••• 179 205		
300	211 276 180 257			148 191 241 325 91 93	461	485 ••
302	165 247 309 231 304		477	95B		
304	109			238		
306	133 171 199 323 •••• 122 215 301 328 66 69	450 463		97 250		
308	113 119 138 240 308			267		490 493
310	61 142 262 67 219 266 294			334	456 476	
312	168 170 261 292 300 132 145A 212 240 285	464 472 ••		73 216 221 158		
314	64 117 160 317 319 ••• 187 200 265 320	336 463		223 271		•• 483
316	281 127 152 163					
318	84 175 176	453 454 475		214 314		
320	139 204 222 243 315 326 74 80 164 279	452				
322	134 177 195 129 196 220	460 ••				478
324	128 188 289	471				
326	228 234 311 316 ••••• 85	466 348 465		166		494
328	89 146 254 268	344				
330	77 130 274 182 209 298			151		
332	266 114					
334	119 244	469 ••	495			
336	203 251 258 332 63 270		489			
338		344	497			
340	272 307					
342		335 458				
344	206 245 79		497 486			
346						
348						
350	248	473				
352	308 99					
354		457				
356		462				
358						
360						
362	233					
364						
366						
368						
370						

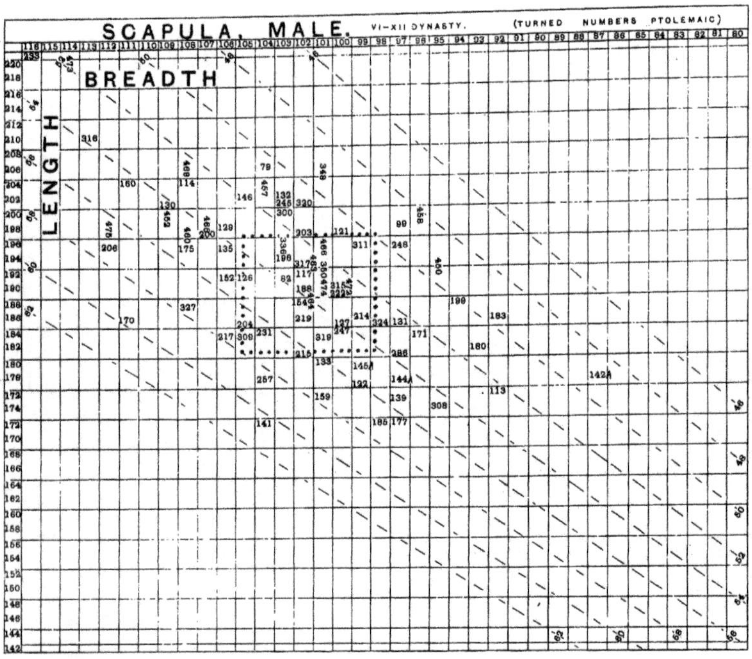

INFRASPINOUS HEIGHT	VI–XII DYN	PTOL
129	320	
128		
127		458
126		469
125		
124	245 311	465 473
123	233 316	348 457 466
122		
121		
120		450
119	171 327	
118	317	
117		
116	146β	
115	180 • • • •	463 472 475
114		
113	196 300 324	350 464
112	183 206 248 315	474
111		460
110	152 175 185 215 214	
109	154 188 286	452
108	160 231	
107	200 204 309	336
106	217	
105	222 • • • •	
104	170	
103	247 319	
102	177 257	
101	199	
100	308	
99		
98		
97	219	
96		
95		
94	159	
93		
92		
91		
90		
89		
88		
87		
86		
85		
84		
83		
82		
81		

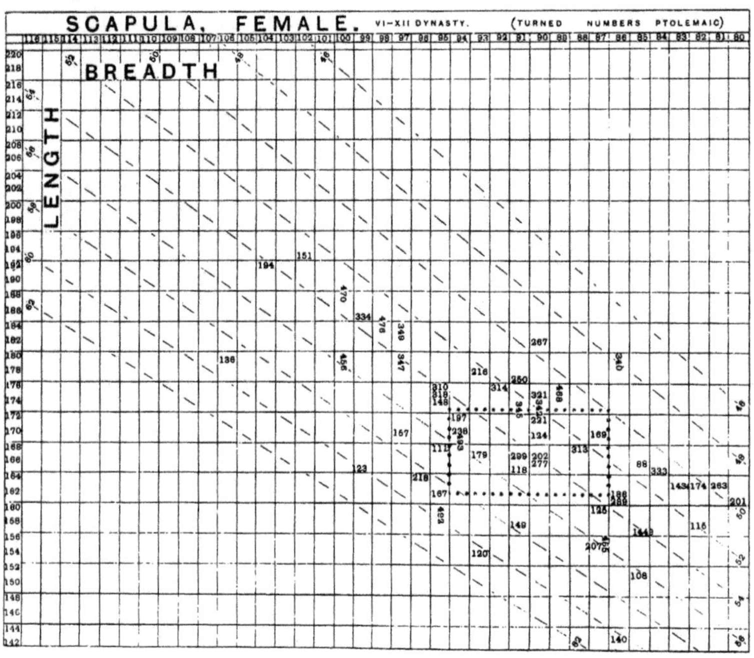

INFRASPINOUS HEIGHT	VI–XII DYN	PTOL
128		
127		
126		
125		
124		
123		
122		
121	151	
120		
119		
118		476
117		
116		
115		
114		456
113		
112		
111	194	
110		340
109	146	
108	216	470
107	260	
106	136 314	342
105		
104	313	
103	263 • • • • • • • •	
102	186 197 218 321	
101		468
100	334	
99	179 310 318	
98		
97	157 167 202 221 267 277	349
96	169 201 238	
95	• • • • • • • • • •	347
94	174 230 144	
93		493 345
92	207 299 333	
91		
90		455
89	149	
88		
87		
86		
85	143	
84		
83		
82		492
81		

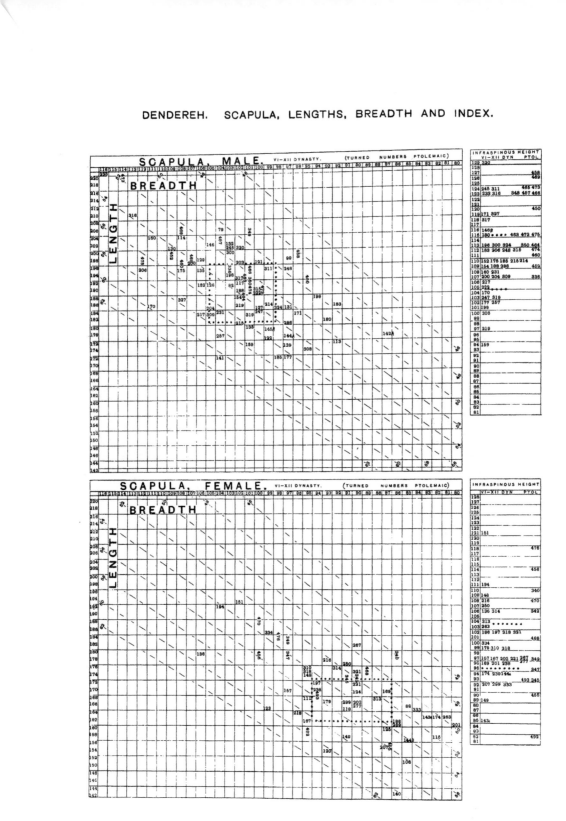

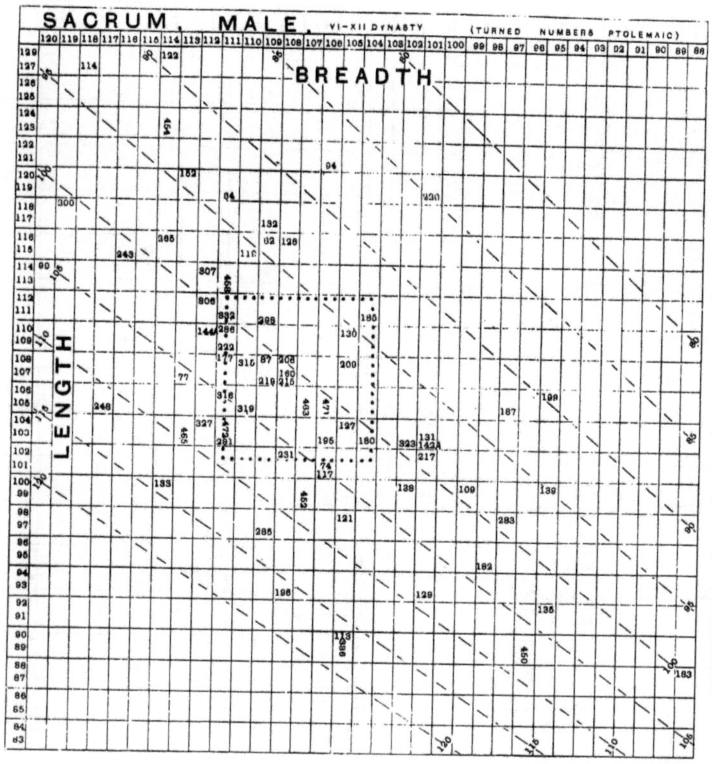
SACRUM, MALE. VI–XII DYNASTY
(TURNED NUMBERS PTOLEMAIC)
BREADTH
LENGTH

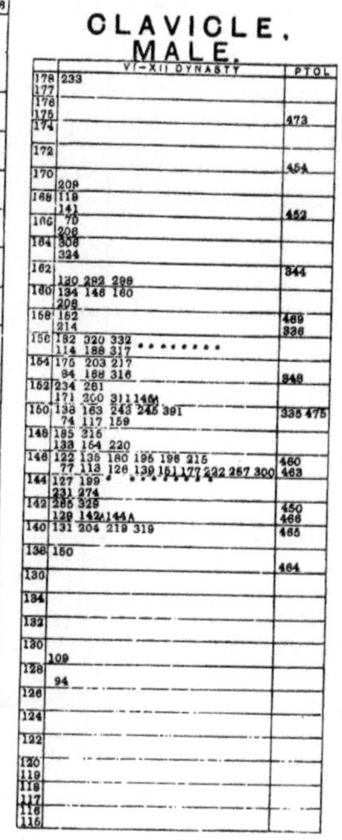
CLAVICLE, MALE.
VI–XII DYNASTY
PTOL

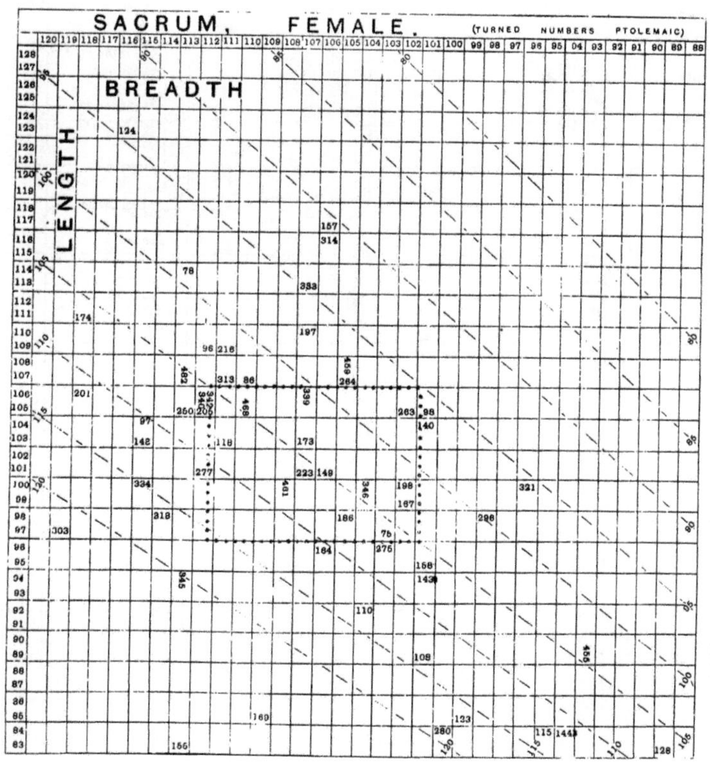
SACRUM, FEMALE. (TURNED NUMBERS PTOLEMAIC)
BREADTH
LENGTH

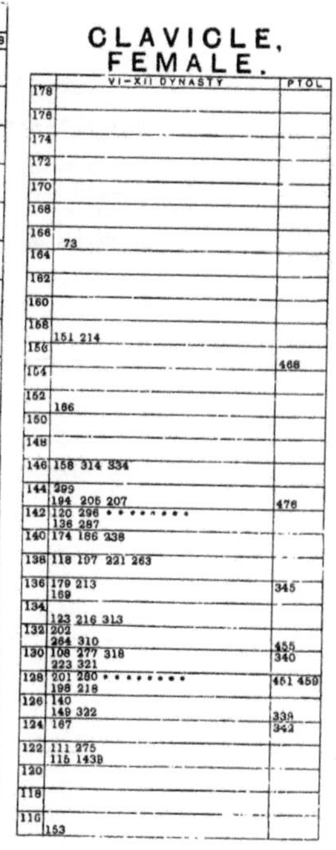
CLAVICLE, FEMALE.
VI–XII DYNASTY
PTOL

	FEMUR, MAX.			FEMUR, OB.		
	VI–XII DYNASTY	PTOLEM	RO	VI–XII DYN	PTOLEM	RO
531 530	248 228			228		
529 528 527 526 525	233			233		
524 522 520		457				
518 516						
514 512 510						
508 506						
504 502 500						
498 496	119 306 99			99 306		
494 492 490	77 206 307	460 473				
488 486	89 332			77 206 307 332 89	473 460	
484 482 480	244 67	462	489	119 244	462	489
478 476	289 209 251 285 63 245 176 234 259 268 324	469	495	67 251 289 63 209 285 324	469	495
474 472 470	268 270 114 188 315 85 146 B •••••			245 176 234 259 315 85 114 268 288		
468 466	254 301 291 170 196 84 132 204 279	458 ••••		188 254 270 301 •••• 148 146B 291	458	
464 462 460	265 316 152 261 266 203 133 311 320	454 475		170 196 204 132 152 265 279 261 316		
458 456	222 142A 129 130 177 294 302 180 160 171 195 ••••	335 348	497	203 222 266 84 311 320 302 133 142A 130 177 195 294	475 •••• 454	
454 452 450	282 163 200 243 300 319 240 64	453 471 ••••		180 160 163 171 282 319 ••••••• 129 300 243	335 348	
448 446	262 122 80 175 281 117 168 327	344 336 464	480	240 64 200 262 80 122 175 168	453 471 ••••••	497 480
444 442 440	82 154 219 286 87 258 317 326 66 127 212 156	465	487	117 327 219 286 281 154 317 214 82 87 258 326	336 344 464 465	487
438 436	144A 187 220 274 •• 141 247 165 304	466 •••• 450		66 144A 127 156 212 220 274 141 187 •••• 165	466	
434 432 430	83 142B 308 113 126 69 215 323 199 185	463		247 83 126 304 308 69 113 142 199 215 283 323	450 •••• 463	
428 426	217 309 329 61 211 109	452 474		217 185 211 330 109 309 329	452 474	
424 422 420	231 278 184			61 278 231		
418 416	255			184		
414 412 410	94 293		496	255 94		
408 406	135 183	350		293 135 183	350	496
404 402 400	312			312		
398 396		338				
394 392 390					338	
388 386						
384 382 380						
378 376						
374 372 370						
368 366						

	TIBIA, MAX.			TIBIA, AXIAL			FIBULA		
	VI–XII DYNASTY	PTOL	RO	VI–XII DYNASTY	PTOL	RO	VI–XII DYNASTY	PTOLEM	RO
456 455 454									
452 451 450	99								
448 446	248								
444 442 440	306 228								
438 436				228					
434 432 430	272						248		
428 426	307 332	460		99					
424 422 420	244 251		489	306			99		
418 416	114	473						460	
414 412 410	119 288 245 289 206	457 462					272 307		
408 406	291 259 89 188 265 268 302	348		272 307	460				
404 402 400	63 196 209 234 80 138 203 254 ••••••• 176 148	469		332		489	245 244 251		
398 396	222 163 317 132 266 311	••••		188 244 251 196 114	462 457 473		206	473	
394 392 390	142A 195 301 324 170 282 127 319 204 66 285 316	475 454 453		206 119 234 259 288 312 245 89 289			188 222	457	
388 386	74 286 67 152 175 262 126 243 315 160 168 240 •••••••			291 63 209 265 74 203	348		265 146	469 348	
384 382 380	113 117 133 220 171 208 261 327 85 129 320 130 139	335 465 458 •••	497	80 138 266 254 176 •••••• 146 B	469		142A 311 317 319 152 160 195 196 •••	453 •••• 458	
378 376	300 215 84 219 147 200 323	471 344		222 311 66 163 317 170 301 195 324	••••		130 243 261 133 234 132	454	
374 372 370	156 87 263 330 144A 187 214 145A 177 •••••••• 122 199	464 450 336 350		132 266 133 319 127 142A 285 286 208 243 282	475 454		126 127 316 113 258 301 308	344	
368 366	142B 121 141 180 154 278	•••• 474	487	67 152 316 315 113 175 •••••• 126 168 204 282	453		200 66 122 168 171 ••• 330 85 286 327	335 336 471 ••	
364 362 360	83 165 247 329 61 69 109 276 185 217 274	462 46 472		117 160 220 320 129 139 261 308 85 130 327 171 240 258 147 200 300	458 335 • 465 471 344 •	497	323 320 141 177 215 220	464	
358 356	255 76			330 215 323 84 87 156 177 219	450		144A 217 214 199 283 180 185 ••••• 87	450 466 472 350 •••• 452 474	
354 352 350	211	463		•••••• 144A 199 122 187 121 141 154 283 214	464 336 350 ••••	487	61 219 83 156 187 247		
348 346	203 135 184 94			142B 255 145A 165 83 180 329	452 472 474 466		154 276 109 186		
344 342 340	312			217 69 61 185 274					
338 336	71 188 183	338		109 276 71 78			212 94		
334 332 330			496	211	463		135		
328 326				94 293 184			180	469 338	
324 322 320				312 135					
318 316				183	338	496			
314 312 310									
308 306									
304 302 300									
298 296									
294 292									

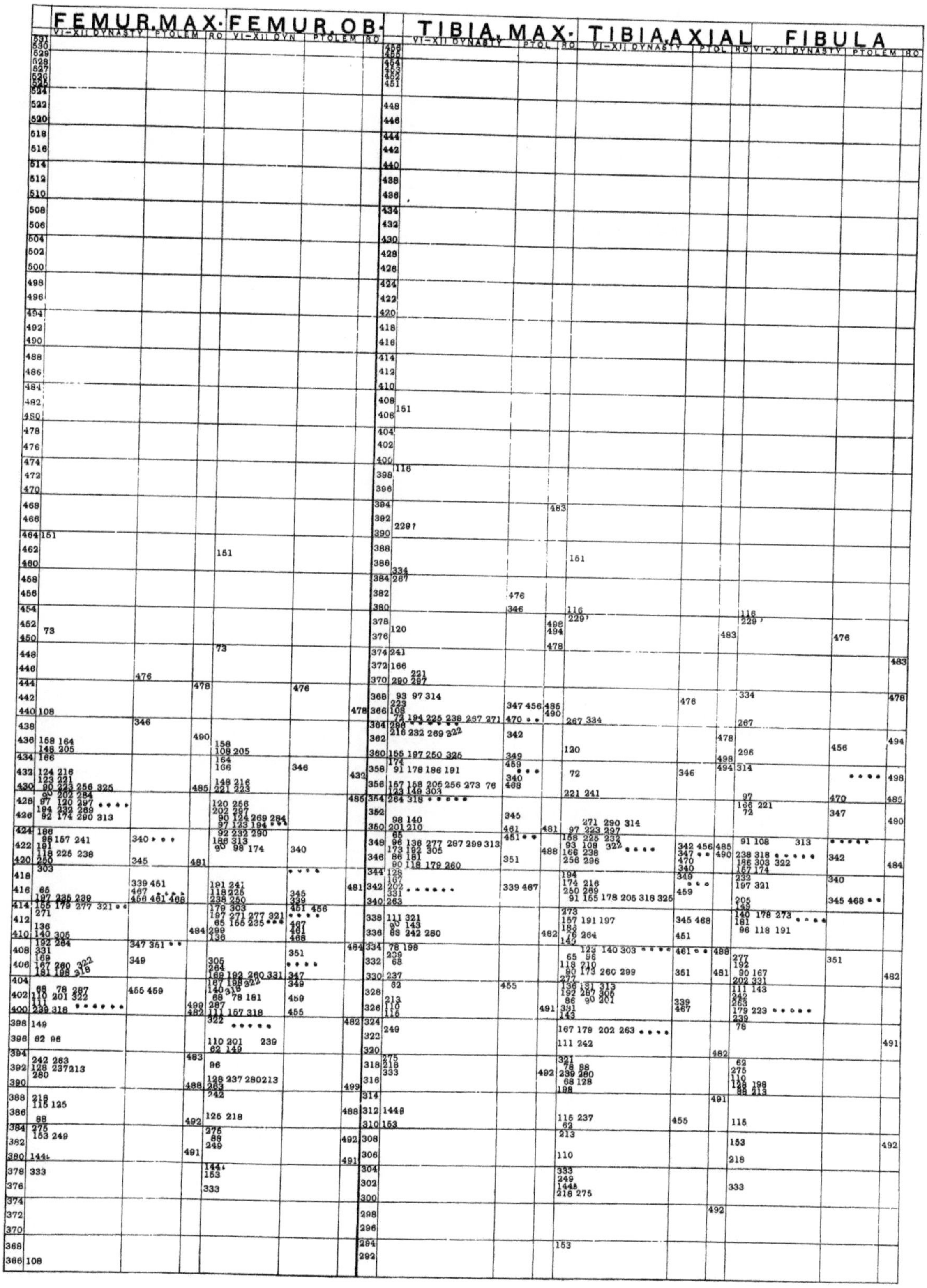
FEMUR. MAX.
VI–XII DYNASTY
PTOLEM
RO
FEMUR. OB.
VI–XII DYN
PTOLEM
RO
TIBIA. MAX.
VI–XII DYNASTY
PTOL
RO
TIBIA AXIAL
VI–XII DYNASTY
PTOL
RO
FIBULA
VI–XII DYNASTY
PTOLEM
RO

For EU product safety concerns, contact us at Calle de José Abascal, 56–1°, 28003 Madrid, Spain or eugpsr@cambridge.org.

www.ingramcontent.com/pod-product-compliance
Ingram Content Group UK Ltd.
Pitfield, Milton Keynes, MK11 3LW, UK
UKHW051028150625
459647UK00023B/2854